CONTEMPORARY RESEARCH IN LEARNING

SELECTED READINGS

Edited by

JOHN R. BRA

Univer

AN INSIGHT BOOK

D. VAN NOSTRAND COMPANY, INC.
PRINCETON, NEW JERSEY
TORONTO   LONDON
NEW YORK

D. VAN NOSTRAND COMPANY, INC.
120 Alexander St., Princeton, New Jersey
(*Principal Office*)
24 West 40 Street, New York 18, New York

D. VAN NOSTRAND COMPANY, LTD.
358, Kensington High Street, London, W.14, England

D. VAN NOSTRAND COMPANY (Canada), LTD.
25 Hollinger Road, Toronto 16, Canada

Foreword

The editorial conception guiding the selection of readings for this book has been to provide the reader with coverage in depth of a central issue in the contemporary literature of psychology. In this way he can acquire an immediate acquaintance with the major findings, methods, and personalities engaged with the problem. He will find himself in the midst of problems still moving toward solution, forced to listen to contending theories and conflicting findings, and asked to master new concepts, ideas, and formulations. Thanks to the editorial skill which produced this book, the student will be exposed to original papers usually denied him by reason of unavailability, lack of bibliographical skill, and lack of sophistication with the problem.

This book is one of a second grouping of selected readings volumes in the general Insight series. Unlike the Enduring Problems books edited for the beginning and undergraduate student, the group of which this book is a part will serve the advanced student and scholar. These selections presume an acquaintance with vocabulary, theoretical positions, and methodology. Readers with these qualifications will appreciate the topic coverage and elucidation provided by these collections.

Suggestions for Use

These books can be used by the student in either of two ways. They are organized so that the instructor can treat them in further depth through lecture or discussion. They may serve as seminar material for a group of students sharing responsibilities. Secondly, the student may find the volume a suitable handbook for guiding research papers and term projects into the literature area of his interest. It is also expected that students having area examinations at the graduate level may find these readings valuable as guides to study.

Finally, it may be safely presumed that researchers and teachers will themselves find these volumes useful. The assembly of materials in depth always carries with it the possibility of comparison and contrast from which new ideas and relations may emerge.

iii

Preface

The articles selected for inclusion in this volume afford a survey of some of the major theoretical issues that have been of concern to psychologists working in the area of learning. They all bear, in one manner or another, on the attempt of some psychologists to account for behavior by means of a model based on conditioning principles without reference to cognition.

For example, the place-vs.-response learning studies were once believed to provide a crucial test between conditioning and cognitive views. Restle has summarized this literature and has also made a provocative reinterpretation of the data using a mathematical model. Similarly, the phenomena of sensory preconditioning and transposition have been regarded by some as presenting data difficult to incorporate within a conditioning framework. The Seidel article presents an excellent review of the sensory preconditioning work, while that by Riley gives an interesting reinterpretation of transposition phenomena.

With but few exceptions (Guthrie's being the outstanding example), theories derived from conditioning models have tended to consider learning as an incremental rather than an all-or-none matter. The Estes article represents an important challenge to the incremental view. Spence's paper on emotionally based drive furnishes an extension of conditioning principles to make predictions possible, even in complex verbal learning of man.

The findings of stimulus generalization, secondary reinforcement, and partial reinforcement experiments have been controversial matters in themselves. In addition, stimulus generalization and secondary reinforcement have often been used as explanatory concepts by conditioning-model advocates. Therefore, the excellent reviews of Mednick and Freedman, Myers, and Lewis are included in this collection.

It is hoped that the careful reader will be able to detect many interrelationships and possibilities for cross-references among the eight articles of this volume. The editor has attempted to select papers that would be likely to stand as important contributions to the literature for some time to come. He hopes that he has succeeded.

JOHN R. BRAUN

Bridgeport, Connecticut
April, 1963

Contents

1

Discrimination of Cues in Mazes: A Resolution of the "Place-vs-Response" Question*

FRANK RESTLE[1]
Michigan State University

Whether rats in mazes learn turning responses or places is a question which has often been subjected to experimental test. Data from different experiments conflict, and attempts at a definitive answer seem only to add to the confusion. This paper will defend the thesis that the place-vs.-response question is wrongly formulated, and that the data which fail to decide between place and response learning give an unequivocal answer to a question properly stated.

The place-vs.-response question has been approached largely through the use of the T maze, rotated in its visual surround. A typical arrangement showing runs reinforced in "place" and "response" learning is shown in Fig. 1, along with the fixed-maze problem in which both place and response may be learned. In both place learning and response learning, the maze is rotated on alternate trials at random. The place learner is always to go to the same place in the room, responding consistently

* From *The Psychological Review*, 1957, 64, 217-228, and used here with the permission of the author and the American Psychological Association. When this paper was originally published the author was at the Center for Advanced Study in the Behavioral Sciences.

[1] Dr. Richard L. Solomon suggested and drafted part of this paper (see footnote 2). His guidance and help are gratefully acknowledged by the author.

to extra-maze cues but making different turns on different
trials. The response learner makes the same turn on all
trials, going to different places. One supposed test of
whether place or response learning is more dominant is
to compare rates of learning on these two problems. Another test is to train animals with the maze in a fixed
position (place + response learning), and then rotate the
maze for a test trial. The animal can now either make
the same turn he has learned or go to the same place he
has been going to, but not both. In this *direct opposition*
experiment, the relative number of animals taking each
choice is a test of the relative dominance of place and
response.

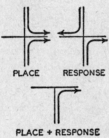

PLACE   RESPONSE

PLACE + RESPONSE

Fig. 1. *Runs reinforced in place, response, and place + response
(fixed maze) learning. Only one T maze is present on a
given trial.*

In 1946, Tolman, Ritchie, and Kalish (23) proposed
that in such a situation place learning is more natural
and primitive for the rat than response learning, and place
will dominate response in all tests. Their experiment supported the hypothesis, but some later repetitions have
found response dominating place, or have found no difference.

An answer to these apparent contradictions is here
sought by assuming that maze running depends on a multiplicity of cues, and that the rat learns differential responses to relevant cues in a maze just as he would in
a discrimination box. A theory based on learning in the
discrimination box will be applied to the maze situation.
Since the discrimination theory to be used (15) is very

close to earlier theories of the effect of sensory input on learning in mazes, theories which antedate the place-vs.-response controversy, it is useful to place the recent studies within their historical context and analyze all the data at once.

MULTIPLE CUE THEORY

Hunter (9, 10) and Honzik (8), among others, have proposed that learning and performance in mazes depends upon many cues, in all available modalities and from all sources. Depending on what stimuli are available to the rat, maze learning may depend on visual, auditory, olfactory, tactual, and kinesthetic stimuli. Visual, auditory, and olfactory stimuli may arise from within the maze or outside. The cues used by rats may be not only the specific physical stimuli but also patterns or arrangements of stimuli, so that changes which preserve the arrangement may not disrupt performance.

When a portion of the cues are removed by surgery or screening, or made irrelevant by interchanging maze units, rotating the maze, etc., learning of the maze is retarded, but mazes are often perfectly solved in the presence of known irrelevant cues.

The earlier formulation of multiple cue theory is somewhat refined by considering more recent theory derived from discrimination learning (15). This newer theory distinguishes between relevant cues, which bear a regular relationship to the correct path, and irrelevant cues which are not consistently related to the correct response.

A cue with a constant or predictable relationship to the true path will in the course of learning become "conditioned" to the correct response. All such cues will eventually be learned, and all will play a part in performance. If a certain cue is irrelevant, bearing a changing and unpredictable relationship to the correct response, it cannot be the basis of learning and is only a distractor. Such cues will become "adapted" during learning, and eventually will play no part in performance.

The rate of learning depends directly on the proportion of relevant, usable cues in the total set available.

When learning has been based on a variety of relevant

cues and then some of these cues are scrambled and made irrelevant, the amount of disturbance reflects the relative importance of the newly changed cues. Though irrelevant cues will eventually be adapted, making important cues irrelevant reduces the proportion of relevant cues and thus retards learning. Disruption due to scrambling of learned relevant cues is attributed to the fact that such cues are not adapted, having previously been relevant. Recovery from the disturbance results from progressive adaptation of the scrambled cues.

If the learning program involves constantly introducing new cues which have not been present before, these new cues will always disturb performance, since they cannot have been attached to the correct response and they cannot have been adapted.

In an ordinary multiple-unit maze, the untrained rat responds erratically early in training, producing different kinesthetic stimuli on different trials. As a result, such stimuli are not consistently related to the true path, and alone they cannot be the basis of rapid learning. As performance based on other cues improves, the animal makes more nearly the same movement each trial, producing for himself a regular pattern of kinesthetic stimuli which can serve as partial basis for the learned habit. Highly skilled performance thus depends to some degree on kinesthesis, though such cues do not alone mediate learning to a significant degree.

The above application of the theory of discrimination learning to mazes does not differ in important respects from the assumptions and conclusions of Hunter and Honzik. The main refinement is in attributing the rate of learning to the *proportion* of relevant cues. The earlier writers do not make just this statement, though their statements may be interpreted to this effect.

No attempt will be made in this paper to apply the specific quantitative formulation of discrimination learning to multiple-unit maze learning. The effects peculiar to the *serial* character of maze learning are not reflected in discrimination theory. When a single-unit T maze is used, as in the recent place-response experiments, discrimination theory should apply exactly and quantitative predictions should be correct.

The multiple cue theory can be compared with the results of studies using multiple-unit mazes, with the understanding that specific quantitative values (error scores, trials to learn, etc.) depend both on the discrimination of cues and on serial patterns. An understanding of these earlier studies of maze cues is essential in gaining a clear insight into the place-vs.-response controversy.

THE HISTORICAL CONTEXT[2]

Studies of the sensory control of maze behavior of rats have been reviewed in detail by Munn (14), so only a broad summary will be given here, along with discussions of the main points.

Early studies of the role of sensory processes in maze behavior were motivated by the early conclusion by Small (1901) and by Carr and Watson (1908) that in complex mazes rats form kinesthetically controlled habits which become "automatic." This hypothesis is that kinesthetic cues, arising from one response in the maze, serve as the main cues to the next response in the sequence. Each response is associated with the previous one, and other sensory input becomes unimportant in maintaining performance. This conclusion was based on the erroneous assumption that if one sort of cue is important, others must be unimportant. The technique was essentially one of eliminating a single sense modality at a time, in each case observing that performance remains essentially intact. The only modality not disturbed was kinesthesis, which was assumed to be "the" crucial one. Hunter (11) has shown the flaw in this line of argument.

The "kinesthetic" hypothesis inspired a series of experiments designed to prove or disprove it. These experiments uncovered a wealth of information about the cues which in fact control behavior in various mazes. Fundamentally, the data were analyzed to determine the relative effectiveness of (a) kinesthetic stimuli, (b) intramaze stimuli, such as visual, olfactory, and tactual stimuli from the maze itself, and (c) extra-maze stimuli, such

[2] The bearing of these studies on the place-vs.-response question was pointed out to the author by Dr. R. L. Solomon. This section and the beginning of the next section are based in part on a personal communication from him.

as visual or auditory stimuli from the room containing the maze. Intra- and extra-maze stimuli were broken down into components due to different sense modalities, again with the intention of evaluating each.

The methods used in assessing the role of sensory events in maze behavior were as follows: (a) surgical interference with receptor organs and neural pathways; (b) elimination of stimuli from the intra-maze or extra-maze environment; (c) introduction of distinctive stimuli to the environment; and (d) the controlled rearrangement of intra-maze and extra-maze stimuli.

In general, the results of these experiments were as follows:

(1) Simple alternation mazes can be learned by the rat on the basis of kinesthetic cues alone, but more complex mazes cannot be learned in any reasonable number of trials without the aid of visual, olfactory, or auditory cues. Removal of kinesthetic cues by surgical means does not greatly affect maze performance if intra- or extra-maze cues are left intact. However, once a maze performance is perfected on the basis of intra- or extra-maze cues, removal of such cues does not destroy the performance completely. As one would expect from the multiple cue theory, kinesthetic cues are relevant and conditioned to the correct response only when a regular relationship between the last response and the next correct response is established. Such a relationship exists in a simple alternation maze early enough for learning to take place. In more complex mazes, usable kinesthetic cues exist only after the maze is learned on some other basis. Since during learning kinesthetic cues are mostly irrelevant anyway, their removal does not retard learning.

(2) Mazes can ordinarily be learned on the basis of intra-maze cues alone, even if extra-maze cues are made irrelevant by rotating the maze in the room. Such rotation retards learning, however, especially if the maze is elevated and the room contains conspicuous visual cues. If the maze is kept in place in the room and its spatial arrangement is preserved while units of the maze are interchanged to make intra-maze stimuli irrelevant, rats can still solve the problem. Again, interchanging of stimuli retards learning. In many mazes, it should be noted,

all blinds have a common visual appearance, being shorter than true alleys and ending within sight of the rat at the choice point. Interchanging units does not make such stimuli irrelevant. But even if the spatial pattern of the maze is scrambled, if the goal is in a fixed position relative to the extra-maze environment the rat can learn to run to the goal box without following alleys which lead away from the food. Thus, intra-maze and extra-maze cues are each separately capable of sustaining learning and performance in the maze. With one type scrambled, perfect performance can often be attained based on the other type, indicating that irrelevant cues are eventually disregarded. Retardation of learning due to removal or scrambling of important cues is consistently observed.

(3) In elevated mazes, where most of the visual field arises from outside the maze, extra-maze cues are usually more important than intra-maze cues. If the maze is enclosed in a homogeneous room, however, extra-maze cues are relegated to a minor role. Intra-maze cues are generally more important in alley or tunnel mazes, where the rat has at best an obstructed view of the outside. In a unidirectional maze, extra-maze cues are more important than they are in a maze which requires the rat to run in many different directions. The results support the idea that either type of cue may be the more important, depending on the relative amount of relevant stimulation stemming from each source.

(4) In general, two ways of assessing the importance of a certain cue give comparable estimates. One method is to scramble the cue during learning, assessing its importance by the relative retardation in the rate of learning. The other method is to have the rat learn the maze with the cue relevant, then scramble it. The amount of disruption of the perfected habit indicates the importance of the cue. To an approximation, these two methods rank various classes of cues the same way. Removing a type of cue by depriving the animal of necessary receptors, as by blinding or deafening the animal or rendering it anosmic by surgical interference, is not the same thing as scrambling cues experimentally. Blinding, for example, removes both relevant and irrelevant visual cues, whereas rotating the maze makes otherwise relevant extra-maze

cues irrelevant, and does not affect intra-maze visual cues. Thus, exact comparisons between the effects of scrambling and the effects of surgery cannot usually be made.

These findings suggest that kinesthetic cues are unimportant in the learning of complex mazes, but that both intra- and extra-maze cues are important. The relative importance of various types of cues depends on the maze and its surround, for rats seem to use various cues proportionally as those cues are available and relevant. Rats seem capable of overcoming the distraction of irrelevant cues.

The results are consistent with the conception that maze learning and performance depend on multiple cues, and that such cues are discriminated and responses learned to them in accord with the theory of discrimination learning.

"PLACE" AND "RESPONSE" IN SINGLE-UNIT T MAZES

In the light of the earlier extensive studies of the sensory basis of maze running, studies of place and response in T mazes appear as comparisons of extra-maze and kinesthetic cues. The Tolman-Ritchie-Kalish hypothesis that rats learn "places" rather than "responses" means, in the earlier terminology, that extra-maze cues are more important than kinesthetic cues. Since in earlier studies kinesthetic cues were found barely sufficient to permit any learning at all, whereas extra-maze visual cues bulk large in importance when they are available, it would appear that the dominance of "place" learning was indubitable, and the Tolman-Ritchie-Kalish experiment redundant.

It should be noted that Tolman's "place" formulation is inferior to earlier formulations. Tolman does not specify what cues are thought to make up "place" indications, and he does not identify "response" learning as learning based solely on kinesthetic cues. Though intra-maze cues do not seem to be "response" cues in Tolman's sense, it is not clear whether they are "place" cues or not.

Though the hypothesis that place learning will dominate response learning seems to follow in a general way from Tolman's concept of cognitive maps, his position was not really controversial because stimulus-response theorists did not believe response learning would be easier than place learning. The early Carr-Watson hypothesis, that maze habits are mainly controlled by kinesthesis, was by 1946 buried under conflicting evidence, and S-R theories stated that the stimulus components of the maze habits were quite likely to be extra-maze visual cues, especially if the maze is elevated and in a room full of such cues.

From these considerations, one should expect that the dominance of place learning is a foregone conclusion. The existence of a "controversy" is itself a surprise. In order to show the nature of this controversy it is necessary first to consider how place-response experiments have been conducted and what results have been obtained. Since this recent literature has not received a definitive review, a relatively thorough analysis is presented here.

Tests of Place-vs.-Response Dominance

We first consider whether place learning in fact dominates response learning in the single-unit maze. Ten studies have compared the rates of place and response learning in single-unit T mazes or slight modifications thereof. Of these, seven found place learning faster (1, 3, 5, 22, 23, 24, 25), and two found response learning faster (7, 20), while one found that either could be faster depending on the intertrial interval (21). In direct opposition tests (rotation of the maze after the habit is learned on a fixed maze), one study showed that either place or response could be superior depending on the shape of the approach stem (18), another showed that either could be dominant depending on differential cues (27), and two others found response tendencies overriding place tendencies (2, 12). A modification of the opposition test consists of setting up conditions in which the animal alternates. Several studies have asked whether an animal alternates response or stimulus (place) characteristics (4, 6, 13, 26), and the answer has always been that place alternation is stronger than response alternation. These studies used enclosed alley mazes, "place" cues being especially distinctive intra-maze cues.

In summary, if we merely count titles, the impression is received that place tendencies are usually learned faster than responses, and that they are sometimes stronger in opposition tests, especially those depending on alternation. One certainly cannot draw the conclusion that place learning is always dominant, though, for response tendencies dominate in at least some conditions of seven different studies.

Conditions Associated With Place and Response Dominance

Since neither place nor response is uniformly dominant, we may consider the experimental conditions which make one or the other stronger.

Several writers (1, 7, 21, 25) have suggested that the relative dominance of place depends on the amount of differential visual stimulation. This is, of course, the position taken by earlier writers on general maze learning, though place-vs.-response studies are not usually analyzed in terms of this variable. Counting heads in the experimental reports, we see that the use of a homogeneous visual surround (a dome or enclosure, usually made of muslin, which prevents the animal from discerning any uncontrolled stimuli from the room about him) greatly predisposes rats to learn responses instead of places. All four experiments using such domes report response dominance (2, 7, 20, 21), though one (21) showed that response dominance could be neutralized by massing trials. The only other cases of response dominance reported (12, 18) were in plain rooms under low illumination, which may be thought of as approximations to dome-type enclosures. All other studies showing place dominance were done in open rooms (1, 3, 5, 22, 23, 24, 25) or in alley mazes with strong differential cues (6, 13, 26). One study showed that when the two places contrast sharply in illumination, place dominates, whereas when the illumination is more nearly equal, response tendencies dominate.

In summary, place tendencies dominate when visual stimuli at the two ends of the maze are very *unlike*, and response tendencies dominate when such stimuli are relatively *alike*. In every case the domination seems to be quantitative—both place and response tendencies exist, but one is stronger than the other depending on stimulus conditions.

By inspecting the experimental reports we can get some idea of what constitutes a strong place cue for the rat. The most dramatic place dominance was found in two studies (17, 23) in which rat cages were located to one side, nearer one goal than the other. In one of these studies (17) it was found that the rats would not give up responding to one place in the room, despite a number of controls, until the cages were moved, following which almost all the rats reversed. Stimuli such as lights had only a slight effect on performance, compared with the rat cages.

When rat cages are placed directly behind the starting point and are thus not available as place cues, or when the room is devoid of cages, such visual stimuli as windows (in daylight studies) give rise to strong place preferences (1, 3), as do well-lighted rooms with many small objects in them (5, 25). Somewhat less striking but still consistent place dominance was shown in two studies in which one wall of a plain room (the wall behind one goal), was moderately well illuminated, the other wall not being illuminated at all (22, 24). The power of room cues can be estimated by noting the quick learning of a successive discrimination between rooms (19). Attempts to give differential cues inside domes by illuminating a 10-inch disc behind one goal with a 7.5-watt lamp (2, 12) or using 7.5-watt lamps themselves as cues, with (7) or without (20) overhead illumination, did not lead to place dominance. Symmetrical overhead illumination in an empty room produced response dominance with spaced practice (21). A small lamp on the floor below one goal, pointed to throw long shadows on the floor, gave slightly more place than response tendency (18). Ratio of illuminations rather than difference seems to be a crucial variable (27).

In summary, rat cages are very strong place stimuli, windows or objects in a well illuminated room rank next in power, and fairly strong differential lighting of walls of a plain room is also effective. Discs lit by 7.5-watt lamps, or such lamps themselves, are not usually enough to make place dominant over response in an otherwise homogeneous setting.

Some other variables are associated to some degree with place and response dominance. For example, all experiments using pigmented rats, (4, 22, 23, 24) show place dominance, except for one (12) which showed cases of both place and slight response dominance under low illumination. But white rats also show place dominance under good illumination (1, 3, 5, 25), so we may reason that it just happened that experimenters who intended to use strong visual cues also sometimes used pigmented rats to take advantage of their superior vision. The pigmentation of the rat cannot be shown to have any other effect on place and response dominance.

The noncorrection procedure (picking up the rat after an error) seems to lead to better response learning than the correction procedure (allowing the rat to find the food by retracing after an error). Using the place-response studies, the effects of correction cannot be isolated from the visual cue effects mentioned above.

One study (21) indicates that response learning is slowed by massing trials. Little more about massing effects in these studies is known, but most of the studies employ at least moderate trial spacing.

There seems to be no interesting relation between place-vs.-response dominance and either the ages of rats used or the size of the maze employed. The slight tendency for smaller mazes to go with response dominance is more than explained by the tendency of experimenters using domes to use slightly smaller mazes for convenience.

Evaluation of the Place-vs.-Response Controversy

The details of the single-unit T maze experiments quite clearly indicate that there is nothing in the nature of a rat which makes it a "place" or "response" learner. The main factor determining the outcome of place-vs.-response experiments is the amount of extra-maze visual stimulation which differentiates the region around and behind one goal from the region around and behind the other. Such visual cues are relevant in place learning and irrelevant in response learning.

It seems reasonable to conclude that the place-vs.-response controversy, which seemed ill formulated when compared above with earlier maze studies, gives a distorted and confusing interpretation of the experiments designed to settle it.

It should be remarked that in single-unit mazes, kinesthetic cues appear sufficient to support quite rapid learning. This conflicts with Honzik's conclusion that "when all other avenues of stimulation are destroyed, kinaesthesis is helpless" (8, p. 56). Honzik's statement, if taken as applying generally to all mazes including single-unit ones, would be incorrect. The importance of a sense modality depends on the richness and relevance of stimuli in that modality which exist in the maze situation. In single-unit mazes, relevant kinesthetic stimuli apparently abound. In Honzik's 14-unit maze, animals do not make regular enough runs to give themselves a constant set of kinesthetic stimuli on which to build accurate performance. One may also consider Hunter's point that in complex mazes, with left and right turns required in irregular order, simple kinesthetic cues are irrelevant. Attempts to state the relative importance of sense modalities or of intra- and extra-maze cues in general, for all mazes, are akin to the "place-vs.-response" hypothesis in that they fail to incorporate the most important variable, the stimulus situation presented to the animal. Such attempts are, accordingly, doomed to failure.

PREDICTION OF T-MAZE DATA BY THE QUANTITATIVE THEORY OF DISCRIMINATION LEARNING

The single-unit T maze, being devoid of the serial characteristics of more complex mazes, may be thought of as a kind of discrimination-learning apparatus. When the T maze is rotated on random trials as in place-response experiments, extra-maze (place) and kinesthetic (response) cues are uncorrelated.[3] In place learning (see

[3] If the whole maze is rotated as a unit, intra-maze cues are relevant in response learning and are confounded with kinesthetic cues. If the starting stem is moved but the cross-arm is left in place, intra-maze cues are relevant in place learning, and are confounded with extra-maze cues. We shall assume that intra-maze cues combine additively with the cues they are correlated with, and shall not specify what happens to them.

Fig. 1) place cues are relevant, and all others including responses cues are irrelevant. In response learning, response cues are relevant and all others including place cues are irrelevant. In place + response learning, with a fixed maze, both place and response cues are relevant.

We may entertain the hypothesis of cue-additivity; that the set of cues relevant in place + response learning is simply the sum of the place and response cues. This hypothesis can be tested quantitatively, using a theory of discrimination learning (15). In this theory, the rate of learning is set equal to the proportion of relevant cues, and the single number is called θ. The learning curve (or statistics such as total errors to mastery, total errors in n trials, trials-to-criterion, etc.) may be used to estimate θ: and, conversely, given θ the learning curve or any of its statistics can be computed in advance of experimentation. The equations involved and the methods of computation will not be repeated here.

TABLE 1

Median trials to 10-out-of-10 criterion and proportion of relevant cues (θ) in the Galanter-Shaw Experiment

Relevant Cues	Observed		Predicted	
	Trials	θ	Trials	θ
Place	5.0	.34	—	—
Response	33.5	.10	—	—
Place + Response	2.0	.58	3.1	.44

Galanter and Shaw (5) used three groups of rats trained in the same apparatus and surround, under conditions of place learning, response learning, and fixed-maze or place + response learning, respectively. Using median trials-to-criterion[4] as an index of typical performance, the

---

[4] Since retracing and "false-start" responses were counted as errors, animals had a higher probability of making an error than a correct response at the beginning of training. This bias in favor of errors has relatively little effect on trials-to-criterion, which is accordingly used as an index of performance. The parameter θ is estimated from trials-to-criterion by an approximation to the maximum likelihood method.

proportion of relevant cues in each problem was computed, using the equations of discrimination-learning theory. Theoretically, the proportion of relevant cues in the place + response problem should be the sum of the proportions in the other problems: $\theta_{P+R} = \theta_P + \theta_R$. The results of the computations to check this hypothesis are shown in Table 1. Place + response performance is predicted using only data from the place and response groups. Inspection of Table 1 indicates that the prediction is relatively accurate, although, since subjects in the place + response group ranged in trials-to-criterion from 0 to 3, the prediction is at the edge of the obtained distribution of scores.[5]

Scharlock (20) used a maze in a dome with either one light behind one goal or lights behind both. If there was one light it was the only source of differential place cues, so if there were two lights there were no place cues. Scharlock ran place, response, and place + response groups with one light. He also had a control group which made no progress on place learning with both lights— an expected result confirming that with a light behind each goal there were no place cues. One other group, which we may call "response-minus-place," learned a response with both lights on, and thus with no place cues available. Here again we can predict that the place + response group will yield a learning rate, θ_{P+R}, which is the sum of the rates of the place and response groups, $\theta_P + \theta_R$. In addition, the learning rate of the response-minus-place group should be faster than that of the response group, because of the elimination of irrelevant place cues. Since θ_P is the proportion of differential place cues, it follows theoretically that $\theta_{R-P} = \theta_R/(1 - \theta_P)$. The results of computations to check these hypotheses are shown in Table 2. Inspection of Table 2 shows that the predictions are quite accurate. The discrepancies between predictions and observations are not statistically significant.

[5] Dr. Galanter, in a personal communication, noted that the place + response group was run after the other parts of the experiment were completed. In Galanter's opinion, the experimenters were by this time somewhat more skillful, and the place + response group had an advantage. This might account for the discrepancy between prediction and observation.

A third experiment by Blodgett, McCutchan, and Mathews (3) separates location and direction cues. The rat may approach the same location (for instance, the center of the room) from either of two directions if the maze is shifted appropriately. Location and direction are usually lumped as place cues, but in this experiment they

TABLE 2

Errors in 28 trials and proportion of relevant cues (θ) in the Scharlock Experiment

Relevant Cues	Observed		Predicted	
	Errors	θ	Errors	θ
Place	5.53	.216*	—	—
Response	3.84	.296	—	—
Place learning, no place cues (2 lights)	17.50	.000	—	—
Place + Response	2.28	.445	2.00	.512
Response — Place: no place cues (2 lights)	2.84	.366	2.66	.378

* Because of initial biases, the probability of correct response on the first trial is estimated at about .375 for all groups. The correction is made in the fashion shown in (16).

are separated. Seven groups constitute the experiment, with one group learning each problem possible: location, direction, response, all combinations of two relevant, and the combination of all three relevant (fixed maze learning).

The data were reported in terms of "cycles," pairs of trials, which contained at least one error. From this it is not possible to make good estimates of θ, but an effort has been made to attain fair approximations. The estimates, and the corresponding predictions made by adding θ-values of problems with fewer relevant cues, are shown in Table 3. The results seem quite encouraging, under the circumstances.

SUMMARY AND CONCLUSIONS

Consideration of early studies of the sensory basis of maze learning, and review of place-vs.-response experiments, indicate that:

(1) There is nothing in the nature of a rat which makes it a "place" learner, or a "response" learner. A rat in a maze will use all relevant cues, and the importance of any class of cues depends on the amount of relevant stimulation provided as well as the sensory capacities of the animal. In place-response experiments, the importance of place cues depends on the amount of differential extra-maze stimulation.

(2) A multiple-cue theory of maze learning is successful in comprehending the major results of experiments using complex mazes, and the detailed results of place-response experiments using single-unit T mazes.

(3) Useful refinements of classical multiple-cue theory

TABLE 3

Proportion of relevant cues (θ) estimated and predicted in the Blodgett, McCutchan, and Mathews Experiment

Relevant Cues	Estimated θ	Predicted θ
Location	.02	—
Direction	.11	—
Response	.08	—
Location + Direction	.13	.13
Location + Response	.10	.10
Direction + Response	.13	.18
Location + Direction + Response	.18	.21

were taken from discrimination-learning theory. These are that irrelevant cues are adapted during learning, and that the rate of learning depends on the *proportion* of relevant cues.

(4) Quantitative analysis of the results of certain place-response experiments indicates that place and re-

sponse cues combine additively in the place + response (fixed maze) problem.

The writer's general conclusion is that further "definitive" studies of the place-vs.-response controversy, to prove that rats are by nature either place or response learners, would be fruitless since the issue is incorrectly drawn. However, use of the T maze to analyze the stimuli in maze learning holds promise of yielding a consistent quantitative account of how rats find their way. Such studies can build on the earlier work on more complex mazes.

REFERENCES

1. BLODGETT, H. C., & McCUTCHAN, K., Place versus response learning in the simple T-maze. *J. exp. Psychol.*, 1947, 37, 412-422.
2. BLODGETT, H. C., & McCUTCHAN, K., Relative strength of place and response learning in the T maze. *J. comp. physiol. Psychol.*, 1948, 41, 17-24.
3. BLODGETT, H. C., McCUTCHAN, K., & MATHEWS, R., Spatial learning in the T-maze: the influence of direction, turn, and food location. *J. exp. Psychol.*, 1949, 39, 800-809.
4. GALANTER, E. H., Place and response learning: learning to alternate. *J. comp. physiol. Psychol.*, 1955, 49, 17-18.
5. GALANTER, E. H., & SHAW, W. A., "Cue" vs. "reactive inhibition" in place and response learning. *J. comp. physiol. Psychol.*, 1954, 47, 395-398.
6. GLANZER, M., The role of stimulus satiation in response alternation. *J. exp. Psychol.*, 1953, 45, 387-393.
7. HILL, C. W., & THUNE, L. E., Place and response learning in the white rat under simplified and mutually isolated conditions. *J. exp. Psychol.*, 1952, 43, 289-297.
8. HONZIK, C. H., The sensory basis of maze learning in rats. *Comp. Psychol. Monogr.*, 1936, 13, 1-113.
9. HUNTER, W. S., The sensory control of the maze habit in the white rat. *J. genet. Psychol.*, 1929, 36, 505-537.
10. HUNTER, W. S., A further consideration of the sensory control of the maze habit in the white rat. *J. genet. Psychol.*, 1930, 38, 3-19.
11. HUNTER, W. S., A consideration of Lashley's theory of the equipotentiality of cerebral action. *J. gen. Psychol.*, 1930, 3, 455-468.
12. McCUTCHAN, K., RETHLINGSHAFER, D., & NICHOLS, J. W., The role of response and place learning under alternating

hunger and thirst drives. *J. comp. physiol. Psychol.*, 1951, 44, 269-275.

13. MONTGOMERY, K. C., A test of two explanations of spontaneous alternation. *J. comp. physiol. Psychol.*, 1952, 45, 287-293.

14. MUNN, N. L., *Handbook of psychological research on the rat*. New York: Houghton Mifflin, 1950.

15. RESTLE, F., A theory of discrimination learning. *Psychol. Rev.*, 1955, 62, 11-19.

16. RESTLE, F., Theory of selective learning with probable reinforcements. *Psychol. Rev.*, 1957, 64, 182-191.

17. RITCHIE, B. F., Studies in spatial learning: III. Two paths to the same location and two paths to different locations. *J. exp. Psychol.*, 1947, 37, 25-38.

18. RITCHIE, B. F., AESCHLIMAN, B., & PEIRCE, P., Studies in spatial learning: VIII. Place performance and the acquisition of place dispositions. *J. comp. physiol. Psychol.*, 1950, 43, 73-85.

19. RITCHIE, B. F., HAY, A., & HARE, R., Studies in spatial learning: IX. A dispositional analysis of response performance. *J. comp. physiol. Psychol.*, 1951, 44, 442-449.

20. SCHARLOCK, D. P., The role of extramaze cues in place and response learning. *J. exp. Psychol.*, 1955, 50, 249-254.

21. THOMPSON, M. E., & THOMPSON, J. P., Reactive inhibition factor in maze learning: II. The role of reactive inhibition in studies of place learning versus response learning. *J. exp. Psychol.*, 1949, 39, 883-891.

22. TOLMAN, E. C., & GLEITMAN, H., Studies in spatial learning: VII. Place and response learning under different conditions of motivation. *J. exp. Psychol.*, 1949, 39, 653-659.

23. TOLMAN, E. C., RITCHIE, B. F., & KALISH, D., Studies in spatial learning: II. Place learning versus response learning. *J. exp. Psychol.*, 1946, 35, 221-229.

24. TOLMAN, E. C., RITCHIE, B. F., & KALISH, D., Studies in spatial learning: V. Response learning vs. place learning by the non-correction method. *J. exp. Psychol.*, 1947, 37, 285-292.

25. WADDEL, D., GANS, S., KEMPNER, P., & WILLIAMS, A., A comparison of place and response learning in very young rats. *J. comp. physiol. Psychol.*, 1955, 48, 375-377.

26. WALKER, E. L., DEMBER, W. N., EARL, R. W., & KAROLY, A. J., Choice alternation: I. Stimulus vs. place vs. response. *J. comp. physiol. Psychol.*, 1955, 48, 19-23.

27. WEBB, W. B., A study in place and response learning as a discrimination behavior. *J. comp. physiol. Psychol.*, 1951, 44, 263-268.

2

A Theory of Emotionally Based Drive (D) and Its Relation to Performance in Simple Learning Situations*

KENNETH W. SPENCE

State University of Iowa

A number of years ago we instituted at the University of Iowa a series of experiments concerned with the role of aversive motivational factors in learning situations. In addition to the more usual direct manipulation of variables influencing the motivational state of an individual, such, for example, as varying the intensity of a noxious stimulus, degree of motivation was also varied in these studies by employing selected subjects who differed in terms of their performance on a so-called scale of emotional responsiveness or manifest anxiety (31). That these experiments have aroused considerable interest among both clinical and experimental psychologists is readily evident, not only from the large number of published studies that have attempted either to check or extend our experimental findings, but also from the not infrequent critical reactions they have elicited. Now, while some of the criticisms directed against our studies undoubtedly have merit, it has been rather dismaying to discover the extent to which many of them reflect a serious lack of understanding of the structure and purpose of the basic theoretical framework underlying the experiments.

* From *The American Psychologist*, 1958, 13, 131-141, and used here with the permission of the author and the American Psychological Association.

While some of the responsibility for this failure to understand the nature and objectives of the theory can be assigned to the critics, I hasten to acknowledge that our theoretical treatments have been quite inadequate. The major difficulty is that the studies have appeared only in experimental journals in which space limitations have required that theoretical discussions be kept to a minimum. Since each article tended to limit the discussion to those portions of the theory relevant to the particular phenomena being reported, the theory has been presented only in a very piecemeal fashion. Apparently our hope that the interested reader, particularly the critic, would familiarize himself with the theory as a whole by considering all of the articles has not been realized.

THEORETICAL SCHEMA

One of the purposes of this paper is to provide a more systematic presentation of our basic theory, or, to use an expression recently introduced by Cronbach and Meehl (4), of the nomological network underlying our studies. Following this the experimental evidence bearing on the theory will be presented and discussed. Fig. 1 presents

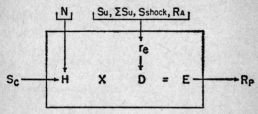

Fig. 1. *Diagram representing portion of theoretical schema relevant to data for classical conditioning.* (*See text for explanation of symbols.*)

the main concepts employed, at least in so far as one kind of learning situation, classical conditioning, is concerned. At the top of the figure are shown the experimentally manipulated independent variables such as N, the number of paired conditioning trials; S_u, the unconditioned stimulus; ΣS_u, the number of previous presentations of the unconditioned stimulus; R_A, score on the anxiety or emotional responsiveness scale. The empirical response measure at the lower right-hand corner is the dependent variable. Inside the rectangle are represented the several theoretical concepts (intervening variables) and the interrelations assumed among them. The arrows indicate the functions relating the dependent response measure to the intervening variables, and the latter to the experimentally manipulated variables. Details of the portion of the theory between the intervening variable E and the empirical response measure (R_p), involving such theoretical concepts as oscillatory inhibition and response threshold, have been omitted since our present purpose does not require them. It is sufficient to state that response frequency (R_p) is some positive monotonic function of excitatory potential E.

That the schema presented in Fig. 1 conforms to the Cronbach and Meehl concept of a nomological net is readily apparent. Thus to quote these writers: "The laws in a nomological network may relate (a) observable properties or quantities to each other; or (b) theoretical constructs to observables; or (c) different theoretical constructs to one another" (4, p. 290). One may readily find examples in our schema of each of these "laws," or as I would prefer to call them, "relations," since the term "law" typically has a narrower meaning than these authors have given it.

The theory takes its start from Hull's basic assumption that the excitatory potential, E, determining the strength of a response is a multiplicative function of a learning factor, H, and a generalized drive factor, D, i.e., $E = H \times D$ (9). We have assumed, further, that the drive level, D, in the case of aversive situations at least, is a function of the magnitude or strength of a hypothetical response mechanism—a persisting emotional response in the organism, designated as r_e, that is aroused by any form of aversive stimulation. That is, aversive, stressful stimulation is assumed to arouse activity under the control of the autonomic nervous system, which, according to some neurophysiological evidence, may act as an energizer of cortical mechanisms. Those of you who are familiar with the theoretical writings of Miller (13) and Mowrer (14) will recognize that this mechanism is similar to one these writers have postulated in connection with their investigations of acquired motivation. Thus they assumed that aversive stimuli arouse a hypothetical pain (emotional) response which, when conditioned to previously neutral stimulus events, provides the basis for an acquired drive of fear.

On the basis of analogy with overt reflexes to noxious stimulation, there were a number of properties that could be assigned to our hypothetical response mechanism. Three, in particular, will be discussed here. The first and most obvious is based on our knowledge that the magnitude or strength of observable reflexes to noxious stimulation (e.g., the corneal reflex to an air puff, the GSR to an electric shock) varies directly with the intensity or degree of noxiousness of the stimulus. Assuming our hypothetical emotional response, r_e, would exhibit the same property, it followed that the level of drive, D, present in classical defense conditioning would be a positive function of the intensity of the US. From the remaining portion of the theory, it could be deduced that the performance level, e.g., frequency of CR's, would vary positively with the intensity of the US employed. At the time of the original formulation of our theory there was some evidence, in particular an experiment by Passey (15), which supported this implication of the theory.

A second implication of our hypothetical mechanism was based on the adaptive property of observable reflexes to noxious stimuli: namely, that such responses characteristically exhibit adaptation or weakening with repeated stimulation. On the assumption that our hypothetical emotional response would behave in an analogous manner, it followed that, if a series of trials employing the US alone were given *prior* to conditioning, a lower level of D would be present during the subsequent conditioning than if no such adaptation trials were given. But if D were lower, the level of performance in the conditioning situation would also be lower following such adaptation trials than without them. This assumption or hypothesis, if you wish, is represented in Fig. 1 by $r_e = f\ (\Sigma S_u)$. At the time of formulation of the theory, we found a study by MacDonald (12) that gave results precisely in line with this implication.

The third implication of our theoretical mechanism was based on the well-known fact or observation that individuals differ in the magnitude of their reflex responses to a given intensity of stimulation. By analogy, again, we were led to assume that individuals would differ characteristically in the magnitude of this response, r_e, to the same intensity of stressful stimulation. If now there were available some means of assessing differences in this emotional responsiveness of individuals, our theoretical schema would lead to the prediction that highly emotional subjects, as assessed by the measuring device, would exhibit a higher level of performance in aversive forms of conditioning than subjects who scored low on the device.

The problem thus became one of attempting to develop a test for identifying individual differences in the responsiveness of this hypothetical emotional mechanism. Such a test, of course, would have to be defined independently of the measures that were to be employed in testing the theoretical network, i.e., the measures of performance in conditioning and other learning situations. It was in connection with this portion of our theory that the Manifest Anxiety or A-scale was developed. The idea of using a self-inventory test that would differentiate subjects in terms of the degree to which they admitted to possessing overt or manifest symptoms of emotionality was suggested by Taylor in a doctoral dissertation (30).

At this point I should like to make a methodological digression and comment on a criticism recently made concerning this aspect of our research. One pair of critics, inspired, but unfortunately not too enlightened, by the excellent article of Cronbach and Meehl (4) on construct validity, insisted that we should have developed our scale for measuring D on the basis of a theory so that, and I quote them, "performance on it might be a basis for inferring drive (differences) independently of the outcome of subsequent experiments" (10, p. 162). While there are a number of highly questionable methodological points in the arguments of these critics, I should like to call attention here merely to the fact that it is simply not true that no theorizing guided us in the development of the A-scale. As has just been recounted, we did have some very definite theoretical notions as to what lay behind differences in level of generalized drive, D, especially in the case of classical defense types of conditioning.

This theory, that D is a function of the strength of the emotional response made by the organism to the noxious stimulation, had already received considerable support. Its extension in the present instance to the individual difference variable logically demanded that we measure the emotional responsiveness of individuals under comparable environmental conditions. Naturally, so-called physiological indices of emotionality, such as, for example, changes in pulse rate or in the GSR, were indicated; and we have conducted some research along this line. However, it occurred to Taylor that it might be both interesting and valuable to investigate the possibility of making use of the presumed behavioral symptoms of emotionality that clinicians have described. That the questionnaire type of test developed turned out as well as it apparently has is to the credit, I think, of the clinical psychologists who selected the behavioral items as indicative of emotionally over-reactive individuals.

In this connection a further comment is in order concerning a surprising question that was asked by these same critics. Thus the problem was posed as to what the consequences would have been for either the theory or the test had the experiments using the A-scale been negative. The answer to the question, at least regards the theory, should be obvious. The implications of the other portions of our theory with respect to our response mechanism, r_e, were sufficiently well confirmed that we would have had no hesitancy about abandoning the A-scale as being related to D in our theory. Since, however, the implications of this aspect of our theoretical net were confirmed, we have continued to employ the A-scale as one operational definition of this emotional responsiveness variable. That a more satisfactory scale, even one of this questionnaire type, can be developed, I have no doubt. Indeed, I would recommend that some of the time and energy now being squandered in the many distorted, even mendacious, criticisms that seem to find such ready acceptance in our current discussion-type journals be directed at this more constructive task. If the main purpose of these attacks is to discredit and eliminate the theory, they will fail in this objective, for the history of science clearly reveals that a theory is usually discarded only when a better theory is advanced. The same goes for the constructs within a theory.

EXPERIMENTAL EVIDENCE

With these methodological remarks out of the way, let us turn now to the experimental evidence bearing on our

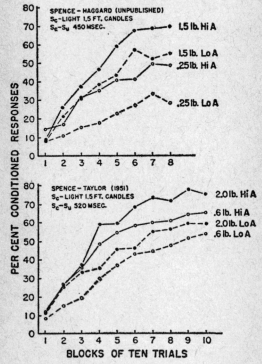

Fig. 2. *Performance in eyelid conditioning as function of A-score and intensity of US.*

theoretical schema. I shall spend the major part of my limited space presenting and discussing the findings of our eyelid conditioning experiments, for it was in connection with data from this type of learning situation that the schema was originally formulated. With regard to performance curves of conditioning, e.g., frequency curves, the implications of the theory are, as we have seen, that level of performance will be a positive function of (a) the intensity of the US, (b) the level of score on the A-scale, and (c) the intensity of an extra stressful stimulation. We shall take up the first two of these variables together; since space is so limited, I shall present only those studies which had the largest sample of subjects and hence have provided the most reliable and stable data.

Eyelid Conditioning Experiments

In Fig. 2 are presented the findings of two experiments (one unpublished; the other, 27), one of which involved 120 subjects and the other 100 subjects. Both studies employed two levels of puff intensity, .6 lb. and 2.0 lbs./sq. in., in the one represented in the lower graph; .25 lb. and 1.5 lbs./sq. in., in the upper graph. Each study also involved two levels of emotionality (upper and lower 20% of subjects on the A-scale). Examination of the curves in both graphs shows clearly that at each of the four puff intensities, the High A group (shown by solid curves) was well above the Low A group (broken curves). Statistical analysis over all of the conditioning trials revealed the differences were significant at the .01 level in the lower graph and at the .025 level in the upper.[1]

A second point to be noted in these data is relevant to the assumption that the learning or habit factor (H) and the drive factor (D) combine in a multiplicative manner to determine response strength. This assumption leads to the further implication that frequency curves of conditioning for different values of the anxiety variable will

[1] Since unequal numbers of each sex were used in both of these studies and because women consistently exhibit a greater difference than men, the curves have been weighted equally for male and female subjects.

exhibit a gradual divergence over the course of training.[2] That this prediction was borne out may be seen by inspecting the graphs. Statistical confirmation of the divergence is revealed by the fact that the trials-×-anxiety interaction terms for both sets of data were highly significant (.005 and .025 levels).

The findings with respect to the intensity of US variable also supported the implications of our theory. Thus it may be seen in both studies that the subjects that had the strong puff performed at a higher level than those with the weak puff. The divergence between the curves is also apparent.

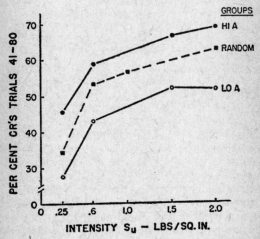

Fig. 3. *Showing relation between conditioning performance and intensity of US for unselected and high and low A-score subjects.*

As an indication of the stability of our findings involving these two experimental variables, Fig. 3 presents data from these same two studies along with some relevant data from four other investigations recently conducted in

---

[2] This prediction must be qualified to the extent that the frequency measure has a ceiling of 100% and thus may not always reflect the continued growth of E. This is particularly the case at high levels of D in which E also is high.

our laboratory (26). Shown on the ordinate of this graph are the percentage of CR's given in the block of Trials 41-80 as a function of the intensity of the unconditioned stimulus employed. The uppermost curve in this graph represents the results for subjects selected from the high end of the A-scale; the lowest curve, subjects selected from the low end. The middle curve represents data obtained in four different experiments in which unselected subjects, so far as A-score, were conditioned under highly comparable conditions to those used with the selected subjects (i.e., similar visual CS and very comparable S_c-S_u intervals). The consistency of the results from experiment to experiment, particularly the relation of the curve for the unselected subjects to those for the High and Low A subjects, is, I believe, quite impressive.

In addition to the data presented in these graphs, four other investigations have reported finding that High A subjects responded at a significantly higher level than Low A subjects in eyelid conditioning (21, 22, 28, 30). One additional study (8) also found superior performance by High A subjects, although the difference in this instance was not significant. A reasonable interpretation of the failure to obtain a significant difference in this latter study, especially to anyone familiar with the variability of individual conditioning data, is that there were only ten subjects in each group.

Mention was made earlier of the fact that in addition to the anxiety scale we have also attempted to employ a number of physiological measures as further operational definitions of our emotional responsiveness variable. One of the most discouraging aspects of this work has been the lack of consistency, i.e., unreliability from day to day, of such measures. Especially has this been the case with the GSR, on which, unfortunately, we concentrated most of our time and energy. Recently, however, we have obtained results (to be published) with these measures that are rather more promising. Using changes in GSR and heart rate made to a mildly noxious stimulus and converting the measures into a so-called autonomic lability score by means of a formula suggested by Lacey (11), two groups of subjects who fell in the upper and lower third of the distribution of such scores were subsequently conditioned. Shown in Fig. 4 are the frequency curves of eye-lid conditioning for these two groups of subjects. As may be seen, the subjects with the high autonomic lability index performed at a higher level than those with a low index. The difference is significant at the .02 level.

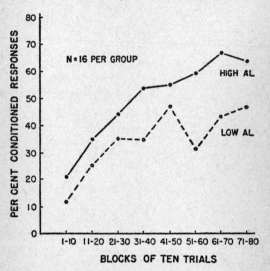

Fig. 4. *Percentage of CR's for the high and low autonomic lability* (AL) *groups in blocks of ten trials.*

In addition to varying performance by manipulating the A-scale and US variables, it should be possible to produce a higher level of conditioning performance by presenting a strong extra stimulus, such as an electric shock, during the course of conditioning. Similarly, after a subject has experienced a strong electric shock just prior to conditioning, the mere threat of further shocks during the conditioning should arouse a strong and persisting emotional response that would raise the level of D and hence the level of performance. We have already published the results of one such experiment with unselected subjects which corroborated, in part, these theoretical expectations (25).

Recently a further experiment (to be published) study-

ing the effects of shock threat on High and Low A subjects was completed in our laboratory. Some idea of the
nature of the findings can be gained from Fig. 5 which

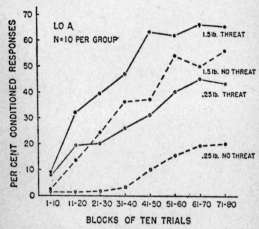

Fig. 5. *Percentage of CR's in blocks of ten trials as a function
of shock or no-shock threat and intensity of the US for
subjects who score low on A-scale.*

presents the frequency curves of conditioning for four
groups of Low A subjects (20th percentile). The two top
curves in this graph are for subjects conditioned with a
relatively strong air puff (1.5 lbs./sq. in.); the lower two,
for subjects who had a weak puff (.25 lb./sq. in.). It will
be seen that at both puff levels the threatened group
(solid curve) was consistently above the nonthreatened
group (broken curve) throughout the whole 80 trials. A
similar experiment with high anxious subjects revealed a
difference between the threat and nonthreat groups
throughout the conditioning in the case of groups which
had a weak puff. In the strong puff groups, however, the
curves for the threat and nonthreat group, after separating in the early trials, came together in the later stages of
the conditioning (last 40 trials). This latter effect undoubtedly results, in part, from the ceiling imposed by
the frequency measure.

Space will not permit a detailed presentation of the experimental evidence with respect to that portion of our theory concerned with the assumption that the emotional response to the noxious US would be weaker if adaptation trials are given prior to conditioning. It is sufficient to state that the original finding of MacDonald (12), that such preadapted subjects exhibited a lower level of performance in conditioning than nonadapted subjects, has been corroborated by Taylor (32). The latter experimenter also found that conditioning performance was inversely related to the intensity of the US employed during the preconditioning adaptation period. Thus the implications of this part of the theoretical network have also received further support.

The final set of conditioning data that I would like to present are concerned with the effect of level of D on differential conditioning. Without going into the theoretical derivation, it may be shown that one of the implications of our theory is that the higher the drive level, D, of the subjects, the greater should be the differentiation between the positive and the negative, i.e., nonreinforced, stimulus in such differential conditioning. Two studies from our laboratory have reported finding that, in five separate comparisons, high anxious subjects showed better discrimination than low anxious subjects (21, 23). Although none of the differences were significant, four closely approached being so. More recently we have investigated the effect of varying the level of D on differential conditioning by direct manipulation of the intensity of the US. The graph in Fig. 6 presents the findings of this study (17) in terms of the frequency of CR's given to the two stimuli, positive and negative. As may be seen, the subjects conditioned with the strong US not only showed a higher level of response to the positive and negative stimuli, but, as predicted from our theory, the difference between the conditioned responses to the two stimuli was greater in the case of the group that had the strong US. Again this latter difference approached, but did not quite reach, statistical significance. Unfortunately, conditioning data are plagued by high individual variability, produced in part by a few subjects who show very little or no conditioning. In an effort to ascertain what the finding would be for subjects who showed considerable conditioning, a separate analysis was made of the upper two-thirds of each of the two groups run in the experiment. In the case of these subjects discrimination was significantly better for the high drive group at the .05 level.

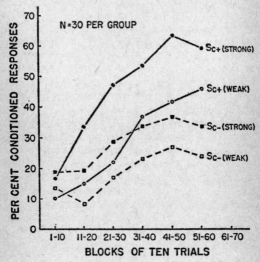

Fig. 6. Percentage of CR's to the positive and negative stimuli for groups conditioned with a strong and weak US.

So much for the findings in our eyelid conditioning studies. On the whole, we believe they are in fair accord with our theoretical schema, including the portion of it that involves the A-scale. While not all of the results have met acceptable levels of significance, the fact that the direction of the differences in such instances has almost invariably been in accord with the theory has encouraged us to continue to hold to it. Attention might also be called here to the fact that this theoretical model, particularly the hypothetical emotional response mechanism, has also been quite successful in connection with a wide variety of other behavioral situations involving noxious stimulation with animals. Examples are to be found in the many studies cited by Miller (13) on the motivating and reinforcing roles of acquired fear in learning situations. The experiments of a number of investigators on the persisting motivational effects of emotionality aroused by electric shock on the consummatory behavior of rats provide yet another example (1, 2, 18, 19).

Complex Human Learning

Turning now to our studies involving the more complex types of human learning, let me begin by saying that it is in this area that the limitations of space in experimental journals for theoretical elaboration have been most unfortunate. Certainly we recognize that these treatments have been quite inadequate, particularly from the point of view of discussing the many factors that complicate efforts at theorizing in this area. By way of example let me mention two important points that need to be recognized but, unfortunately, have not always been so.

First, it should be realized that in order to derive implications concerning the effects of drive variation in any type of complex learning task, it is necessary to have, in addition to the drive theory, a further theoretical network concerning the variables and their interaction that are involved in the particular learning activity. It is perhaps unnecessary to point out here that theoretical schemas for such types of learning are as yet in a very primitive state of development, indeed almost nonexistent. As a consequence of this, one has considerable difficulty in drawing conclusions about the motivational part of the new, combined theory from supposedly negative findings, for the defect may be in the part of the network specifying the action of the variables in the complex learning situation.

The second point is that our theory of the mechanism underlying D was developed in connection with experimental situations involving some form of noxious stimulation. Complex human learning tasks, on the other hand, typically do not involve the use of a noxious stimulus. Whatever stress is present in these situations is usually produced by instructions that aim to create in the subject the desire or need to make as good a showing as possible. While it is true that this stress may be greatly augmented by introducing failure or punishment into the situation, so far as the usual type of human learning experiment is concerned, the question as to whether High A subjects would be more emotional than Low A subjects, and hence have a higher D level, is a moot one. In this connection two alternative subhypotheses have been proposed: (a) the chronic hypothesis: that High A subjects react emotionally in a chronic manner to all situations, whether stressful or not; and (b) the emotional reactivity hypothesis: that High A subjects have a lower threshold of emotional responsiveness and react with a stronger emotional response than Low A subjects to situations containing some degree of stress (16, 20, 25). As may be seen, according to the first of these hypotheses, mild non-threatening situations would produce a differential drive (D) level in subjects scoring at extremes of the scale; whereas according to the second, there would not be a difference. These two examples are sufficient, I believe, to point up the fact that the problems involved in the extension of the theory to these more complex types of learning are quite formidable and that at this stage there necessarily must be a considerable amount of trial and error in our theorizing.

Now it will be recalled that the theoretical schema presented in Fig. 1 assumed that in classical conditioning habit strength to but a single response was established to the CS. In this circumstance, as we have seen, an increase in drive level implied an increase in response strength. In more complex, selective learning tasks, on the other hand, there are, typically, a hierarchy of competing response tendencies. Actually most of the complex learning situations employed with humans involve a number or sequence of such response hierarchies which involve competing responses, e.g., a number of choice points in the maze, whether verbal or spatial. To show what the implications of variation of drive level will be in such competing response situations, let us begin by considering the simplest conceivable case: one in which there is but a single response hierarchy involving two alternative responses. The single choice point maze involving turning left or right is one example of such a situation. If now the habit strength of the correct to-be-learned response is, at the beginning of the learning, somewhat stronger than that of the incorrect response, it may be shown that the higher the drive level, D, the greater will the difference between the competing excitatory potentials be and, *neglecting all other considerations*, the higher should be the percentage of correct responses at the start of learning, the sooner should the learning criterion be attained, and the smaller should be the total number of errors.[3]

The reverse situation, that in which the correct response is at the outset weaker than the incorrect one, is, from the theoretical viewpoint, even more complex. In this instance the stronger the drive, the greater will be the percent choice of the wrong response, or, in other words, the poorer will be the performance at this initial stage. But, as training proceeds, sooner or later the habit strength of the correct, reinforced response will overtake that of the wrong, unreinforced response and from this point on the percent choice of the correct response should in general be higher for the high drive group than for the low drive group. In other words, the performance curves should be expected to cross. Precise predictions about the total number of errors, number of trials, etc. in this situation will depend to a considerable extent upon the particular functions and parameter values assigned to

[3] As discussed in my Silliman Lectures (21), there are a number of other considerations that need to be taken into account in extending the theory to such competing response situations. Thus the particular composition rule (law) assumed in these lectures to describe the manner in which the competing responses interacted with each other led to the implication that the percentage of occurrence of the competing responses is a function, not only of the magnitude of the difference between the competing Es, but also of their absolute level above the threshold L. As a consequence in the low range of E values, there may actually be an inverse relation between performance level (percent choice of the response with stronger E) and the level of drive. Still other considerations involve whether habit strength (H) in learning situations is or is not assumed to be dependent on the reinforcer and whether drive strength (D) determines the inhibitory factor (I_n). Different combinations of these alternative assumptions, including even other possible composition rules, lead to different behavior consequences. Critical evaluation of the different conceivable theoretical models will require considerably more empirical data obtained under a wide variety of experimental conditions than is now available.

the assumed habit and inhibitory factors. Actually we have never got around to working out in detail the implications of the various possibilities for the total learning period even in this simplest case.

Recalling now that such a learning task as the serial verbal or spatial maze involves a number of such competing response hierarchies, we see that the problem of predicting the effect on performance of variation of the drive in such situations becomes even more complicated. On the assumption that anticipatory and perseverative associative tendencies would develop in such a manner as to make the incorrect response the stronger in the case of many of the choice points of a maze, it was hoped that it would be possible to demonstrate that high drive (i.e., High A) subjects would perform more poorly in such serial learning situations than low drive (i.e., Low A) subjects. Two experiments, one with a verbal form of maze (35) and one using a finger maze (5) actually did provide results in agreement with this theoretical expectation. However, as was pointed out at the time, there was a serious discrepancy between the theory and the obtained results in these studies in that the anxious subjects made more errors at all but one of the choice points in both studies. In view of the ease of learning many of these choice points, and hence evidence for little or no strong competing response tendencies, the theory would have led us to expect that the High A subjects would have made fewer errors on them than the Low A subjects. Obviously the theory was wrong in some respect, but just in what way—an incorrect assumption or failure to include an important relevant variable—was not clear.

At this point in our work we realized that such serial learning tasks are, for a variety of reasons, quite unsatisfactory. Among the most important from our viewpoint was the fact that one has little or no knowledge of the relative strengths of the competing responses in each of the hierarchies. Accordingly we abandoned this type of situation and attempted to develop learning tasks in which it would be possible to specify or manipulate in some known manner the relative strengths of the competing responses in each hierarchy. Probably the chief value of these earlier experiments is that they did point up the

fact that a higher anxiety score (and hence possibly a
higher drive level) does not necessarily always lead to a
higher level of performance.

Among the types of learning problems that we turned
to was paired-associates learning. This type of learning
task may be conceived as consisting of the formation of
a set of more or less isolated S-R associations or habit
tendencies. In one type of list, which we have referred to
as a noncompetitive list, an attempt is made to isolate
as much as possible the paired items by minimizing the
degree of synonymity or formal similarity among both the
stimulus and response words. As learning proceeds and
the habit strengths of the stimulus words to their paired
response words increase, high drive subjects should, according to our theory, perform at a higher level than low
drive subjects. An important condition in this derivation
is that the associative connections between each stimulus
word and the nonpaired response words are lower than
that to the paired response word.

Two lists of this type have been employed. In one the
associative connections between the paired words were
initially zero or at least very low. In this type of list it
would be predicted that there would be little or no difference between high and low drive subjects at the start of
learning, but that as learning progressed the curve of correct responses would diverge, that for the high drive group
being the higher. Using nonsense syllables of low association value and low intralist similarity, Taylor has reported
two experiments in which this type of list was employed
(33, 34). The lower pair of curves in Fig. 7 present the
data from one of these studies (34). Both curves, it will
be observed, began at a very low level with the curve for
the High A group (solid line) rising above that for the
Low A group (broken line). An unpublished study from
our laboratory employing nonassociated paired adjectives
has given similar results, although the superiority of the
High A over the Low A subjects was significant only on
a single tailed hypothesis.

The second type of noncompetitive list differs from the
first in that the associative strengths of the paired words
are, as the result of past experiences, considerably above
zero. Under this condition it would be predicted that the

performance curves would, on the first anticipation trial, be considerably above 0% and that the curve for the high drive group would be above that for the low drive group. Employing paired adjectives that had been scaled by Haagen (7) as having high "closeness of association"

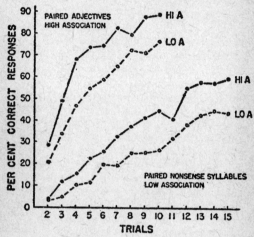

Fig. 7. *Paired-associates learning as a function of A-score under conditions of unusual interword pair competition.*

values, two studies (24, 29) have reported results which support these implications. The upper pair of curves in Fig. 7 shows the findings of one of these studies (29). As may be seen, the initial level of performance was well above 0 and the High A subjects started out and continued at a higher level than the Low A subjects. On the other hand, a recently completed doctoral dissertation (6) using this type of list failed to obtain results in accord with the theory. There was little or no difference between the two groups at any stage of practice.

In contrast to these noncompetitive type lists we have also designed a competitive list which includes some paired items in which the initial habit strength of the stimulus word to call out the paired word is weaker than the habit strengths to one or more other response words in the list. In the case of these items it would be predicted from our theory that high drive subjects would at the start of learning perform more poorly than low drive subjects. Here again we should have emphasized that the theory of paired-associates learning has as yet not been developed sufficiently to predict what will happen beyond the first few trials, and it would have been more appropriate, as far as implications for our drive theory are concerned, if we had used at most only the data from the first four or five trials. Precise predictions concerning performance beyond this point must await the development of a more adequate theory of the variables determining the weakening of these stronger, incorrect responses in paired-associates learning. Two published studies (24, 29) and one doctoral dissertation (6) have reported data with respect to the implication of our theory for this type of list; while all three found, as predicted, that the High A subjects were inferior to Low A subjects in the first four trials, none of the results was statistically significant. However, the implication of the theory that there would be an interaction between level of A-score and performance on the two kinds of lists, competitive and noncompetitive, was confirmed.

Summarizing the results with these paired-associates lists, I would say that the batting average of our theory is fairly high but by no means perfect. It is clearly evident from the data that differences in level of A-score (and hence level of D), if it is a factor determining performance on such tasks, is a relatively unimportant one. Certainly individual differences in verbal learning ability play a much more decisive role. Moreover, there are as yet many factors that play important roles in such complex behavior situations, about which we have as yet little or no knowledge. Among those of a motivational nature is the type of task-irrelevant response that Child and his group have studied (3). We think of these interfering responses as being elicited by drive stimuli (s_D), and hence they would be incorporated in a more complete motivational theory of learned behavior. On the basis of evidence in the literature and some recently completed studies of our own, we believe this factor is especially important when shock is introduced into verbal learning situations.

I should like to conclude this presentation by stating very briefly the purpose of such theoretical schemas as has been presented here. As I conceive them, their primary function is to provide for the unification of what, without the theory, would be a multiplicity of isolated or unconnected facts and laws. Thus, in the present instance, such phenotypically different phenomena as behavior in eyelid conditioning under various stimulus conditions, degree of emotionality as revealed by a personality questionnaire and physiological measures, and such opposite performance differentials in paired-associates tasks as just described have been interrelated by means of the theory. That much work, both of a theoretical and experimental nature, remains to be done in this area of behavior study is clearly revealed by the many gaps and deficiencies in the present attempt. It is my firm belief, however, that progress in the development of this, as in any other scientific field of knowledge, is greatly facilitated by such theoretically oriented research endeavors.

REFERENCES

1. AMSEL, A., The effect upon level of consummatory response of the addition of anxiety to a motivational complex. *J. exp. Psychol.*, 1950, 40, 709-715.
2. AMSEL, A., & MALTZMAN, I., The effect upon generalized drive strength of emotionality as inferred from the level of consummatory response. *J. exp. Psychol.*, 1950, 40, 563-569.
3. CHILD, I. L., Personality. *Annu. Rev. Psychol.*, 1954, 5, 149-170.
4. CRONBACH, L. J., & MEEHL, P. E., Construct validity in psychological tests. *Psychol. Bull.*, 1955, 52, 281-302.
5. FARBER, I. E., & SPENCE, K. W., Complex learning and conditioning as a function of anxiety. *J. exp. Psychol.*, 1953, 45, 120-125.
6. FREDENBURG, NORMA C., Paired-associates learning as a function of anxiety level and shock. Unpublished doctoral dissertation, State Univer. of Iowa, 1956.
7. HAAGEN, C. H., Synonymity, vividness, familiarity, and association value ratings of 400 pairs of common adjectives. *J. Psychol.*, 1949, 27, 453-463.
8. HILGARD, E. R., JONES, L. V., & KAPLAN, S. J., Conditioned discrimination as related to anxiety. *J. exp. Psychol.*, 1951, 42, 94-99.

9. HULL, C. L., *Principles of behavior*. New York: Appleton-Century, 1943.

10. JESSOR, R., & HAMMOND, K. R., Construct validity and the Taylor anxiety scale. *Psychol. Bull.*, 1957, 54, 161-170.

11. LACEY, O. L., The evaluation of autonomic responses toward a general solution. *Ann. N. Y. Acad. Sci.*, 1956, 67, 123-164.

12. MACDONALD, ANNETTE., The effect of adaptation to the unconditioned stimulus upon the formation of conditioned avoidance response. *J. exp. Psychol.*, 1946, 36, 1-12.

13. MILLER, N. E., Learnable drives and rewards. In S. S. Stevens (Ed.), *Handbook of experimental psychology*. New York. Wiley, 1951. Pp. 435-472.

14. MOWRER, O. H., A stimulus response analysis of anxiety and its role as a reinforcing agent. *Psychol. Rev.*, 1939, 46, 553-565.

15. PASSEY, G. E., The influence of intensity of unconditioned stimulus upon acquisition of a conditioned response. *J. exp. Psychol.*, 1948, 38, 420-428.

16. ROSENBAUM, G., Stimulus generalization as a function of clinical and experimentally induced anxiety. Unpublished doctoral dissertation, State Univer. of Iowa, 1950.

17. RUNQUIST, W. N., SPENCE, K. W., & STUBBS, D. W., Differential conditioning and intensity of the US. *J. exp. Psychol.*, in press.

18. SIEGEL, P. S., & BRANTLEY, J. J., The relationship of emotionality to the consummatory response of eating. *J. exp. Psychol.*, 1951, 42, 304-306.

19. SIEGEL, P. S., & SIEGEL, HELEN S., The effect of emotionality on the water intake of the rat. *J. comp. physiol. Psychol.*, 1949, 42, 12-16.

20. SPENCE, K. W., *Behavior theory and conditioning*. New Haven: Yale Univer. Press, 1956.

21. SPENCE, K. W., & BEECROFT, R. S., Differential conditioning and level of anxiety. *J. exp. Psychol.*, 1954, 48, 399-403.

22. SPENCE, K. W., & FARBER, I. E., Conditioning and extinction as a function of anxiety. *J. exp. Psychol.*, 1953, 45, 116-119.

23. SPENCE, K. W., & FARBER, I. E., The relation of anxiety to differential eyelid conditioning. *J. exp. Psychol.*, 1954, 47, 127-134.

24. SPENCE, K. W., FARBER, I. E., & MCFANN, H. H., The relation of anxiety (drive) level to performance in competitional and noncompetitional paired-associates learning. *J. exp. Psychol.*, 1956, 52, 296-305.

25. SPENCE, K. W., FARBER, I. E., & TAYLOR, ELAINE., The relation of electric shock and anxiety to level of performance in eyelid conditioning. *J. exp. Psychol.*, 1954, 48, 404-408.

26. SPENCE, K. W., & ROSS, L. E., Experimental evidence on the relation between performance level in eyelid conditioning and anxiety (drive) level. USN Office of Naval Research *Tech Rep.*, 1957, No. 5 (Contract N9 onr-93802).

27. SPENCE, K. W., & TAYLOR, JANET A., Anxiety and strength of the US as determiners of the amount of eyelid conditioning. *J. exp. Psychol.*, 1951, 42, 183-188.

28. SPENCE, K. W., & TAYLOR, JANET A., The relation of conditioned response strength to anxiety in normal, neurotic, and psychotic subjects. *J. exp. Psychol.*, 1953, 45, 265-272.

29. SPENCE, K. W., TAYLOR, J., & KETCHEL, RHODA., Anxiety (drive) level and degree of competition in paired-associates learning. *J. exp. Psychol.*, 1956, 52, 306-310.

30. TAYLOR, JANET A., The relationship of anxiety to the conditioned eyelid response. *J. exp. Psychol.*, 1951, 41, 81-92.

31. TAYLOR, JANET A., A personality scale of manifest anxiety. *J. abnorm. soc. Psychol.*, 1953, 48, 285-290.

32. TAYLOR, JANET A., Level of conditioning and intensity of the adaptation stimulus. *J. exp. Psychol.*, 1956, 51, 127-131.

33. TAYLOR, JANET A., The effects of anxiety level and psychological stress on verbal learning. *J. abnorm. soc. Psychol.*, in press.

34. TAYLOR, JANET A., & CHAPMAN, J. P., Paired-associate learning as related to anxiety. *Amer. J. Psychol.*, 1955, 68, 671.

35. TAYLOR, JANET A., & SPENCE, K. W., The relationship of anxiety level to performance in serial learning. *J. exp. Psychol.*, 1952, 44, 61-64.

36. TAYLOR, JANET A., & SPENCE, K. W., Conditioning level in behavior disorders. *J. abnorm. soc. Psychol.*, 1954, 49, 497-502.

3

A Review of Sensory Preconditioning*

ROBERT J. SEIDEL[1]

Human Resources Research Office, The George Washington University

The paradigm for SPC was established by Brogden (1939), as was the name "Sensory Preconditioning." The procedure consists of the following three stages: (*a*) repeated contiguous unreinforced presentation of intersensory stimuli, (*b*) establishing a response to one of them, and (*c*) testing transfer of response to the other stimulus. Unfortunately, a control which is necessitated by this procedure has not been utilized in a number of experiments (Bahrick, 1952; Brogden, 1939; Karn, 1947). That is, equal exposure to the test stimulus must be given to both experimental and control groups. Lacking this control, the eventual difference between the group initially presented with paired stimuli and the control group could be attributed to differential familiarity with the test stimulus. Consequently, according to Reid (1952), these early studies by themselves are not conclusive.

The present study is a review of the existing data in this area with an attempt at reconciliation of certain of the more apparent inconsistencies. A descriptive analysis of the experimental setting will be offered; and, later, research will be suggested to clarify the existing body of

* From *The Psychological Bulletin*, 1959, 56, 58-73, and used here with the permission of the author and the American Psychological Association. When this paper was originally published the author was at the University of Pennsylvania.

[1] The author gratefully acknowledges the criticisms and analyses offered by William A. Shaw, Ronald H. Forgus, and Howard Ranken during the preparation of this manuscript.

information concerning sensory preconditioning (SPC). Within this approach the paper is directed toward a general consideration of three questions: (a) Is sensory preconditioning, as substantiated by the existing data, a phenomenon to be dealt with by learning theory? (b) If so, what laws of learning does it follow? (c) What are some of the problems which the learning theorist faces in attempting to integrate the data of SPC into his system?

THE EXPERIMENTAL EVIDENCE

Animal studies. The initial experiment on "sensory preconditioning" was done by Brogden (1939). Eight experimental animals were presented with 200 pairings of a bell and a light. Secondly, one of these stimuli was used as a CS in a shock-avoidance setting until a criterion of avoidance was reached. During the test trials the other stimulus was presented and responses to extinction were recorded. The control animals which had not been exposed to the preconditioning pairing gave significantly fewer Rs to the unreinforced stimulus.

Subsequently, Reid (1952) performed an experiment with 16 pigeons. He trained them in a modified Skinner box to peck for food reward at a signal. In the test situation, pecking Rs were counted to the other stimulus which was presented without reward. The design was modified so that the control and experimental groups were given equal amounts of exposure to the buzzer and light during pretraining; however, for the Control Ss the stimuli were not paired but presented separately. With the Ss equated in this manner, no significant differences were obtained between experimental and control groups in number of pecking Rs to the test stimulus (either buzzer or light). Reid does summarize results of an unpublished study, using pigeons, which was done by Mac-Phersen in which Brogden's original data were confirmed; however, this study did not equate amount of exposure to the test stimulus for the two groups.

Bahrick (1952, 1953), using rats in an avoidance situation, obtained somewhat ambiguous results. He did find that high drive (14-hour food deprivation) during preconditioning led to greater positive transfer effects than did low drive (satiated); but the confusing outcome was that the control group (under high D) showed positive transfer to as great a degree as the Low Drive experimental group (Bahrick, 1953). A possible explanation for this occurrence may lie in Bahrick's use of the same apparatus for exposure and training. Perhaps there was a sufficient number of cues in the apparatus other than the buzzer to mediate the transfer effect to the light. This possibility may plausibly account for Reid's data, also.

Clearcut positive results have been obtained recently in an avoidance training investigation by Silver and Meyer (1954). Unlike Bahrick, however, they used an exposure apparatus which was distinctly different from that used in the other two phases of the experiment. These authors, using rats, found no significant differences among three control groups, one of which had had pretraining to the test stimulus alone (light or buzzer), one to the training stimulus alone (buzzer or light), and one with no pretraining experience. Apparently, differential exposure to the test stimulus was unimportant. These findings were subsidiary to the main purpose which was to relate sensory preconditioning to classical conditioning by showing that the same optimal temporal relationships hold for connection of the intersensory stimuli to occur as for the CS-UCS in the Pavlovian paradigm. The three experimental situations in preconditioning were: simultaneous, forward (.5 second between stimuli), and backward (.5 second between stimuli, but the training and test conditions were reversed). The results partially support their hypothesis of similarity of the two procedures since "forward" sensory preconditioning resulted in greater positive transfer effect in the test avoidance training than either of the other experimental conditions. The latter two did not differ from one another in transfer effect. The fact that the experimental groups as a whole gave more avoidance Rs in the test situation than did the controls indicates that "backward" preconditioning exists. Yet does such a temporal relationship between CS-UCS exist for classical conditioning? Without considering this PC phenomenon necessarily analogous to what has been called "backward" conditioning, at this point one might raise the question of a possible difference between the two in temporal parameters. (Coppock's S-R analysis [1958] to be covered later presents a *forward* conditioning interpretation of such an occurrence in SPC.)

Finally, a recent study by the author (1958) extended Bahrick's findings regarding the role of specific responses as possible mediators in SPC. Hooded rats were exposed to the PC stimuli when food-deprived, and later were split into hungry, thirsty, and satiated groups during avoidance learning (and transfer). All three experimental groups showed the *same* degree of positive transfer when compared to the control group (initially exposed only to the test stimulus). The reader will note that the experimental animals showed this equivalent effect despite differences in degree of similarity between the autonomic response-complex present during the preconditioning period and that present during the training-testing phases. It seems also possible then, that in SPC, unlike conditioning, the role of the response is an unimportant one.

Human studies. Karn's study (1947) most resembles Brogden's original design. This author used fingerflexion avoidance training. The 12 experimental Ss (college students) received 50 simultaneous presentations of buzzer and light; all 24 Ss were then trained to criterion to avoid shock by responding to the buzzer; and finally, all were given 10 unreinforced trials to the light. The control group had no pretraining. The results agree with Brogden's data, but suffer from the same flaw, unequal exposure to the test stimulus (favoring the Experimental Ss).

Brogden's 1942 study incorporating the GSR as the CR met this lack and the results turned out negative. But the outcome was attributed by the author to lack of a reliable measure of conditioning; and hence, the experiment was not a valid test of SPC. In the rest of his experiments, which were somewhat more successful, Brogden (1947, 1950; Brogden & Gregg, 1951; Chernikoff & Brogden, 1949) also controlled for possible differential effects.

In one study where Brogden (1947) utilized reaction time measure instead of GSR, he was successful in obtaining the SPC effect. The training, transfer, and extinction test procedures were: 30 trials to light; 10 trials to tone; 10 extinction trials to light. Included were three control groups: (*a*) Given no pretraining (preconditioning) period. This condition provided a test for sensory generalization (based upon unequal exposure to the test stimulus). (*b*) Given exposure to the test stimulus alone equal to that of the experimental groups. This was the usual SPC control condition. (*c*) Given no pretraining and no transfer test to the tone. This group acted as the SPC control condition for the extinction test of reaction time to the light. All Ss were told to respond to the light only and they would be shocked if they were too slow. Actually, no shock was given. The instructions were given after S had been told to be seated and E "accidentally" had presented the preconditioning stimuli while "fixing" the apparatus.

The transfer test was successful in showing SPC. In this test Control Groups (*a*) and (*b*) did not differ from one another even though (*b*) had the advantage of sensory generalization. The extinction test was not successful. It was based upon the assumption that the unreinforced (no shock) tone presentations should have extinguished the shock-expectancy to the greatest degree for the experimental group, next for Control Groups (*a*) and (*b*), and least for Control Group (*c*). The first three groups showed similar marked extinction (latency increase) to the light while Group (*c*) showed none. Apparently, the 10 unreinforced tone trials, regardless of prior associations, were sufficient to extinguish the expectancy.

Chernikoff and Brogden (1949) repeated the experiment using electronic equipment, and a diffuse tone source, all of which seemed to increase the efficiency of the experiment since positive transfer results were obtained with only 10 Ss per group whereas Brogden had used 42. Also, the percentage of Ss responding in the test series was twice that of the other study. Another variable in this experiment was instructional variation. One experimental group was given the same instructions as in the previous study, while two others were told "not to respond" or to "do what seems natural" in the test situation. Only the group given the old instructions evidenced a significant difference from the controls.

In another experiment (1950) Brogden utilized a diffuse source for both tone and light in preconditioning. This time he failed to get successful results with the usual measures. By adding the procedure of measuring absolute auditory thresholds to the preconditioning tone at the end of the experimental sessions, he obtained positive results. He found that the presence of the light with the tone led to greater "lowering" of the auditory threshold for the experimental group than for the controls. The "lowering" is put in quotes since again the data are subject to contamination by the S's possible deliberate pressing of the key even when he was in doubt about hearing the tone. This is quite possible since: (a) he was instructed to respond to tone if present even when in doubt; and (b) he had previously experienced the light and tone simultaneously. This again points up the need for an involuntary response. With regard to the second point, it has long been known that facilitation takes place when one of these stimuli is supplemented by the other (Child & Wendt, 1938). It is possible that in this study the difference in the facilitation effect (lowering of the tonal threshold) between control and experimental groups was a result of the excess paired presentations of tone and light given the experimental group.

Brogden and Gregg (1951) repeated the threshold procedure in six experiments with variations on: (a) sequence of threshold trials (with and without light), (b) number of preconditioning pairings, (c) steps in obtaining threshold, and (d) illumination (increase or decrease). No significant t ratios were obtained for the above variations, but the experimental group as a whole showed the same results as the earlier study. In recalling the proposed relationship between sensory preconditioning and classical conditioning, it should be noted that the strength of a CR is a function of the number of reinforced trials. Although the exact value of this finding cannot be determined since his data are confounded with a possible facilitation effect, Brogden's data indicate that no such relationship between frequency of exposure and association strength exists in SPC. Brogden also summarized two unpublished studies which support the above positive findings.

A recent attempt at sensory preconditioning with human subjects was made by Bitterman, Reed, and Kubala (1953), who wanted to show that SPC produces as stable an effect as does classical conditioning. Their rationale rests on a sensory integration approach to preconditioning, and they hoped to indicate that a Hullian S-R interpretation could not predict the same results. The S-R argument presumed is that the need reduction following PCS (preconditioning stimuli) would be less than that following the CS; consequently, the sE_R would be weaker following a given number of sensory preconditioning trials than for the same number of conditioning trials.

While their results show no difference in response to extinction between PCS and CS, their data should be evaluated cautiously. First, a difficulty in interpreting their findings stems from the fact that the two PCSs were lights differing in position on a panel. Technically, then, this procedure deviated from the usual one since no intersensory relation was attempted. Moreover, the response measured was the GSR, something which requires extreme care when conducting any sort of conditioning experiment. Seated in a semidarkened room, the preconditioning group was presented with the training and generalization stimuli, sometimes with the CS alone and sometimes paired with the PCS, so that the termination of one coincided with the onset of the other. The conditioning group, on the other hand, was presented with each stimulus on separate trials for the same total number of pretraining trials. Extinction for all Ss to both the CS and generalization stimulus (the other PC stimulus for the PC group) followed training session.

Following upon the use of the GSR and this procedure, two possible weaknesses seem to discount these results. To begin with, a GSR is elicited by a wide variety of stimuli, and was most probably present during the pretraining period; hence, the preconditioning paradigm was not followed. In order for a valid procedure to have been used, it would have been necessary first to extinquish the GSR to the experimental stimuli. Secondly, since a GSR probably did occur to light itself, it is quite possible that a summation effect occurred in the preconditioning group. This would mean that a greater GSR could have been elicited to both lights in the preconditioning period than for each light presented separately in pretraining (the condition for the control group). Thus, contrary to the implication of Bitterman, et al., that the stimuli were initially neutral, it seems probable that they were not. Further, the authors asserted that stimulus generalization could not explain the results. However, if the GSR and summation did occur in the manner outlined above, then the preconditioning group should have been conditioned to a greater degree to light stimuli than the conditioning group. Consequently, it is quite possible that greater stimulus generalization could account for the fact that the so-called preconditioning group showed greater generalization in extinction (one measure of preconditioning) than did the conditioning group. Unfortunately, there was no measure of GSR reported for the pretraining period for either groups so that, although highly probable, the evaluation requires additional data for substantiation.

The latest SPC study (Coppock, 1958) to appear was concerned with "pre-extinction" and involved the use of GSR in classical conditioning (shock as UCS). Although the data shed some light on the meaning of the foregoing experiment, the results raise questions related to the interpretation of GSR in SPC as a mediating response for S-R theory.

The experiment consisted of four experimental groups and a control group. The latter was exposed to the PC stimuli (light and tone) separately on randomly alternated trials. Two of the other groups, PC and IPC, were analogous to the forward and "backward" PC groups in Silver and Meyer's study. The interstimulus interval in the present study, however, was 1 sec. as compared to .5 sec. in the other; and Coppock referred to the inverted stimulus presentation as IPC (inverted PC) rather than "backward."

The two pre-extinction groups (PE) were treated like PC initially. Then one group, IPE, was immediately given an equal number of *inverted* exposures of the PC stimuli (like IPC). The other group, SPE, was presented with the first stimulus alone (analogous to unreinforced CS). Coppock's predictions based upon an S-R mediation analysis were: (a) IPE > SPE, (b) SPE ≥ C, dependent upon success of pre-extinction, (c) IPC > C, and (d) PC > C. His S-R analysis of SPC will be discussed later in the Theory Section.

The results did not completely confirm the proposed S-R hypotheses. The nonparametric comparisons made by Coppock revealed (a) PC > C, (b) SPE > C, (c) IPE > SPE, but (d) IPC did not differ significantly from C. Since the experimental effects were found to be independent of GSR reactivity, per se, and of procedural variables, it is not clear why the IPC group should have shown *training*-extinction effects while the SPE Ss exhibited no *pre*-extinction effects. Unfortunately, certain additional statistical comparisons were not made which would have provided a basis for more thorough theoretical evaluation (viz., S-S vs. S-R) in the pre-extinction setting. For example, it is apparent from the graph of the transfer data that IPE was equal to and possibly superior to PC. Also, SPE seemed equal to PC. Certainly if "extinction" is to be meaningfully applied in this experiment, whether from S-S or S-R viewpoints, equality of SPE and PC prevents theoretical difficulties. In addition, unless it is assumed that the SPC association was maximum in the PC group, S-S theory should have predicted IPE > PC since the IPE group had twice as many pairings of PC stimuli. Finally, according to S-S theory IPC should have done almost as well as the PC group. (Reversal of S-S appearance could have weakened the expectancy slightly.)

It was stated at the outset of this analysis that Coppock's study (1958) shed some light on the ambiguities in the GSR experiment of Bitterman, et al. (1953). As noted earlier in the discussion, Coppock found equivalence in GSR reactivity among all groups at various stages of the experiment and that the treatment effects were independent of GSR magnitude, per se. While one cannot necessarily infer between experiments in this regard, such a finding does lend somewhat more credence to Bitterman's findings.

As one final point, it should be noted that in Coppock's experiment the GSR did not follow the customary S-R curve of extinction. Here again, as in Seidel's experiment (1958), the role of a specific response in SPC seemed irrelevant to the degree of association of the PC stimuli.

Apart from the theoretical problems, Coppock's IPC group (1 sec. interstimulus interval) yielded data contrary to those previously obtained in a comparable condition, (cf. p. 59). Silver and Meyer's "Backward" PC group (.5 sec. stimulus interval) showed mediation equal to their simultaneous PC group (1954). What basis may exist for the discrepancy may only be speculated upon at this point: voluntary (avoidance) vs. involuntary (GSR) response, rats vs. humans, difference in temporal intervals (.5 vs. 1 sec.). Clearly, this problem needs further investigation.

One experiment (Wickens & Briggs, 1951) used an identifying response during exposure to preconditioning stimuli. This one presents a strong case to show that SPC is merely an instance of "mediated stimulus generalization" (MSG), and that contiguity of the PC stimuli is unnecessary to obtain the desired transfer effect. One group of college students was exposed to 15 contiguous presentations of tone and light, while another group was given 15 separate presentations of tone and 15 of light in random order. During the PC period the Ss were asked to give a verbal recognition response ("Now") to the stimuli. Both groups showed the same significant advantage in transfer of an avoidance R over the control groups which had given the verbal response to a tone 15 times or to a light 15 times.

On the surface the hypothesis seems to have been substantiated, but at least two points should be examined before the conclusion is accepted. If the identifying response is considered as instrumental in kind, then it follows obviously that the above-noted transfer effect stands as an example of S-R learning. However, the generalization that the concept SPC is in like manner an aspect of S-R learning (via mediated stimulus generalization), although suggested by, does not necessarily follow from a single experimental outcome. In fact, if one assumes that the identifying response acted to "set" the Ss to connect the two stimuli, one would expect the obtained transfer differences to occur. Stated in another way, the

Wickens and Briggs study showed that the mediating response is a sufficient condition in SPC. In order to show that the response is both a necessary as well as a sufficient condition to effect mediation, it would be essential to eliminate nonresponse induced "sets" as possible mediators. An example of the latter would be the increase in pronouncedness of the PC stimuli by delimiting the quality and quantity of other stimuli available to S (enhancing attention value, per se). Further, to compare MSG and SPC directly, the above study should have included two experimental groups (pure SPC) exposed to the two stimuli minus the identifying response. Experimentation noted earlier pertinent to the role of possible responses during the latency period of SPC and MSG will be discussed further subsequently.

One other related set of experiments concerns mediate association and requires consideration as a possible verbal S-R analogue to mediated stimulus generalization. The general principle of mediate association requires that previous associations between two ideas will facilitate the establishment of one of these with a third hitherto unrelated idea. This concept took the experimental form of learning paired associates. Peters (1935) used various pairs of meaningful and nonmeaningful verbal and motor tasks to investigate the concept. The sequences of associations frequently involved using the response as the common item (A-B, C-B, A-C). Once the stimulus was the common element (A-B, A-C, B-C) and once the response in the first pairing became the stimulus in the second (A-B, B-C, A-C). In no instance did the t test show the expected facilitating effect. The only procedure which even approached significance in this direction was the last one noted above, A-B, B-C, A-C, in which Peters used months (B), numbers from 1-12 (A), and letters (C).

A more recent experiment by Bugelski and Scharlock (1952), with the latter procedure and nonsense syllables as the learning material, produced positive results. Important to note is that here the t test again failed to yield significance. However, the order effect in the expected direction was significant. Unfortunately, the individual results were not available in Peters' article so that the order effect could not be tested in his data. Nevertheless, if one adopts tentatively the suggestion offered by Bugelski and Scharlock that the order of association is important, the phenomenon fits neatly into the classical mediating generalization framework. The sequence A-B, B-C, A-C would be expected to yield facilitation of A-C, whereas A-B, C-B would not and could be considered similar to backward conditioning.[2] The SPC data, although by no means clearcut, suggest that temporal ordering of PC stimuli (and thus also of the unobserved responses) may not be important. Both the IPE and IPC groups in Coppock's study (1958) and the "Backward" PC group in Silver and Meyer's experiment (1954) could be considered the analogue in SPC to the inverted C-B condition. The IPE and Backward PC groups showed the SPC effect while the IPC group did not. Although not conclusive, these results provide an indication that sensory preconditioning may not be simply an instance of S-R learning as is mediated generalization. Certainly, a more detailed comparison of the temporal parameters governing the instances of mediated S-R learning and SPC is needed.

Before going on to theoretical implications, it would be well to summarize the empirical findings. At this point, SPC seems generally substantiated as a phenomenon in learning. Further, there are indications that the required conditions for its occurrence seem to be little more than repeated stimulus contiguity. The above analysis hints at a lack of importance in temporal relationship between PC stimuli. Brogden's data (Brogden & Gregg, 1951) suggest that number of repetitions (i.e., analogous to Hull's N) do not operate in SPC as in S-R learning. Similarly, Coppock's study (1958) suggests that extinction in SPC does not follow the usual curve related to number of unreinforced CS repetitions. In addition, Coppock's results, those of Bahrick (1952, 1953) and of the author (1958) reveal that the existence of a response during the PC period is unimportant for SPC to occur.

[2] Razran (1956) to the contrary, notwithstanding, recent experimental literature indicates that so called backward conditioning is either an artifact of conditioning procedures (Harris, 1941) or an unstable, weak, transient effect (Spooner & Kellog, 1947).

These facts must be taken into account when one attempts to class sensory preconditioning as an instance of a given conceptualization of learning (i.e., S-S or S-R theory).

THEORETICAL INTERPRETATION

Most of the experimenters have not attempted to theorize about the nature of sensory preconditioning with the exception of Brogden, however, who interpreted his results in terms of Guthrian theory; and he hypothesized an unknown UCR and CR to the neutral stimuli.

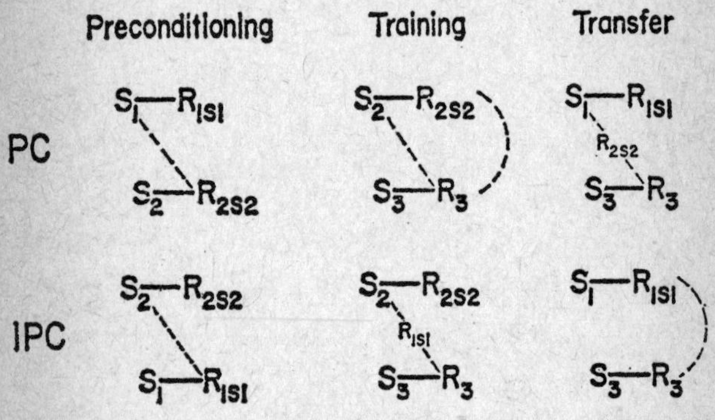

Fig. 1. An S-R Conditioning Analysis of SPC.

Wickens and Briggs (1951) and Silver and Meyer (1954), in agreement on the apparent lack of reinforcement in the SPC situation, have attempted an S-R analysis of the learning process in terms of "mediating stimulus generalization." According to Silver and Meyer, the buzzer and light are actually unconditioned stimuli which lead to "not directly observed" unconditioned responses. After frequent pairing, each of these stimuli comes to elicit equally difficult-to-observe conditioned responses. The resultant in transfer from this initial cross-conditioning, the reader will recall, is that in test trials one should expect positive transfer effect.

Coppock's S-R analysis (1958) differs slightly from the

cross-conditioning approach in that he assumed that in accord with conditioning principles the temporal relationships between S_1 and S_2 during PC determine which response-complex could provide the response-produced stimulus as a basis for mediation. This means, as shown in Fig. 1, that the S-R mediation process differs between Coppock's PC and IPC groups. As pointed out by Coppock (1958, p. 218) the IPC mediator existent during training was the response-produced stimulus of a CR (R_1s_1) which was undergoing extinction during that stage. On the other hand, the usual PC group has a UCR as a base for the response-produced mediator (e.g., R_2s_2). Note that, as a result of his traditional S-R analysis, Coppock labeled the CR-mediation group *inverted* PC rather than "backward" PC as did Silver and Meyer. His analysis has the advantage in that it is less ambiguous to predict from the UCR-CR distinction than from the cross-conditioning analysis that PC > IPC. Further, Coppock could predict that the IPE group, benefiting from the added CR-mediation after extinction of PC, should show greater transfer than a group having undergone simple extinction of preconditioning connections (SPE). On the other hand, neither approach is adequate to account for SPC data that reveal preconditioning *independent* of the response during the PC period (Bahrick, 1953; Coppock, 1958; Seidel, 1958).

In formulating his mediation analysis of SPC, Osgood also abandons the concept of reinforcement as a necessary condition for learning. In fact, after raising the fact of no extinction after many secondarily (at most) reinforced trials of mere bombardment by stimuli, he concludes that sensory preconditioning provides "one of the strongest arguments against reinforcement theory" (1953, p. 462).

Osgood's S-R explanation differs from the above, however, since he suggests that "a common perceptual reaction" (e.g., attentional) is elicited initially to the novel stimuli. "If one of these . . . is now . . . conditioned to a new reaction, the self-stimulation produced by the mediation process . . ." is inferred (p. 461). The obvious difficulty with his interpretation, to agree with Osgood himself, is that nothing of the proposed process is directly apparent in the organism's behavior. Osgood is forced to draw upon analogous evidence from conditioning (e.g., Shipley, 1933) to substantiate his point. However, as noted earlier whether or not these analogies are correct awaits further experimentation in the areas of SPC and MSG to establish as fact the existence of similar stimulus and response relationships in both types of procedure.

As implied by the discussion in the previous section, there appears to be some inconsistency between any S-R analysis of SPC and the analogous evidence cited as support for mediation. With reference to Osgood, although in all of his discussion of the mediation process he states that it is some fraction of previous instrumental behavior, it is difficult to see how such a conceptualization could apply to SPC. No instrumental response is called for in this paradigm, nor is any one differentially reinforced if it does occur. Further, from data discussed, when autonomic responses are made consistent or recurrent with the PC pairing, they apparently have no influence on the association of the two stimuli. If it is asserted that the autonomic responses are not important for mediation but the unobserved UCR's are, one simply begs the question. Why is one inferred response and not the other—the existence of which has more certainty (i.e. through food deprivation or direct GSR measurement)—important for mediation? Furthermore, it would be inconsistent or at least theoretically not parsimonious for Osgood to accept autonomic mediation in one learning instance and to deny it in a second situation where it has an equal possibility to mediate transfer.

An S-S contiguity point of view is proposed by Birch and Bitterman (1949) who feel, "The results of the sensory pre-conditioning experiments require us to postulate a process of afferent modification (sensory integration) . . . which takes place independently of need reduction" (p. 302). They later assert that "the latent learning experiment may be understood as a complication of the sensory pre-conditioning experiment . . ." (1951, p. 360). For the essential condition of sensory integration they postulate, "When two afferent centers are continuously activated, a functional relation is established between them such that the subsequent innervation of one will arouse the other" (p. 358).

To this writer, the key phrases in the above seem to be "functional" and "such that" since in these words lies the linkage between the mediated S-R and the afferent integrations. These verbal ambiguities lead to the ultimate conclusion that the difficulty in deciding upon the correct functional explanation for the mediating process resolves itself into a pseudo-problem for psychology. Perhaps neurologists will some day provide the answer concerning whether or not the central connections are between afferent-efferent or afferent-afferent neurons. As a start in this direction, Harris (1948) has hypothesized that a type of neural summation occurs when intersensory stimuli (e.g., visual and auditory) are paired. His review of the physiological evidence led to the hypothesis that there is high probability of such summation taking place in the mid-brain and brain stem. The intersensory facilitation noted in psychological studies could then be accounted for as the behavioral correlate of this neural integration. Further, through some fractionated intermediary response, common initially to both sound and light, sensory preconditioning is supposed to occur. In this way, Harris attempts to provide justification for a neural locus of an attentional or perceptual mediator (similar apparently to that of Osgood). The physiological data reviewed by him, however, seem to provide an equally plausible basis for an S-S or S-R psychology.

There is one different type of mediated-response hypothesis which deserves mention. Hebb (1949) has proposed a neural associationistic theory which includes the development of alternate neural routes in the CNS as a correlate of perceptual learning. The response which he gives as an example of a mediator in the formation of a visual percept is the scanning eye movement from angle to angle along the sides outlining a visually presented object. Clearly, performing any type of instrumental response can be differentiated from the mediating response in Hebb's theory. The eye movement can occur independently of what instrumental response the S must perform in any given task. In this sense, such an independent mediator is also different from Osgood's "detached responses" which are stated to be in some measure part of previous instrumental behavior. Consequently, it seems plausible to suggest that, if any type of mediating response takes place in sensory preconditioning, it may be of the Hebbian variety rather than the usual instrumental type seen in mediated generalization and mediate association. The rationale for such a proposal should become more apparent in the following section.

A Comparison of Mediated Generalization and Sensory Preconditioning

At this point it might be well to note more clearly the rationale which, it is felt, forces a cautious approach upon any attempt at relating these concepts. As was mentioned in the introduction, one characteristic unique to the SPC learning paradigm is the lack of any response requirement during the latency or critical period. Other procedures which have been used (i.e., place vs. response, latent learning) to test the relative merits of S-S and S-R theories all require, and sometimes reward, specific responses in such a stage. As is evident from the Wickens and Briggs experiment discussed above, this distinction is not readily apparent in the analysis of the paradigm for mediated stimulus generalization. Indeed, in order to better understand both SPC and MSG, a step by step procedural comparison should be helpful.

Consider specifically the breakdown in Table 1. To illustrate the comparison, reference is made to Shipley's study (1933) on mediated stimulus generalization, which Osgood (1953) cites as a classic example of both MSG and SPC. In order to make the comparison more applicable to S-R learning in general, an outline of the Wickens and Briggs study (1951) was included in the chart. Like SPC the experiments involved three stages, but the structure of these stages seem to be observably different from SPC. Shipley first paired a CS_a (faint light) with a definite UCS_b (tap-on-cheek) to condition a CR_1 (eyeblink). The Wickens and Briggs procedure differed somewhat from that of Shipley by utilizing instrumental learning during the first stage. The Ss were required to give a common response ("Now") to the paired CSs (light-tone presentation) or to either CS separately. While these are easily identified as straightforward conditioning or instrumental learning procedures respectively, such a description of the corresponding SPC stage seen in Table 1

TABLE 1

Comparison of procedures in MSG and SPC

Stage	MSG			SPC		
	S	R	Reinforcement	S	R	Reinforcement
1 (Shipley)	CS_a-UCS_b	CR_1	Specified	NS_1-NS_2	None Required	None Apparent
(Wickens and Briggs)	CS_1-CS_2 CS_1, CS_2	CR_1 CR_1	Specified Specified			
2 (Shipley)	CS_b	CR_2	Specified	CS-UCS (NS_1)	CR_1	Specified
(Wickens and Briggs)	CS_1	CR_2				
3 (Shipley)	CS_a	CR_2 mediated	—	CS (NS_2)	CR_1 mediated	—
(Wickens and Briggs)	CS_2	CR_2 mediated	—			

seems inaccurate. During the preconditioning period, Ss are simply *exposed* to contiguous stimuli such as buzzer and light, heretofore in conditioning studies presumed to be neutral stimuli (e.g., NS_1 and NS_2). Note that no instrumental or manipulatory or unconditioned response is required or imposed on the subject. What is more, if any response is made, unlike MSG, no recognition of it by the experimenter is given through reward or punishment.

In the second stage of his experiment, Shipley conditioned CR_2 (finger withdrawal) to CS_b, previously UCS_b (tap-on-cheek). Wickens and Briggs followed a similar procedure. At this stage in SPC one PC stimulus is used as CS_1 in a similar conditioning or instrumental learning procedure. Next, Shipley presented the faint light without further conditioning and this stimulus, CS_a, elicited CR_2, finger withdrawal, in some Ss. Wickens and Briggs obtained positive transfer effect in both their experimental

groups (separate or contiguous presentation of stimuli).
In SPC the final stage is a similar transfer test wherein
NS_2 is used to elicit CR_1.

Note that in Shipley's study, the Wickens and Briggs'
investigation and in MSG experiments in general some
specified response and conditioning is imposed initially.
The attempt at generalization to SPC of the same type
of mediation process rests upon the assumption that
some unobserved or unobservable UCR occurs to both
NSs. Consequently, as noted earlier, Silver and Meyer
(1954) and similarly Wickens and Briggs (1951) hypothesize that any SPC effect is explained as a mediated
resultant of a type of cross-conditioning between NS_1
and NS_2 established in the preconditioning period. In
the training period although only NS_1 is used as CS_1,
an entire stimulus complex is presumed present composed
of NS_1, its stimuli derived from its UCR, and those from
its CR (UCR to NS_2). And, since these stimuli from
its CR are similar to those produced by the UCR of
NS_2, in test trials one should expect positive transfer
effect.

It remains an empirical question, however, concerning:
(a) whether or not SPC and MSG are operationally distinguishable concepts, and (b) whether or not either one
or both can be subsumed under the principles of conditioning. With regard to the latter point, there are at least
the three sources of published data discussed previously
which appear opposed to a conditioning interpretation
of SPC. First, there is the finding that stable backward
SPC exists—to as great a degree as simultaneous SPC;
and, secondly, Brogden (1951) has reported that apparently in SPC the strength of the preconditioning association is not a function of N (number of PC pairings).

Thirdly, the role of the response in SPC seems unimportant. Although Bahrick's results noted earlier were
not definitive for SPC, he did obtain a *positive* transfer
effect in his test situation for all groups. This generalization occurred despite the fact that the rats were exposed
to PC stimuli under hunger and thirst motivation, but
trained and tested on an avoidance problem when satiated for hunger and thirst. Bahrick's data, as a result,
suggest at least two difficulties for an S-R interpretation

of mediation in SPC. The autonomic responses present during exposure, which might have mediated the transfer, were either nonexistent or present in only a slight degree during training and testing. Even more striking, is the fact that the autonomic processes *dominant* during training and testing (sympathetic processes) were opposed to those present during the initial pairing of the PC stimuli. Despite both conditions positive transfer occurred. Furthermore, in the SPC study (Seidel, 1958) cited earlier, the writer substantiated Bahrick's finding in a design which included degrees of similarity between autonomic responses present during preconditioning (the exposure period) and those present during the training-testing stages. As was pointed out in the analysis of that experiment, the most probable mediating responses must have been either the autonomic response-complex, per se, or that complex combined with other unobserved responses. In either case, differences among experimental groups should have appeared if response-produced mediation were involved. Apparently, these two experiments indicate that even when a given response is specifically made consistent with the PC stimuli and thereby allowed the opportunity of serving as the basis for mediation, it has no effect in the SPC paradigm. In addition, the finding that the GSR in SPC does not seem to follow the normal extinction curve argues against an S-R interpretation of SPC.

The caution advised in attempting to subsume SPC under S-R learning theory by calling it an example of conditioning seems clearly justified. From the above data it appears that number of repetitions (i.e., N), temporal order, and specific responses have little effect on the establishment of stimuli association in SPC. On the other hand, the importance of these factors in conditioning is well-established empirically.

Still to be considered is the question (*a*) whether or not SPC and MSG are operationally distinguishable concepts. Returning to the analysis of Shipley's MSG study, it will be recalled that in Stage 1 a faint light (CS_a) was conditioned to elicit an eyeblink (CR_1). Since at this point the link between light and tap-on-cheek (UCS_b) was established, presumably conditioning provided the

basis for mediation. In like manner Wickens and Briggs
established S-R connections initially. Ostensibly at least
the SPC operations (Table 1) do not establish such links.
In addition, since SPC data appear in contradiction to
certain conditioning principles, it is implied from the
foregoing discussion that although MSG would fit S-R
theory, it should not yield data consistent with SPC.

There is an indirect suggestion of such a possibility if
one considers the studies (Bugelski & Scharlock, 1952;
Peters, 1935) on mediate association (A-B, B-C, A-C)
as a verbal parallel to the MSG paradigm. The data gathered so far from these studies indicate that a certain order
of presentation of S and R in each stage is essential to
the attainment of facilitation effects (mediate association) in the third stage. If it is recalled from Table 1
that MSG involves conditioning as the basis for mediation, it is apparent that a similar type of order (the CS-
UCS order) should be of prime importance in the
achievement of mediated generalization. In fact, while
this order principle seems to govern both mediate association and mediated stimulus generalization, as noted
above, it apparently does not hold for SPC. A feature
unique to the preconditioning procedure which seems
related to this difference is the previously mentioned
absence of any required instrumental or conditioned response during the preconditioning period. In addition to
the possible difference in temporal parameter governing
SPC and MSG, other SPC findings discussed offer the
suggestion that N and mediating-response factors are
not the same either.

What this over-all comparison of MSG and SPC indicates is that, although both paradigms yield similar transfer effects in some instances, SPC alone appears governed
by a different set of laws from that of classical conditioning. It is emphasized that this is a tentative working hypothesis suggested by both partial and indirect sources
of data. Whether or not S-R concepts are able to account
for SPC and whether MSG and SPC are actually two
names for a single learning process or reflect different
types of learning await a systematic parametric comparison between the two concepts. Furthermore, if learning
is a two-stage process as Mowrer has already suggested, it

may be that such a comparson could yield the parameters for these factors. At any rate, in the most conservative sense, one might simply state that the SPC studies have given results different from those previously gotten in conditioning or those implied by any S-R mediational learning hypothesis.

CONCLUSIONS

If SPC is to be explained by the same principles as classical conditioning, as Reid has suggested (1952) in addition to following the laws of conditioning, sensory preconditioning should be present in an organism simple enough to make symbolic functioning an untenable interpretation. From the available comparative literature reviewed by this writer, SPC does seem to exist in such organisms.

It is noteworthy that Bahrick and Reid used the same apparatus for preconditioning and training, and these authors found that presenting the control group with only the test stimulus in preconditioning resulted in the same degree of transfer for experimental and control groups. The writer, as well as Silver and Meyer, on the other hand, utilized two distinctly different pieces of apparatus for these conditions; and they obtained significantly different degrees of transfer between experimental and control animals. The apparent paradox seems obviated if one recognizes that in the preconditioning setting the contiguous sensory stimuli are not limited to those which the experimenter has designated. Rather, the sensory associations are formed among the particular situational cues to which the animal attends. These sensory associations, thus, constitute a stimulus complex, in which the tone and/or light represent but one or two components of the totality. Thus, it is proposed that the important stimuli for the organism in the preconditioning situation are constituted by the stimulus complex to which it attends; and all that the experimenter can hope to do is to heighten the probability that the stimuli in which he is interested will be included in the complex of interest to the rat. Consequently, there exists the need for additional animal studies with control of the exposure variable and apparatus similarity, both of which bear on the subject of more definite identification of the stimulus.

At the outset of the paper, the initial question asked was whether or not sensory preconditioning required independent consideration as a phenomenon in learning. Although the data are by no means exhaustive, they do suggest that it tentatively does require such consideration. In addition, regarding the second question of the pertinent laws for sensory preconditioning, whether the parameters of preconditioning and S-R learning differ or are the same should be further investigated in the paradigm specified above. However, it is apparent at this point that the role of the response in SPC is a minor one (Bahrick, 1953; Coppock, 1958; Seidel, 1958).

Concerning the third question of the problems posed for the learning theorist, one issue clearly defined at present is that reinforcement as classically understood (Hull, 1943) seems to be an unnecessary condition for SPC to be effective. The value of this contribution is not to be underestimated. Indeed, the very concept of reinforcement (drive reduction) as developed by Hull and his supporters has been the center of a major controversy in learning theory for many years. To this end, the sensory preconditioning research has proved fruitful. This point is epitomized by the fact that Osgood (1953), an S-R reinforcement theorist, has conceded that the SPC data provide a strong case for the elimination of reinforcement as a necessary condition for learning. Further, if the writer's autonomic interpretation of Osgood's mediational analysis of learning is correct, the SPC data seem to pose difficulties for the latter's peripheral mediation hypothesis. At present, a more tenable approach would be the Hebbian-type analysis proposed by the writer or the S-S view offered by Birch and Bitterman. Finally, if one entertains the possibility for two-factor learning, a systematic comparison of MSG and SPC, which at present seem to reflect different processes, should prove fruitful for learning theory. Thus, granted the need for more research, the sensory preconditioning paradigm already seems to have provided a valuable building block for the theoretical development of psychology.

REFERENCES

BAHRICK, H., Latent learning as a function of the strength of unrewarded need states. *J. comp physiol. Psychol.*, 1952, 45 192-197.

BAHRICK, H., Sensory preconditioning under two degrees of deprivation. *J. comp. physiol. Psychol.*, 1953, 46, 39-42.

BIRCH, H. G., & BITTERMAN, M. E., Reinforcement and learning: The process of sensory integration. *Psychol. Rev.*, 1949, 56, 292-308.

BIRCH, H. G., & BITTERMAN, M. E., Sensory integration and cognitive theory. *Psychol. Rev.*, 1951, 58, 355-361.

BITTERMAN, M. E., REED, P. C., & KUBALA, A. L., The strength of sensory preconditioning. *J. exp. Psychol.*, 1953, 46, 178-182.

BROGDEN, W. J., Sensory pre-conditioning. *J. exp. Psychol.*, 1939, 25, 323-332.

BROGDEN, W. J., Tests of sensory preconditioning with human subjects. *J. exp. Psychol.*, 1942, 31, 505-517.

BROGDEN, W. J., Sensory pre-conditioning of human subjects. *J. exp. Psychol.*, 1947, 37, 527-539.

BROGDEN, W. J., Sensory conditioning measured by the facilitation of auditory acuity. *J. exp. Psychol.*, 1950, 40, 512-519.

BROGDEN, W. J., & GREGG, L. W., Studies of sensory conditioning measured by the facilitation of auditory acuity. *J. exp. Psychol.*, 1951, 42, 384-389.

BUGELSKI, B. R., & SCHARLOCK, D. A., An experimental demonstration of unconscious mediated association. *J. exp. Psychol.*, 1952, 44, 334-338.

CHERNIKOFF, R., & BROGDEN, W. J., The effect of different instructions upon the occurrence of sensory preconditioning. *J. exp. Psychol.*, 1949, 39, 200-207.

CHILD, J., WENDT, G. R., The temporal course of the influence of visual stimulation upon the auditory threshold. *J. exp. Psychol.*, 1938, 23, 109-127.

COPPOCK, W. J., Pre-extinction in sensory preconditioning. *J. exp. Psychol.*, 1958, 55, 213-219.

HARRIS, D. J., Some relations between vision and audition. USNMRL Rep. No. 135, July, 1948.

HARRIS, J. D., Forward conditioning, backward conditioning, pseudo-conditioning, and adaptation to the conditioned stimulus. *J. exp. Psychol.*, 1941, 28, 491-502.

HEBB, D. O., *The organization of behavior.* New York: Wiley, 1949.

HULL, C. L., *Principles of behavior. An introduction to behavior theory.* New York: Appleton-Century-Crofts, 1943.

KARN, H. W., Sensory preconditioning and incidental learning in human subjects. *J. exp. Psychol.*, 1947, 37, 540-544.

OSGOOD, C. E., *Method and theory in experimental psychology.* New York: Oxford Univer. Press, 1953.

PETERS, N. M., Mediate association. *J. exp. Psychol.*, 1935, 18, 20-48.

RAZRAN, G., Backward conditioning. *Psychol. Bull.*, 1956, 53, 55-70.

REID, R. L., A test of sensory pre-conditioning in pigeons. *Quart. J. exp. Psychol.*, 1952, 4, 49-56.

SEIDEL, R. J., An investigation of the medition process in preconditioning. *J. exp. Psychol.*, 1958, 56, 220-225.

SHIPLEY, W. C., An apparent transfer of conditioning. *Psychol. Bull.*, 1933, 30, 541.

SILVER, C. A., & MEYER, D. R. Temporal factors in sensory preconditioning. *J. comp. physiol. Psychol.*, 1954, 47, 57-59.

SPOONER, A., & KELLOGG, W. N., The backward conditioning curve. *Amer. J. Psychol.*, 1947, 60, 321-334.

WICKENS, D. D., & BRIGGS, G. E., Mediated stimulus generalization as a factor in sensory preconditioning. *J. exp. Psychol.*, 1951, 42, 197-200.

4

Stimulus Generalization*

Sarnoff A. Mednick[1]
and Jonathan L. Freedman
University of Michigan
Yale University

Stimulus generalization (SG) is an empirical phenomenon which has, of late, been seeing heavy duty as an
explanatory construct in many disparate situations. It
has been used in theoretical explanations of discrimination learning (Spence, 1936), of transposition (Spence,
1937), verbal learning (Gibson, 1940), psychoanalytic
displacement (Miller, 1948), the behavior of brain-dam-
aged individuals and schizophrenics (Mednick, 1955,
1958a), cross-cultural research (Hull, 1950a), projective
techniques (Moylan, 1959), and psychotherapy (Magaret, 1950). It seems likely that these explicatory uses of
SG are only a beginning. Inasmuch as we are probably

* From *The Psychological Bulletin*, 1960, 57, 169-200, and
used here with the permission of the authors and the American
Psychological Association.
[1] This paper was made possible by grants from the National
Science Foundation (G-3855) and the American Philosophical
Society (Grant No. 2132) to the senior author. Freedman was
at Harvard University when this paper was written; Mednick
was at the Institute of Personality Assessment and Research,
University of California, Berkeley. The authors wish to thank
Tallulah Brown Maki for the important questions and criticisms
she raised as a member of a seminar on stimulus generalization
conducted by the senior author at Harvard University. Judson S.
Brown, Norman Guttman, and Leo J. Postman gave the writer
the benefit of their criticism of a preliminary draft of this paper.
Roger Shepard's comments were of great help in preparing the
mathematical theories section. Penny Reveley contributed in-
valuable editorial assistance.

never exposed to exactly the same stimulus situation more than once, all responses to stimulus "repetition" might justifiably be attributed to SG. This "intellectual imperialism" is condoned and encouraged by suggestions that differential reaction time responses (Gibson, 1939) and most of psychophysics (Brown, Bilodeau, & Baron, 1951) may in large part be understood in terms of SG. While we have some sympathy for these viewpoints, the purpose of this article is to provide a concise summary of empirical findings concerning research on SG and to discuss evidence bearing on some important issues.

Organization of the article. After first defining SG we shall review the area of sensory generalization. Here we will be referring to generalization along stimulus continua that can be measured on a physical scale (e.g., distance, intensity, size). Next we will discuss the effect of variables such as drive and degree of training on SG. We shall conclude with a discussion of issues around which much research has revolved.

Definition. Stimulus generalization can be said to occur when a response, previously trained to be elicited by Stimulus 0, can also be elicited by test stimuli similar to 0. The gradient of stimulus generalization (GSG) can be said to be observed if the strength of these generalized responses (measured by frequency, latency, etc.) varies as an orderly function of the physical difference between the test stimuli and Stimulus 0. (This is what we will mean when the terms SG and GSG are used in the remainder of this article.) Through loose usage, these terms have been invested with a rather large number of different connotations. We are in agreement with Brown, et al. (1951) who have pointed up the importance of distinguishing "between the *empirical phenomenon of generalization* on the one hand and *theories or hypotheses about generalization on the other.*" The use of the terms in a hypothetical manner connotes nonobservable instigative factors while the use of the terms in an empirical manner connotes nothing more than SG and GSG as operationally defined above. Unless the term SG is specifically otherwise qualified, we shall be referring to the empirical usage.

SENSORY GENERALIZATION

In the main, studies in this area use both the classical and the instrumental conditioning paradigms. After initial conditioning, tests for generalization are made by presenting stimuli which vary in their similarity to the conditioned stimulus (CS). Usually SG testing is continued over a series of extinction trials with some reinforced (booster) trials with the CS interspersed to maintain response strength. Following the custom of the Russian and American literature, the original CS will be denoted Stimulus 0 and generalization stimuli (GS) as Stimulus 1, Stimulus 2, Stimulus 3, etc., in terms of their ordinal similarity to Stimulus 0.

Spatial Generalization

Studies by Bass and Hull (1934), and by Grant and Dittmer (1940), made use of a tactual-vibratory conditioned stimulus applied directly to some point on S's body (Stimulus 0). Shock to the right wrist was used as the unconditioned stimulus (UCS); the galvanic skin response (GSR) served as the conditioned response (CR) and generalization response measure. Tests for generalization were made by applying the tactual-vibratory stimulus to points on S's body at varying distances from Stimulus 0. Thus, instead of varying the disparity between the CS and the UCS with changes in the physical properties of the stimulus, they varied the point of application to the body. A typical situation in the Bass and Hull study had S's left shoulder as Stimulus Point 0, while three other points 16 inches apart on the body were used as generalization test points (small of back, left thigh and left calf). Seventy-four per cent of the trials during generalization testing were reinforced booster trials with Stimulus 0. The other 26% were SG test trials with Stimuli 1, 2, and 3. Measurable GSRs were noted upon application of Stimuli 1, 2 and 3; the amplitude of responses to these stimuli decreased as a function of the distance of the stimuli from Stimulus 0. Thus, SG and GSG as defined above were observed. In a second part of the study, E trained all the stimuli (0, 1, 2, 3) to an equal level, extinguished the response to Stimulus 0 to one-fourth of this level and tested 1, 2, and 3 for the generalized effects of this extinction. A gradient of generalization of the effects of extinction was found.

Grant and Dittmer's study paralleled that of Bass and Hull, except that only the back (shoulder to waist) and the dorsum of the right hand were stimulated and the UCS was administered to the left wrist of the group that had the GSR measured on their right hand. They spaced their four tactual-vibratory stimulus points four inches apart on the back and one inch apart from the wrist to the index finger. The gradients under these conditions were concave upward.

In an attempt to test the applicability of SG findings of conditioning experiments to verbal learning situations, Gibson (1939) carried out a study somewhat similar to the Bass and Hull investigation. Two groups were used, one having the tactual-vibratory stimuli placed 4 in. apart across their backs and the other having them placed 4 in. apart down their backs, forming two separate generalization continua. Ss were instructed to indicate verbally when the tactual-vibrator was applied to Stimulus Point 0 and to inhibit verbal responses when stimulated at the other stimulus positions. The reaction time of the verbal response was measured by means of a voice key. For both the vertical and horizontal continua the GSGs of frequency of responses showed significant differences between Stimulus Points 0 and 3, 1 and 3, and 0 and 1. No significant gradient of reaction times was obtained. In fact, the average latency of response to the GSs was less than that to Stimulus 0. Gibson explained this as probably being due to the instructions inhibiting long-latency "false" responses to the GSs. Another interesting finding was an upturn at the end of the GSG when vibrators were distributed horizontally; in the horizontal position, Points 0 and 3 were bilaterally symmetrical and this symmetry of location is offered as an "explanation" of the upturn. This explanation was also used by Anrep (1923) when his dogs showed similar responses to bilateral symmetrical stimulation; Anrep concluded that symmetry was an effective elicitor of generalization responses and that stimulation of the point bilaterally sym-

metrical with Stimulus 0 was as effective as stimulation
of the 0 point itself.

It might be maintained that this voluntary verbal response situation is too different from conditioning to be
considered an instance of SG and that all Gibson observed was a failure to discriminate Stimulus 0 from the
GSs. However, before training, she tested S's ability to
discriminate between the stimulus points. The group that
discriminated better was the one which later generalized
more, casting doubt on any "failure of discrimination"
hypothesis. It could also be argued that the so-called generalization responses were nothing more than chance
errors which were due to hurrying the response. This argument might have some weight if it were found that
speed of reaction and number of generalized responses
were positively related. However, there was no such relationship. This same finding for a voluntary response
SG study is reported elsewhere (Mednick, 1955). In
fact, the group that had slightly longer reaction times was
the group that generalized more. In any case, Gibson's
operations fulfill our initial definition of SG.

In an attempt to demonstrate spatial generalization
in a sensory modality other than tactual, Brown, Bilodeau
and Baron (1951) devised a procedure for testing for
SG along a visual-spatial continuum. Their apparatus
consists of a horizontal row of seven lamps and a reaction
time key for S. S is told that this is a test of reaction
time and that when the center lamp, Stimulus 0, is
flashed, he should release the reaction key as quickly as
he can. He is warned that the other lamps will also be
flashed and that he should not respond to these peripheral
lamps. After a series of training trials with Stimulus 0,
the testing period begins. This period consists of test
trials with the peripheral lamps interspersed among booster trials with Stimulus 0. In two separate experiments
symmetrical gradients were found. No tests for significance were made. Here again, however, the latency data
showed no consistent trends. Brown, et al. concur with
Gibson's interpretation of the lack of a latency gradient
when the generalization of a voluntary response is being
tested.

This method has been used as a measure of SG in a

number of studies. Its use as a measure of SG may be questioned on several grounds. First a study by Slater-Hammel (1955) using a similar apparatus has shown that reaction speed to peripheral visual stimulation decreases as a function of its peripherality. Similar results are reported in Woodworth (1938). Because of the inhibitory instructions used with this method, relatively long reaction times might possibly be expected to be related to reduced responsiveness. (It should be made clear that typically such a relationship has not been found.) Thus it is conceivable that some part of the observed gradient could be attributed to this factor. A second problem concerns the fact that instructions rather than reinforcements produce the major behavioral variations. In view of this, it cannot be said that experiments using this apparatus and method make precise tests of Hull's theory. This is a fact and should be carefully noted, but it does not rule out consideration of the method as one producing "generalization-like effects." These "generalization-like effects" (the term commonly used by Brown and his associates) have proven to be surprisingly parallel to the effects resulting from classical conditioning-generalization studies.

Andreas (1954) pointed out that the empirical gradients reported by Brown, et al. under conditions of inhibitory instructions might be due not only to gradients of associative strength, but could also be ascribed to gradients of inhibitory tendencies (here he is talking in nonempirical "instigative" terms). He tested to see if gradients could be obtained using this type of apparatus without the inhibitory instructions. While the gradients he reports are somewhat irregular, they do show a statistically significant decrement suggesting that positive gradients underlie the observed gradients. Unfortunately, reaction times were not reported so that gradients of latency in the "non-inhibitory instructions" situation could not be observed.

Brown, Clarke and Stein (1958) also criticized the method because the "instructions must be phrased to condone implicitly but not encourage false reactions." They have devised a new procedure using the same basic apparatus which eliminates this problem. The lamps are identified as horses and each trial as a race. S's task is to guess whether the horse (lighted lamp) will win or lose. During training all the lamps but the center lamp win with equal frequency (20%). The center lamp wins more frequently than the others (80%). During the test trials Ss show a gradient-like pattern of the "win" response with a peak at the center lamp and decreasing frequency of guesses as a function of distance from the center lamp.

Despite the objections, several studies have been reported which have made use of the procedure with the inhibitory instructions. Mednick (1955) repeated the Brown, Bilodeau, and Baron study, extending the stimulus continuum by adding two lamps at each end of the stimulus board for a total of 10 generalization lamps. He reports a regular, statistically significant gradient of frequency of response. No regular latency gradient was obtained though latency measures were taken.

The failure of studies involving the generalization of voluntary responses to find latency gradients has been of some interest to researchers in this field. It has probably attracted such attention because of the relative ease with which latencies of voluntary responses may be measured (as compared with latencies of GSR responses). Gibson's explanation of this failure has been generally accepted. As briefly pointed out above, she suggested that with inhibitory instructions, potential long latency responses would be withheld if a GS were the test stimulus, but would be allowed to occur to the CS. On the basis of this, Rosenbaum (1953) suggested that the usual gradient might be obtained with latency data if Ss were given a set to respond very quickly, thus counteracting the effect of the inhibitory instructions. Mednick (1958c) attempted to establish such a set in his instructions to S and found that by only using the data of the 30 Ss with the fastest reaction times, he obtained a relatively consistent positively accelerated gradient of latency. In contrast, the gradient of the 30 slowest Ss was extremely inconsistent. This study was then replicated on a separate group and the findings were consistent with the hypothesis that the faster Ss would demonstrate a "typical" latency gradient of generalization. In a study of the GSG as a function of age in children, Mednick and Lehtinen

(1957), using this apparatus, predicted and found that younger children were less restrained by the inhibitory instructions and demonstrated a latency gradient. These two studies seem to support Gibson's interpretation of the failure to find latency GSGs. Other studies using the Brown, Bilodeau, and Baron apparatus, or some modification of it, have investigated the effect of level of manifest anxiety and experimental naivete on SG (Mednick, 1957) summation of GSGs (Bilodeau, Brown & Meryman, 1956), the central tendency effect of GSG (Gewirtz, Jones, & Waerneryd, 1956), the correlation of SG with ethnocentric attitudes (Arnhoff, 1956, 1957), and intelligence (Arnhoff & Loy, 1957). Most of these studies will be discussed below under appropriate headings.

Conclusions: From these studies we might reasonably assert the following with respect to SG along a spatial continuum:

1. With human Ss, GSGs can be obtained for both voluntary and involuntary response dimensions with statistically significant gradients regularly observed.

2. In voluntary response situations, with inhibitory instructions, using latency as the response measure, GSGs have not been regularly observed. However, some recent studies have supported explanations of this failure and have reported gradients.

Pitch Generalization

In studies of pitch generalization, some special problems present themselves. If frequency is varied (keeping intensity constant) apparent loudness varies concomitantly. Thus, stimulus intensity dynamism may become a complicating factor. Secondly, human Ss have had extensive experience in differentiating pitch so that simple use of cps to characterize points on a pitch similarity continuum seems naive. There are points on the pitch similarity continuum which are well separated in terms of cps, but are actually difficult for Ss to discriminate, e.g., octaves.

Hovland (1937a) handled these problems by establishing a jnd scale using four points separated by 25 jnds as his test stimuli. He varied intensity in order to equate for apparent loudness. In this study (CR was GSR; UCS was electric shock), a regular GSG was observed with significant differences between test points. In a repetition of Hovland's study, Littman (1949) used an improved GSR apparatus. In the early test trials, generalization was complete (responses to test stimuli as great as responses to Stimulus 0) with a significant GSG only appearing in the fourth cycle of SG testing. Littman explains the relative irregularity and extreme height of his plotted gradients as possibly being due to his Ss being less acclimated and less experienced in the GSR-shock situation than were Hovland's Ss. In support of Littman's interpretation, Mednick (1957) has since shown that generalization responsiveness is indeed greater for relatively naive Ss.

In view of the complications involved in testing in more than one octave, Humphreys (1939) questioned the use of as broad a range of test stimuli (153-1967 cps) as employed in the Hovland studies. He restricted his test stimuli to 1000-1967 cps (only 25 jnds). Under 100% reinforcement conditions (such as were used by Hovland and Littman), he noted a concave upward gradient. Those Ss receiving 50% reinforcement produced a GSG that was quite elevated. He also found that the octave of Stimulus 0 had an unexpectedly strong response eliciting power (octave effect). A study by Wickens, Schroder, and Snide (1954) also made use of the Hovland paradigm except that only the three lowest tones were employed (153, 468 and 1000 cps) and each S was tested on only one GS. Regular GSGs were observed. Le Ny (1957a, 1957b) employed the same tones as Hovland but required a voluntary key-pressing response. He found regular gradients.

Garmezy (1952) used two sets of five tones, one ranging from 500 to 560 cps and the other ranging from 700 to 760 cps. Ss were trained either on 515 or 715 cps and were tested with all the GSs in that set. The response consisted of pushing or pulling a handle. Conditions of reinforcement were varied and smooth regular gradients were produced by all conditions of training.

The octave effect was also reported by Blackwell and Schlosberg (1943) who studied rats running for food and away from shock in a straight alley maze. Ss were trained to run to all stimuli (10, 8, 7, 5, and 3 kc.) and extinguished on all but the 10 kc. stimulus. A gradient of latency of response was produced with a reversal at 5 kc., the octave of 10 kc. A second study aimed at minimizing the secondary harmonic effects at the octave produced an even more apparent octave effect.

In a study of the effect of various attitudes upon SG, Razran (1949a) made use of a pitch continuum. With his dental cotton technique, he conditioned salivation to the Tone C and tested with the Tones F, B, e, a, d′, g′, c#², and f#². While attitude (cooperative, noncooperative) affected conditioning, it did not influence generalization. In Table 1 (p. 823) Razran presents the percent generalization of each of the attitude groups for each of the generalization pitches. Razran suggests that the data indicate that he failed to observe anything other than a very rough two step gradient. However, inasmuch as attitude had no effect on generalization, we are able to combine the data for all the attitude groups for each of the generalization stimuli. Thus, we may reprocess the reported data to plot a GSG along a continuum of unusual breadth, almost four octaves. The resultant gradient is very regular and steeply descending.

Jenkins and Harrison (1958) made use of an operant conditioning method for studying SG in pigeons which was suggested by Guttman and Kalish (1956). They conducted two experiments in pitch generalization on the effect of differential training (CR extinguished to absence of CS) on SG. They found that differential training produced steeper gradients than nondifferential training.

The following may be reasonably asserted regarding SG along a pitch continuum:

1. Regular and reliable gradients are observed.

2. Augmented responsiveness to the octave of Stimulus 0 has been noted.

3. As with some other continua, initial generalization test trials often elicit augmented SG responsiveness. This is often observed in studies utilizing a noxious UCS. It would be desirable for such studies to institute a pseudo-conditioning control to see what role sensitivization is playing in this situation.

4. Humphrey suggests that in view of the complications inherent in working with pitch SG (particularly the oc-

tave effect), future research work should consider such continua as hue. However, in view of the quirks of the $\Delta\lambda/\lambda$ incremental hue discrimination curve, nonmonotonic gradients are not to be unexpected in studies of this continuum also.

Intensity Generalization

In a theoretical article, Hull (1949) discusses an aspect of intensity generalization studies which should be initially clarified; other things remaining constant, an organism will react with greater amplitude, frequency, and speed to a stimulus of greater intensity. Since all studies of intensity generalization use training stimuli of different intensity from the generalization test stimuli, according to Hull's postulate, tests for generalization should show strength of reactivity to be a joint function of SG and stimulus intensity. Hull predicts different forms of observed gradients for test stimulus intensities ranging above and below the CS. He predicts convex upward gradients when test stimulus intensities range above the CS, and concave upward gradients when test intensities range below the CS. His postulate also leads to the prediction that the general trend of the gradient originating at a relatively strong stimulus intensity and generalizing toward weaker stimulus intensities will have a greater downward slope than will the gradient extending in the opposite direction between the same stimulus intensities.

The fact that the shape of a curve may be modified by scale transformation mitigates the importance of Hull's notions unless there is some specification of the stimulus and response units. This question is discussed again in the section on the shape of the gradient.

Intensity of direct light source. Hull finds confirmation for his postulate of the joint action of SG and stimulus intensity in a study by Brown (1942). This study may be considered with a group of experiments in which Ss were trained to respond to a certain intensity of direct light (as opposed to intensity of reflected light) and tested with other intensities. Brown's study tested the adient pull of rats to the stimulus of a screen of 0.2, 5, or 5000 apparent foot-candles illumination which, in turn, was associated with food. In accordance with Hull's prediction, the GSG (of a maze-running, harness-pulling response) was steeper for "high intensity trained" animals (trained on a high intensity stimulus and tested for SG on lower intensities, CS being the highest stimulus) than for "low intensity trained" animals (trained on the lowest intensity stimulus and tested on higher intensities, CS being the darkest stimulus). These terms, "high intensity trained" and "low intensity trained" will be used henceforth to denote groups trained respectively at the upper or lower extremity of the stimulus continuum used in the specific study.

Fink and Patton (1953) in part of a larger study, also found greater slope of GSG for high intensity trained rats than for those low intensity trained, using rate of water drinking as his response measure with two degrees of direct light (56 foot-candles apart) as the stimulus dimension. Frick (1948), using only high intensity trained rats in generalization test trials with varying degrees of illumination (20 to .02 foot-candles), found a concave upward gradient.

In an experiment with preschool children, Spiker (1956b) differentially reinforced a white (positive) and a blue (negative) light for a lever-pressing response. He then tested for generalization with three additional white lights; half of the Ss were high intensity trained and half were low intensity trained. The gradient for the high intensity trained was, in accordance with Hull's prediction, significantly steeper than the gradient for low intensity trained.

These studies, varying intensity of a direct light source, generally support Hull's principle of stimulus intensity dynamism.

Intensity of reflected light source. Another group of studies yielding results somewhat incompatible with those reported above, used intensity of reflected light as the generalization continuum. Raben (1949) trained rats to run in the brightest of five painted runways (varying in steps of 0.33 log units) and then tested for GSG of response latency in subsequent test sessions. She noted that the GSG went from convex upward in the first session (contrary to Hull's prediction) to concave upward in the fourth: this change paralleled a progressive decrement in SG responsiveness. Grandine and Harlow (1948) trained monkeys to get food from under a block of a certain brightness and tested for generalization with blocks of varying brightness by the simultaneous comparison method. They found a significantly decreasing GSG on the first trial; the authors state that the obtained GSGs did not differ significantly from a straight line.

Montgomery (1953), hypothesizing an exploratory drive which can be satisfied by exposure to a novel stimulus situation, extinguished exploratory behavior of rats in one maze and then tested for generalization of extinction to other mazes which varied in the intensity of the light reflected from their surfaces. He obtained an essentially straight line gradient by plotting percentage response decrement against difference of maze illumination. Schlosberg and Solomon (1943) trained rats to establish a black-white discrimination and then tested generalization to five degrees of relative brightness. They found a straight line gradient.

In an ingenious adaptation of the Brown, Clarke, and Stein (1958) method, Bass (1958) used variations in the grayness of the projected silhouette of a jockey on a running horse as her SG continuum. Every exposure of the silhouette represented another race; S was required to guess whether the horse would win. The Stimulus 0 horse won 80% of its races, while the other three horses (Stimuli 1, 2 and 3) won 40% of their races. It was assumed and found that the tendency to guess "win" would generalize from Stimulus 0 to the GSs as a function of their distance from Stimulus 0 on the grayness scale. This method could be readily adapted for use with children.

In general, studies using the intensity of direct light source as a continuum tend to support Hull's stimulus intensity dynamism principle; studies using reflected light tend to show ambiguous or negative evidence. Inspection of the two groups of studies suggests that the variations in reflected light (in the range of intensities thus far employed) have not produced as compelling a difference in intensity as variations in the intensity of a direct light source.

Intensity of sound. Hovland (1937b) tested for generalization of a CR to varying degrees of intensity of a tone; CS frequency was 1000 cps, the GSs were each 50 jnds apart and placed 40, 60, 74, and 86 dbs. above the threshold. Human Ss were used with PGR as CR and electric shock as UCS. Hovland trained half of the Ss to low intensity, half to high, with a counterbalanced design. While he does not plot differential gradients for low intensity trained as opposed to high intensity trained, it is apparent from inspection of the reported data that the slope of the gradient for the high intensity trained group is greater than that for low intensity trained. Fink and Patton (1953), studying learned drinking responses in white rats, found that the GSG for high intensity trained Ss tended to have steeper slope than that for low intensity trained Ss.

Miller and Green (1954) tested for generalization of extinction effects along a continuum of buzzer intensity. Using rats motivated by shock to run to a buzzer signal along a T maze, they reported a GSG with greater slope for high intensity trained animals. The gradient of extinction trials for the low intensity trained group approached a horizontal line, which result is explained in part by the greater number of trials which this group took to learn as compared with the high group.

From studies of sound intensities, the theory of SG responsiveness as a joint function of SG and stimulus intensity is supported.

Drive intensity SG. Stimulated by some studies showing indirect evidence of the generalization of responses to proprioceptive stimulation associated with specific durations of food deprivation, Yamaguchi (1952) explicitly designed a factorial study to test for this phenomenon. He deprived rats of food for from 3 to 72 hrs. during training and tested for generalization along the continuum of proprioceptive stimulation resulting from different degrees of hunger at each deprivation level. He found significant GSGs; the slope of the GSG of the high intensity trained group was significantly greater than the slope of the GSG for those that were low intensity trained. What is of special interest is the fact that generalization could be measured along this unusual continuum.

Some new interpretations. Johnsgard (1957), following up some work by Bragiel and Perkins (1954), has presented evidence suggesting that it is the degree of stimulus-background contrast rather than absolute stimulus intensity which is the variable producing the stimulus intensity dynamism effect. Johnsgard had rats run on an elevated runway to stimulus cards of varying reflectance placed before a screen of relatively medium intensity. He made more accurate predictions of number of responses and of latency from consideration of the contrast of stimulus card and background than from the absolute intensity of the stimulus card.

Perkins (1953) has also suggested a new interpretation (with supporting evidence) of the observed effects of stimulus intensity. He maintains that during the conditioning procedure an inhibitory response is built up to the absence of the CS, i.e., response is inhibited at those times that CS intensity equals zero. The inhibitory GSG originating at the point of zero intensity dampens response strength to the relatively weaker intensities of the CS. He further points out, in agreement with Heyman (1957), that in the typical maze running, direct light-intensity study, another factor to be considered is the fact that S is experiencing the highest possible intensity of the stimulus at the moment of reward. Since the animal usually gets the reward near the light source, it makes sense that he should respond with greater vigor to higher stimulus intensities. This interpretation may also explain the ambiguity of the findings in the reflected light intensity studies.

Hull (1950b, 1951, 1952) himself, has presented a revision of his original ideas on stimulus intensity dynamism. This revision has received little research attention. The revision suggests that intensity enters as a variable both during training (affecting $_sH_R$) and during response evocation. (In the earlier paper no effect on $_sH_R$ was postulated.) This revision actually has only a minor effect on his earlier predictions. Heyman (1957) in an excellently conceived study, evaluated the revised position. He used high intensity and low intensity trained rats approaching and pushing open a door covered with grey stimulus paper of appropriate reflectance. He found regular GSGs with slope and shape in agreement with Hull's predictions. He did not find that habit strength $(_sH_R)$ was affected by the intensity of the training stimulus. His results suggest that Hull's earlier position is better able to predict his results than the revised model.

Conclusions. The following conclusions may be reasonably asserted regarding SG along an intensity continuum:

1. Statistically significant gradients are regularly observed.

2. The slope of the GSG for Ss trained at high intensity and tested with GSs of low intensities is steeper than that for Ss trained with the CS at low intensity and tested at high intensity.

3. It is possible that studies using reflected light as the stimulus continuum do not have enough effective intensity differences, in comparison with direct light studies, to yield results in accordance with Conclusion 2.

4. Some recent work suggests that stimulus background contrast is an important variable determining the effective intensity of the stimulus.

Size Generalization

A number of experiments have investigated generalization along the dimension of stimulus size. The basic paradigm is similar to that of other SG studies; S is trained to respond to a CS of a given size and is then tested for generalization to stimuli above and/or below the CS on the particular size dimension being employed. According to most theoretical formulations, the amount of generalizations should be inversely proportional to the distance of the given stimulus from the CS. Although this expectation is, to a large extent, supported by the data, there are various factors which complicate the situation and which make it difficult to obtain regular gradients.

The two earliest studies were conducted by Gulliksen and by McKinney. Gulliksen (1932) used size and direction of angles as the stimuli and the moving of a handle to the left or right as the response. A gradient along the size dimension was reported. McKinney (1933) employed geometric line drawings that varied in the total length of the lines used. The results show "that the percentage of transfer decreases as the amount of alteration increases" (p. 857).

More recently, a series of experiments has been conducted employing circles of varying areas as stimuli. All of these studies used an apparatus designed by Grice, consisting of a straight alley maze 24 in. long with a starting box at one end and the stimulus at the other end. The stimulus circle has a small door through which a rat may reach the feeding dish. The maze can be rotated so that S does not have to be replaced at the end of a trial.

In the initial study by Grice and Saltz (1950), five white circles (79, 63, 50, 32, and 20 sq. in.) were used. Ss were trained either to the largest or smallest circle, and were tested on all stimuli in an extinction situation. Bidirectional GSGs were obtained.

Kling (1952) investigated generalization of extinction using the Grice apparatus. Ss were trained to respond to two different stimuli which were presented singly. One of the two stimuli was then presented alone for 15 non-reinforced trials. Testing consisted of a presentation of the other stimulus. The measure of generalization was the latency of the first response to the test stimulus. Smooth gradients were obtained for generalization from large to small and from small to large.

Margolius (1955) repeated Grice's experiment varying the number of reinforced trials during the training periods, and employing only the 79 sq. in. stimulus as the CS. Using the mean latency of the first three test trials as a measure, smooth gradients were obtained. Two other measures—number of responses in 30 trials and number of responses in 60 sec.—also produced regular gradients which weren't as precise as the latency gradient.

A study by Brush, Bush, Jenkins and Whiting (1952) is quite similar to the three just discussed. With pigeons as Ss, an illuminated spot of varying size on a pecking target in a Skinner box was used as the stimulus. Generalization was tested on both sides of the CS; rate of response was the response measure. Asymmetrical gradients were produced, that on the larger side being higher. However, if the log of size was substituted for absolute size, the gradients become more symmetrical. Jenkins, Pascal, and Walker (1958) also used this operant technique and report smooth and fairly regular GSGs.

Quite a few studies have investigated SG using the height of the stimulus as the independent variable. Grandine and Harlow (1948) trained monkeys to find food in a dish under a block of a given height. The Ss were then presented with the CS and a stimulus of a different height. The choice of the nonrewarded stimulus was considered an SG response. First trial data yielded regular GSGs.

A study by Buss (1950) followed one of the basic concept formation paradigms. Ss were presented with blocks of various heights, colors, areas, etc., and were made to respond "vec" or "non vec" to each block. Two response keys corresponding to the two possible responses were provided. During a short training period all "vec" responses to tall blocks were reinforced. Generalization gradients were produced along the height dimension both by number and latency of the "vec" responses. This is one of the few experiments in this area, or in fact in the whole area of stimulus generalization, in which human Ss, making a voluntary response, produced a gradient based on latency. It is interesting to note that there were two positive responses (i.e., lifting either key), rather than a single positive response and inhibiting instructions as in comparable studies. Two other studies (Buss, Weiner & Buss, 1954; Buss, 1955) making use of the same basic method and varying mode of reinforcement also produced smooth GSGs.

Rosenbaum (1953) using psychiatric and normal Ss, employed rectangles of light of various heights as the stimuli. The response consisted of moving a slider along a wire. Strong and weak shock as well as a buzzer were used to increase the speed of the response and to heighten anxiety. Regular gradients of amplitude were reported for all conditions except for the group of normal Ss that received the buzzer. A nonsignificant reverse gradient of latency was found, i.e., latency varied inversely as a function of GS dissimilarity. Unfortunately, during the testing session three CS booster trials were regularly presented between test stimuli. This would tend to prepare S for the test stimulus and constitutes a factor whose influence in the experiment is difficult to assess.

In a study by Botwinick (1953), Ss were trained to a small rectangle and were tested for generalization to three larger rectangles. The response consisted of moving a handle to the right. The measures used were frequency, amplitude and latency. For the first trial, first 10 trials and for the first 20 trials gradients were reported for frequency and amplitude. Using all trials, a gradient was found for latency, as well as for the other measures.

Grant and Schiller conducted a study with the GSR as the response measure, and shock as the UCS. A rectangle of light 1 in. $\times$ 12 in. was the CS and rectangles of 9, 10, 11, 13, 14, and 15 in. were the test stimuli. A gradient was reported based on first trial data, but a reversal occurred on the largest stimulus (1953).

In general, regular gradients have been observed for generalization along the size dimension. In some cases, however, reversals and asymmetries have been observed. These have uniformly occurred in cases where Ss have been trained to a relatively small CS and tested on larger GSs. It seems likely, as pointed out by Grice and Saltz, that this is due to a general effect which tends to augment responsiveness to larger stimuli. In view of the fact that large stimuli appear brighter than small stimuli, the effect may be indirectly due to stimulus intensity dynamism.

An alternative or complementary explanation could be based on the problem of defining equal distances between stimuli. If equal physical distances are used, it is evident that the psychological distances between the smaller stimuli are greater than those between the larger stimuli. This would make the larger stimuli closer to each other and to the CS than are the smaller stimuli, producing an elevated gradient. Brush et al. (1952), have demonstrated that using logarithmic scales tend to compensate for this effect.

Conclusions. From these studies, we can reasonably assert the following with respect to SG along the dimension of size:

1. For both human and infrahuman Ss, for both voluntary and involuntary response measures, for measures based on frequency, amplitude and in some instances latency of response, regular GSGs are observed.

2. The use of a slider response for human Ss, such as used by Gulliksen, Rosenbaum, and Botwinick, provides excellent amplitude and frequency data. However, latency GSGs are not observed.

3. A group of studies from widely separate laboratories which made use of the Grice apparatus have obtained highly consonant and meaningful results. This recommends this method quite highly for animal work.

Drive Stimulus Generalization

In this area we ask: (a) whether a response can be trained to the proprioceptive stimulation arising from a deprivation state; and (b) if so, will generalization of this response occur to proprioceptive stimulation which arises from similar deprivation states. In an attempt to answer these questions, Yamaguchi (1952) used a modified factorial design, Skinner box bar pressing response, and varying degrees of internal response to food deprivation as stimuli, with rats as Ss. He found generalization along this drive stimulus continuum.

Temporal Generalization

Pavlov (1927) demonstrated that dogs could learn to respond to a time interval as a conditioned stimulus. Several studies have subsequently investigated SG along this dimension. Czehura trained four dogs to respond to a one second silent interval between two tones differing in pitch. He then tested responsiveness to three additional durations of silent interval—3, 9, and 26 sec.— observing a regular gradient.

Rosenbaum (1951) trained rats to press a bar every 60 sec. to obtain food pellets. During testing, seven additional intervals were used—14, 30, 45, 75, 90, 105, and 120 sec. Using a latency measure of response strength, a significant gradient, decreasing in height as the CS was approached, was obtained; past the 60 sec., Stimulus 0 point, latencies tended to remain at the same level as those for the CS interval. The lack of a regular gradient beyond the CS interval was interpreted as the result of S being set to respond at 60 sec., at which point internal stimulus cues would be maximal. Therefore, for intervals greater than 60 sec. response latencies would not be expected to increase. A question which can be raised regarding this study is the positioning of the animal. As the testing interval approached the CS interval, the animal could have been moving closer to the bar, so that proximity would result in decreased latency. After 60 sec. the animal might have remained poised at the bar resulting in the observed plateau.

A further study of the temporal dimension was that by Fink and Davis (1951) with human Ss giving a voluntary key-pressing response to three series of tones of differing duration. Muscle action potential data was also recorded. In one series, Ss were told to respond to all tones and were presented with tones of 2, 2.25, 2.5, 3.0 and 4.0 sec. In the second series (both given to all Ss) only two-second tones were presented. During testing, 10 trials were given with the two-second durations, then 10 trials with the other four durations. Fairly regular convex upward gradients of both muscle action potential and key pressing were obtained. It is of interest in this study that the key pressing response yielded results which were directly comparable to the results obtained from the muscle action potential response. These results on muscle action potential in a sense support the use of voluntary response measures with human Ss. Fink and Davis discuss the problem of choosing an interval scale that is most appropriate for the independent variable. They suggest that any measure is as good as another if followed consistently; logs are of particular value for human Ss when the temporal intervals used are very small.

A final study in this area is that by Mednick (1959), who used taped tones differing only in duration (CS = 2.7 sec., GSs = 3, 3.3, 3.6, 3.9 sec.). Twenty CS training trials were given and a regular generalization gradient of a voluntary key pressing response was found during testing.

It may be concluded that regular, statistically significant GSGs may be obtained along a temporal dimension. It would seem to be advantageous for Es to adopt a consistent method of presenting gradients in terms of the interval scale expressing the independent variable. Log units appear to be the most generally applicable.

Hue Generalization

Utilizing a modified version of the Skinner automatic key-pecking pigeon apparatus, Guttman and Kalish, are conducting a series of careful investigations of SG along the hue continuum. The stimulus is produced by a monochromator and displayed on the translucent pecking key. Typically, the pigeon is brought to a high level of responsiveness by means of a variable interval reinforcement schedule and generalization testing is carried on under extinction conditions. Regular gradients are almost invariably obtained with this technique. It also has the advantage of enabling E to obtain GSGs from individual Ss.

In an early experiment Guttman and Kalish (1956) studied the relationship between the degree of discriminability of changes in a stimulus continuum and the shape of the generalization gradient along that continuum. One might predict an inverse relationship between the incremental discriminability of a continuum (as measured by $\Delta\lambda$) and the amount of generalization. However, these variables were found to be relatively independent of each other. Kalish (1958) adapted this apparatus for humans and found an inverse relationship between generalization and discriminability along the wave length continuum. The differences in procedure and Ss between the Guttman and Kalish (1956) and Kalish (1958) studies makes it difficult to explain these opposing results.

In a later study on summation of gradients (Kalish & Guttman, 1957) the method proved successful in producing regular GSGs along the hue continuum. An outstanding doctoral dissertation by Honig (1958), using the same basic procedure investigated problems in transposition and stimulus preference. Of special interest is the finding that stimulus preference may be predicted from knowledge of the underlying generalization gradients. Hanson (1957) had pigeons learn to peck at a key for one wavelength and not to peck for another. The pigeons were then tested for generalization along the wave length continuum that surrounded these two stimuli. As might be expected, generalization responsiveness on the side of the negative stimulus was greatly reduced. What is surprising is that the discrimination training did *not* reduce the total amount of generalization responsiveness. Instead the entire GSG seemed to move up the continuum away from the negative trained stimulus. The maximum point of the curve was also displaced in this direction. In an informative paper on the problem of the scaling of the independent variable, Guttman (1956) reports on some current work from his laboratory.

VARIABLES INFLUENCING GENERALIZATION

Stimulus Generalization as a Function of Drive Level

Studies in this area have concerned themselves with the effect of hunger, sex, and fear-anxiety on the GSG.

Hunger. Brown (1942), using the straight alley maze, rat-pulling-harness apparatus, varied the number of hours of pretest food deprivation. He noted regular gradients with the amplitude and speed of response varying directly with number of hours of food deprivation. The GSG of the high drive group also tended to be steeper. In a later study of similar design (Brown, 1948), these findings were replicated. An additional condition of strong electric shock produced results which suggest that the gradient of avoidance (shock) behavior is steeper than that for approach (hunger) behavior.

Rosenbaum (1951), studying generalization along a temporal dimension, using a modified Skinner box, varied drive by depriving two groups of rats for 22 hours and then feeding one group a small quantity of food just before testing. He noted no significant differences between the GSGs of his two groups when the fed group received only 4 gms. of food. When this amount was increased to 10 gms. in a second experiment, the difference between the groups was significant. The unfed group demonstrated greater SG responsiveness.

The more pigeons are deprived of food the more generalization responsiveness they exhibit (Jenkins, Pascal, & Walker, 1958). The pigeons were tested using operant techniques with the size of the pecking key serving as the generalization continuum.

None of these studies utilized a factorial design; this factor would tend to complicate the interpretation of their findings due to the possibility of a drive stimulus SG effect. Despite this, their results make it reasonable to conclude that increased time of food deprivation will lead to increased SG responsiveness.

Electric shock. Rosenbaum (1953) used three degrees of noxious stimulation (strong shock, weak shock, and buzzer) to produce varying levels of drive state with human Ss. While the weak shock and buzzer conditions did not produce differing results, the strong shock resulted in considerably elevated gradients.

In one of the series of studies on displacement, Murray and Miller (1952) compared the GSG under three levels of electric shock, finding greater generalization responsiveness for the greater shock condition. Brown (1948) reported a similar finding. Relatively strong shock produced relatively elevated gradients.

Sex. Testing the effects of testosterone proprionate upon the copulatory behavior of sexually inexperienced male rats exposed to "incentives" of varying degrees of "appropriateness," Beach (1942) measured responsiveness on a 5 point scale. A rough gradient may be observed from his data. The greater the dose of testosterone proprionate the less the incentive need resemble a receptive female in order for it to elicit a response and the stronger the response to the incentive. Macerone and Walton (1938) obtained similar results.

Situational factor. Mednick (1957) compared the GSGs of experimentally naive and experimentally sophisticated Ss finding that the naive Ss demonstrated greater SG responsiveness than the sophisticated Ss. Inasmuch as this effect was especially marked in Ss who scored high on the Taylor Manifest Anxiety Scale he interpreted this finding in terms of situational drive arousal.

It may be reasonably concluded from the above evidence that any condition which will increase the drive state will result in increased SG responsiveness.

Individual Differences in Generalization

The study of individual differences is concerned with a search for correlates of SG reactiveness. The bulk of the work has dealt with developmental factors, personality variables, schizophrenia, and brain damage. In most instances the intent is utilization of SG as an explanatory concept. Thus an excess in SG reactiveness is seen by some writers as an important basis of the disorder of thinking in schizophrenia.

However, there is another possible direction that this research might take. Basic problems in learning could be attacked by this method. If a theory hypothesized SG as an important variable promoting learning in a given context, then a group evidencing a high level of SG reactiveness would be expected to perform well in such a context. For example, Gibson (1940) hypothesized that SG is behind the interference arising in the learning of serial lists of high intralist similarity. A group showing reduced SG reactiveness should learn a high intralist similarity list with little interference (relative to its performance on a low intralist similarity list). Mednick (1955) has shown that individuals with cortical brain damage evidence reduced SG reactiveness. On the basis of this result, Carson (1958) hypothesized and demonstrated that cortically brain damaged individuals showed relatively little decrement in learning as a function of increasing intralist similarity. In studies of this type, it is necessary that the effect be shown in the interaction term since simple differences between groups could be due to a myriad of other factors.

Manifest anxiety. Mednick (1957), comparing high and low scoring college students on the Taylor Manifest Anxiety Scale (MAS) found that the highly anxious Ss showed more spatial generalization. Studies by Hilgard, Jones, and Kaplan (1951) on eyelid conditioning, Wenar (1953) on temporal conditioning, and M. T. Mednick (1957) on PGR conditioning and mediated generalization, have also demonstrated greater generalization reactiveness on the part of high anxious Ss. In the study by M. T. Mednick it was found that conditioning level of the anxiety groups was directly related to degree of anxiety. In order to evaluate generalization responsiveness independent of conditioning level, she compared anxiety groups equated for conditioning level; the nature of her findings was not changed. It is important that all studies attempting to demonstrate group differences in SG responsiveness either equate their groups for conditioning level or use a measure of relative generalization (ratio of generalization response to conditioned response).

A study by Buss (1955), on psychiatric patients found no differences as a function of MAS scores; he suggests that the MAS is not an appropriate test for psychiatric patients. Fager and Knopf (1958) agree with Buss' conclusion on the basis of their experiment with psychiatric patients. They found no relationship between MAS scores and SG.

Clinical groups. On the basis of clinical observation, Schilder (1939) first remarked on the difficulties schizophrenics have in tasks involving differentiation. Bender and Schilder (1930), studying conditioned withdrawal from shock, noted extreme over-generalization by schizophrenic Ss. Cameron (1951) has spoken of over-inclusion and the broadening of the GSG on the part of schizophrenics. Garmezy (1952), studying generalization along the dimension of pitch, found that schizophrenics demonstrated more relative generalizations than normals. This effect was especially marked under conditions of socially administered punishment. Mednick (1955), using the dimension of space, found that schizophrenics generalized more than normals. Dunn (1954) tested schizophrenics with social and non-social materials and found relatively greater generalization for schizophrenics with the social materials. The "social" generalization continua were very cleverly constructed, in one instance, consisting of changes in the angle of elevation of the pointing arm of a scolding mother. Rosenbaum (1953) utilized psychiatric patients in a generalization study, but did not compare them with the normal Ss in the study. However, inspection of the reported data suggests that there was little apparent difference in generalization between the groups. Mednick (1958a) has presented a learning theory approach to research in schizophrenia which leans heavily on SG theory.

Eriksen (1954) compared size generalization in "hysterics" and "psychasthenics" as defined by extreme scores on the appropriate MMPI scales. The "hysterics" demonstrated more generalization. Both groups show more generalization when instructed that they could avoid the UCS (electric shock) than when told it was unavoidable.

Personality tests. Arnhoff (1956) reported that high generalizers showed more ethnic prejudice (E scale), but on replication of his study (1957) he found the difference did not hold up. In this laboratory, similar fluctuating results have been observed across a group of four studies using the highly related F scale (authoritarianism). Analysis of the subscales of the F scale indicates that the Projectivity subscale consistently holds up. High "projectors" tend significantly, to be high generalizers. In the process of carrying out generalization research at this laboratory, various additional personality measures have been incidentally correlated with generalization responsiveness. We will mention these briefly. No relationship has been noted between SG responsiveness and field independence (Witkin, 1954) or need achievement (McClelland, Atkinson, Clarke, & Lowell, 1953); on the other hand, those low in achievement imagery (Iowa Picture Interpretation Test, Hedlund, 1953), tend to generalize more than those high in achievement imagery (Mednick, 1958b).

Age. Mednick and Lehtinen (1957) found that SG responsiveness varied inversely as a function of age in school children; no relationship was found for adults in a separate study by Mednick (1955). With the younger children, Mednick and Lehtinen noted a latency gradient while none was noted for the older children. In line with these results, Reiss (1946) found generalization along a gradient of homonymy to vary inversely as a function of age in children.

Brain damage. In a study of patients suffering from a variety of types and locations of cortical brain damage, Mednick (1955) noted extreme curtailing of generalization responsiveness. These results are similar to those of Smith (1951) who noted decreased transfer (based on deficiency in SG responsiveness) from Ss with corpus callosum damage. Goldstein's (1941) concept of the "concreteness" of the brain damaged may also be based on

some retardation in SG responsiveness. A study by Mednick and Wild (1958) on cerebral palsied children indicates an accompanying deficiency in SG responsiveness.

Degree and Type of Training

SG has been regarded as a spread of habit strength
from the CS to the GSs. Thus, one of the variables that
might influence the GSG is level of habit strength of the
CR. Experiments in this area have manipulated either
amount or distribution of reinforcement of the CR.

Number of reinforced trials. The earliest relevant data
comes from Pavlov's laboratory and is reported by Razran
(1949b). Using dogs as Ss, the salivary CR, and an as-
sortment of stimuli as CS, Pavlov found, in a number of
different experiments, that the amount of generalization
to test stimuli increased with increased number of training trials to the CS.

Beritoff (1924), experimenting with dogs, reported a
"spread of generalization," that is, as training continued,
tones further and further removed from the CS could
elicit the response. However, after three days of training
generalization ceased to spread. There was considerable
variation among Ss; no statistical analysis was reported.

In a study by Hovland (1937c), different groups were
given 8, 16, 24, or 48 reinforcements. Generalization occurred at all levels of training; relative generalization (i.e.
ratio of generalized response to conditioned response
strength) increased with training and then decreased. Ss
receiving 16 reinforcements generalized not only more
than those receiving less reinforcement, but also more
than those receiving more reinforcement. It was also
found that the more reinforcement Ss received, the more
rapidly the generalized response extinguished. Hovland
(1935) conducted a similar experiment, the results of
which again indicate that relative generalization increases
from 8 to 16 reinforcements and then decreases.

Razran (1940) experimented with the conditioned salivary response in humans using the increase in weight of
cotton dental pads placed in S's mouth as the response
measure. Conditioning consisted of short periods during
which Ss ate while the appropriate CS was presented. In
the tests for generalization, which were held at the end of

each of the eight training sessions, different colored lights, buzzers and monosyllabic words were substituted for the CS. There was generalization to each stimulus at each degree of training. Relative generalization increased with training and then declined; the decline was more marked when single stimuli were used as CS than when combinations of stimuli were used. The interpretation of the results of these experiments is somewhat difficult. For one thing, while Razran states that there were from 2 to 16 Ss in each study, 22 of the 26 studies had only 2 Ss. Further, when summarizing the various results he takes the mean of a group of percentages based on differing numbers of Ss.

In a study of Spiker (1956a) children were trained to push a lever in order to get marbles which they could exchange for toys. Pushing the lever was rewarded with marbles only when a particular color of light was presented in contiguity with the response; each correct response was rewarded. Two groups of Ss, equated for response frequency, were given either 12 or 24 training trials. At the end of the training period generalization was tested with different colored lights. The group that received more reinforcement responded to the generalization test stimulus more often.

The experiments discussed so far dealt with the effect of amount of reinforcement on the amount of generalization, the latter being tested with only a single GS. An excellent study by Margolius (1955) investigated the relationship between number of reinforcements and the gradient of generalization. Using the Grice apparatus, Ss (white rats) were trained on a 79 sq. cm. circle and tested on circles of 63, 50, 32, and 20 sq. cm. Groups of Ss were given different numbers of reinforcements ranging from 4 to 104. In testing for generalization, three measures were used: number of responses in 30 trials, latency of the first three test trials, and number of responses in 60 sec. Absolute and relative generalization increased with training, the smoothest gradients being obtained from the latency measure.

In the studies reported, SG responsiveness increased as a function of the number of reinforced training trials. On the other hand, those studies using human Ss and

PGR or salivary CR measures found relative generalization increasing up to a point and then decreasing. Margolius studied rats running in the Grice maze apparatus and reported a direct relationship between relative generalization responsiveness and number of reinforced training trials. These differences in results are ascribable to too many differences in procedure and sampling to allow for unequivocal interpretation. However, there is a possible interpretation. The conditioned PGR is highly sensitive to the effects of adaptation, far more so than reinforced maze running on the part of hungry rats. After 24 or 48 reinforced trials, a gross overall adaptation of the PGR would not be unexpected. This could easily have masked any possible advantage that the generalized response was gaining from increased training.

Distribution of reinforcement. In a study by Humphreys (1939), the percentage of reinforcement of the CR was varied. With tones as stimuli, PGR as CR, Ss received either 100% or 50% reinforcement. All Ss received the same number of trials. The 100% reinforced group produced a negatively accelerated gradient; the 50% reinforced group responded almost equally to all stimuli, including the CS, though there was a slight decrease in responsiveness to the stimulus farthest removed from the CS. In a subsequent repetition of this study which made use of a voluntary response Humphreys found essentially the same results (1948). Humphreys concluded that it is reasonable to predict a positively accelerated GSG for the 50% reinforced group when the gradient becomes more marked. This group also generalized more than the 100% reinforced group, despite the fact that the latter received twice as many reinforcements. In explanation, Humphreys points out that the 50% group was concerned about the shock during the generalization trials, while the other group was not. Another possible explanation of the results is that the extinction situation was more similar to the training situation for the partially reinforced group than it was for the 100% reinforced group (i.e. from 50% reinforcements to no reinforcements is less of a change than from 100% reinforcements to no reinforcements).

THEORIES OF STIMULUS GENERALIZATION

Neurophysiological Formulations

While intuitively it would seem that SG is a phenomenon which affords fertile ground for explanation couched in terms of neurophysiology, little attention has been devoted to such attempts. Pavlov (1927) first put forth the notion that SG is due to a fading wave of excitation irradiating from the spot on the cortex stimulated because of the presentation of the CS. As a result of this wave of excitation, stimuli whose cortical representations are contiguous to that of the CS also possess the potentiality of eliciting the CR. Due to the fading strength of the wave, the response eliciting power of these stimuli decreases as a function of their distance from the cortical representation of the CS.

Loucks (1933) and Denny-Brown (1932) have developed analytical arguments which seem to cast doubt on the "irradiation" hypothesis. Even more damaging, however, is the data from a study by Grant and Dittmer (1940). They point out that the cortical representation of the hand is considerably greater in area than that of the trunk of the body. From this, they infer that irradiation will suffer a greater decrement between two comparable points on the hand than between two points on the trunk. Their data showed the gradient for the trunk to be slightly steeper. Grant and Dittmer also point to the Bass and Hull study as tending to refute the irradiation hypothesis. Bass and Hull (1934) report a smooth gradient going from shoulder to feet. In terms of irradiation theory this is extremely surprising since the cortical representations of the thigh, calf and foot are interposed between the cortical representation of the waist and buttocks. Some aberrancy in the GSG should be observed as a result of this. While these data and analytic arguments cast strong doubt on the usefulness of the irradiation hypothesis as it stands, it certainly is appealing for heuristic reasons and may prove important in some modified form.

Wolpe (1952) has attacked the problem from the standpoint of excitation of common neural pathways. He gives an example from experiments on pitch generalization. It is known that tones which are similar to each other in terms of cps will tend to excite overlapping parts of the relevant end organ of hearing. Further, this end organ overlap is mirrored at higher neural levels such as the medial geniculate body and the cerebral cortex. Thus, a response learned to one of these tones may be called forth by the other tone by means of these common stimulated pathways. Tone A might stimulate Nerve Endings 1, 2, and 3 with a peak at 2. Tone B will stimulate 3, 4, and 5, with a peak at 4. Any response called forth by Tone A will also be elicited by Tone B because of Common Pathway 3. A problem which quickly arises in this formulation is the usual finding of octave generalization, i.e., incremented response to the octave of the CS despite the fact that the tones are well separated on the cps dimension. Wolpe explains this as being the result of overtones having the frequency of the CS being produced by presentation of its octave. This explanation suffices for this aspect of the Humphreys (1939) experiment (which Wolpe cites by way of illustration) but does not explain the Blackwell and Schlosberg (1943) finding of a strong-octave effect in rats despite extensive precautions taken to minimize the appearance of such overtones. Wolpe would also have some difficulty explaining increments of generalization response to symmetrical stimuli (Gibson, 1939; Anrep, 1923). Further, the Humphreys experiment, cited by Wolpe, itself contains data damaging to his theory. Humphreys' experiment fully replicated an earlier experiment by Hovland except for one important detail. Hovland tested across the pitch dimension using a range of 4 tones from 1967 to 153 cps. Humphreys only tested between 1967 and 1000 cps. Since the representation of 1967 and 153 cps are more widely separated on the hearing end organ than 1967 and 1000 cps, we are clearly in a position to predict that in the instance that 1967 was the CS, the 1000 cps test tone of the Humphreys study should elicit more relative generalization than the 153 cps tone of the Hovland study. As it happens the relative generalization strength of Humphreys' 1000 cps tone was .72; the relative generalization strength of Hovlands' 153 cps tone was .70. Humphreys suggests that this similarity of response strengths might be ascribed to a "frame of reference" effect since the tones were both end points of the pitch dimension in their respective studies. These data and such an explanation are not compatible with the Wolpe position.

The common pathways notion is similarly damaged by consideration of the dimension of intensity. Since degree of intensity of a stimulus is not reflected in the firing of a specific neurone it is not clear how common pathways can develop in the intensity dimension.

Form of the GSG

There have been a number of attempts to specify the form of the GSG. These attempts have often made the explicit or implicit assumption that a form exists which is invariant across dimensions. In addition, many have maintained, with Hovland, that "the form of the gradient is of considerable importance in psychological theory" (1937b). Certainly such work as Spence's analysis of transposition, Miller's displacement theory and work on summation of gradients could proceed from firmer foundations if the form or forms of the GSG were better delineated.

Unfortunately there has not been good agreement regarding the shape. In fact, just about all reasonably imaginable shapes have been proposed as "the" form of the gradient (including no constant form at all).

While this question of shape has consumed paragraphs in many a discussion of experimental results, it has only occasionally assumed the status of a central problem. This is perhaps as it should be for the true shape may well be an ephemeral treasure. One dismaying notion is the ease with which any obtained shape may be altered by simply manipulating the units of the axes. It seems clear that without some specification of stimulus and response measurement scales, discussion of the shape of obtained gradients must proceed very cautiously. This fact has been pointed out by Guttman in an interesting treatment of this and other SG problems (1956).

An approach to the problem of the shape of the GSG in terms of a mathematical model is presented by Shepard (1958a) and discussed below.

Mathematical Formulation of SG

The application of mathematical models to SG has been impeded by the absence of a satisfactory independent variable, i.e., a mathematically precise measure of psychological similarity of stimuli. Recently, however, there have been two kinds of attacks on this problem. One of these, proposed by Bush and Mosteller (1951) is based upon a set-theoretic model, and views a stimulus as a collection of elements. The similarity of two stimuli is defined in terms of the fraction of these elements that the two stimulus-sets have in common.

Following Estes (1950) they maintain that the probability of a response to a given stimulus is equal to the proportion of elements in that stimulus conditioned to that response. The probability that any new stimulus will elicit this response is proportional to the similarity of the new stimulus to the conditioned stimulus. An index of similarity is determined by application of a set-theory equation to previously obtained data. By introducing further assumptions about the effects of reinforcement and extinction on the primitive elements, set-theoretic models of this kind have been shown to account for certain ways in which generalized response probabilities change during the course of discrimination learning (Green, 1958; Restle, 1955). However, Bush and Mosteller conclude that their model cannot make any experimentally testable prediction about the shape of the GSG since the index of similarity (that is presumed to govern SG) is "very much organism determined" and, hence, has no invariant relation to the distance between stimuli along "such physical dimensions as light or sound intensity, frequency, etc." Restle and Beecroft (1955) have pointed up the similarity "between the Hull-Spence theory and the Bush-Mosteller mathematical model in the study of stimulus generalization" as it is affected by differences in anxiety level.

Shepard (1957) has proposed a model for SG that regards a stimulus as a point in metric space. The similarity of two stimuli is defined in terms of the distance between these stimulus points in their common space. He supposes that stimuli differing along a single physical dimension (e.g. tones of various frequencies) can be identified with points in a "psychological space" in such a way that the distance between points is invariantly related to SG. Such a curve in psychological space differs from the rectilinear physical scale by some "continuous, differentiable transformation." Therefore, although the GSG is postulated to have an invariant form in this psychological space, when this space is retransformed back into the "physical space" (e.g., into the physical scale of frequency) the form of the GSG becomes irregular and depends upon the position of the CS.

He then asks this question: Given the physical scale with its empirically determined but irregular gradients of SG, is it possible to recover the psychological space and, hence, a unique GSG having the same form for all positions of the CS? Shepard's contention is that for any given experimental procedure the GSG has a unique form that is independent of the position of the CS and of the physical dimension along which the test stimuli are arrayed.

His procedure attempts to discover the unique function that will convert the conditional response probabilities from experiments on SG into psychological distances. On the basis of several paired-associate experiments in which the stimuli vary along such physical dimensions as size, brightness, color and shape, he concludes that the GSG under this kind of experimental condition is concave upward (Shepard, 1958a, 1958b). In addition, though, he concludes that the shape of the GSG depends upon the distribution of reinforcement so that, if the S is reinforced only part of the time, the GSG departs from the pure exponential form and becomes more "bell-shaped," i.e., convex upward in the vicinity of the CS. This conclusion is supported by Humphreys' results (1939, 1948). Although this model accounts for the observed form of the GSG (when that gradient is plotted against psychological distance), it does not attempt an account of the changes in the degree of SG during discrimination learning. In this respect, then, the metric model is less general than the set-theoretic models, like Bush and Mosteller's which incorporate a learning mechanism. Perhaps the two types of approach will eventually be combined so as to account both for the shape of the GSG and for the temporal course of SG.

Summation of Generalized Response Strength

A theorem of Hull's (1939) which has excited much interest but little research suggests that overlapping GSGs originating from two or more points on the same continuum will summate and result in incremented generalization responsiveness in the area of overlap. Bilodeau, Brown and Meryman (1956) studied generalization along a visual-spatial dimension with a task in which Ss gave an instructed voluntary response. They found a summative effect between two positive points separated by 16° of visual angle but not between two points separated by 32° of visual angle. They are careful to point out that while their procedures have a formal correspondence to the methods assumed by Hull, they do not meet all of his assumptions. Guttman and Kalish (1957) point out that the Bilodeau, Brown and Meryman experimental design permits summation to be observed at six different points on the gradients. It occurs at only one of these, the single point between the training stimuli. This latter finding is repeated in the data presented by Guttman and Kalish. They used the pigeon pecking apparatus exposing different hues on the pecking key to test for generalization. Their method comes closer to satisfying the conditions for summation as assumed by Hull (e.g., reinforcement used to build up habit strength rather than instructions) than that of Bilodeau, Brown and Meryman. Thus, while in both studies summation seems observable at points between the training stimuli, it is disturbing not to find it at any of the other possible points on the gradient.

THE LASHLEY, WADE-HULL CONTROVERSY AND SOME NEW INTERPRETATIONS

Hull (1943) postulated that as a result of the reinforcement of a response to a stimulus, gradients of associative strength develop to non-conditioned stimuli which produce empirical GSGs. In an uneven article which, however, contains penetrating criticisms demanding response, Lashley and Wade (1946) present a strong attack on this Hullian postulate as well as other aspects of research on SG. One point lies at the basis of their criticism; this is their assertion that the empirical phenomena of SG do not mirror underlying gradients of habit strength developed during conditioning, but instead represent a "failure of association." By this they mean that the reason S responds to the GS in the test period is that S has not yet been conditioned to respond differentially to the E-defined relevant aspect of the CS. It is only during testing that the GSG develops, and this is only because of S's attention being directed to the E-defined dimension.

Hull's (1947) otherwise effective and informative answer to the Lashley and Wade paper failed to deal with the important "failure of association" argument. Brown, Bilodeau, and Baron (1951) fractionate the argument and dismiss it as circular and untestable. They point out that the only way one can know when S has failed to learn to respond to a particular stimulus element is when S does not respond differentially to that characteristic. However, this failure to respond differentially is the operational definition of SG. Since these two are defined by identical operations, Brown, et al. argue that the Lashley-Wade criticism is circular. However, if this criticism were to suggest a specific differential test, it could avoid this property of circularity.

The "failure of association" notion is in one sense similar to Estes' learning theory since it proposes that only certain elements of the stimulus situation are associated with the response on any one learning trial, due to the specificity of S's attending responses. If, in a test trial, E changes only one small aspect of the stimulus, S will respond to the aspect to which he had attended and which remains unchanged. However, if, during training, S has by chance attended to the E-defined relevant element of the stimulus then S will not respond when that element is changed; no SG will be observed. In these terms a specific prediction may be made. The greater the number of conditioning trials the greater the likelihood of S attending to the relevant stimulus element and thus the greater the likelihood of differentiation of the CS from the GS. Thus, generalization would be expected to decrease as a function of the number of conditioning trials. As pointed out above quite the opposite result has been regularly observed. This is seen as very telling evidence against the failure of association position.

Growing from the failure of association argument is the assertion that the GSG is a product of the test period and develops as a result of S's attention being directed to the E-defined relevant dimension. Lashley and Wade assert that no falling GSG will be observed unless the CS is contrasted with a GS so that the relevant dimension is made manifest to S. Since underlying gradients of response strength cannot develop in the conditioning period "training with one stimulus fails to produce a significantly greater strength of association with that stimulus than with others on the same dimension." Lashley and Wade specifically suggest the method of single stimulus training (followed by a single test with a GS) as a crucial test. Such a test has since been repeated many times over, resulting in occasional reports of first test trial gradients. The Grandine and Harlow (1948) study was specifically designed with the Lashley and Wade restrictions in mind. Regular GSGs were observed on the first test trial. However, in this instance it should be noted that Grandine and Harlow are in the minority. Most experiments have not found a falling gradient on the first test trial. More often there is no difference between the CS and the GSs.

Razran (1949) has proposed another interpretation of generalization phenomena. He suggests that there are two types of generalization: "(a) *pseudogeneralization* and (b) *true generalization*." The Lashley-Wade *failure of association* position refers to pseudogeneralization phenomena where S, because of age, infirmity, or circumstances, is unable to note distinguishing characteristics of the CS. "The relation of pseudogeneralization to true generalization is not unlike that of the undifferentiated total action of the young foetus to the structured whole activities of the fully developed individual."

In his "subsequent testing hypothesis" Razran further asserts that "generalization develops, not during the original training of the conditioned stimuli, but during the subsequent testing of the generalization stimuli." This hypothesis is similar to the Lashley-Wade position on this matter. Razran is suggesting that during training no tendencies or propensities to generalization are built up. During testing with the GSs, Ss will "categorize or rate the new stimulus on some sort of crude similarity-dissimilarity scale" consisting of two or three steps.

The present writers hold a view somewhat intermediate between that of Lashley, Razran and Hull. Before developing this view it may be helpful to analyze some of the assumptions of what we will call, for want of a better name, the Hull position. It should be made clear that this elaboration of Hull's statements is the writers' responsibility. It is not impossible that in order to draw a sharper contrast they have in certain instances exaggerated Hull's position.

Vigorous generalization responses are routinely observed on the first test trial following single stimulus training. Inasmuch as such responses would not occur in the absence of this training and the degree of such training has a marked effect on the degree of generalization behavior, the phenomenon of stimulus generalization is probably best seen as resulting from the operations involved in training.

On the first test trial following training (generally acknowledged to be the "purest" measure of SG) one should expect to find a regular descending GSG. Instead, the GSs usually elicit almost as much response strength as the CS ("complete" SG). Hull suggests that this is due to strong responsiveness occurring immediately after training (not necessarily a convincing argument in view of the action of reactive inhibition which would tend to lower responsiveness) and to unextinguished reactions to irrelevant situational stimuli such as apparatus clicks. Wickens, Schroder and Snide (1954) attempted to extinguish such responses to an irrelevant aspect of the stimulus before beginning SG testing, but nevertheless found complete SG on the first test trial.

The expectation of a descending GSG on the first test trial carries with it some assumptions. First, one must assume that SG responsiveness develops as a consequence of training. This seems to be an acceptable assumption.

The second assumption is that training results in a gradient of apportionment of potential responsiveness along the relevant stimulus continuum. For example, it is expected that if Ss are trained to salivate to a tone of 1000 cps and each S is presented once with a tone at some other point on the cps continuum, the extent of each S's response will be proportional to the physical or jnd distance of his test stimulus from the training stimulus. If S is to respond in a proportional manner (i.e., respond more to 1400 cps than to 1800 cps) it must be assumed that he came to the first test trial with associations between specific stimulus values on a physical or jnd scale and certain levels of response strength. That is, it must be assumed that before the first test trial he already had a certain number of drops of salivation set aside for 1400 cps and a smaller number reserved for 1800 cps.

However, there is another possibility. What if, following training, S set up associations between generalization responses and an *ordinal* scale of stimulus values rather than a jnd or continuous physical scale? That is, what if the extent of S's response to a given GS was proportional to the *number of stimulus units* that separate that GS from Stimulus 0 (with number of stimulus units defined in terms of the population of stimulus units S has experienced within the immediate experimental situation)? This would explain the fact that almost complete SG is usually observed on the first test trial; the first GS that S experiences that is on the same continuum as Stimulus 0 will be, at that point, only one stimulus unit from Stimulus 0, and will elicit a relatively large response. For example, let us say that in an experiment on pitch generalization, Stimulus 0 is 1000 cps and one S receives a 1400 cps GS and another S receives an 1800 cps GS on the first test trial. For each S in terms of his experience in the experimental situation, his GS will be only one unit removed from Stimulus 0. With continued testing S's GS units hierarchy will change until he has experienced the full range of GSs used in the experiment. At this point a regular descending GSG would be expected. This would in turn explain another typical finding of generalization experiments, a regular descending GSG is usually only found at a relatively late stage of testing. Also, it is typically observed that the slope of the GSG increases with continued testing.

Let us take another situation where some differential predictions may be made. The Hull position, as stated above, would tend to predict that the amount of responsiveness elicited by a GS will be determined by its distance from the CS along a physical or jnd scale without regard to what other GSs, if any, are presented in the experiment. In terms of the alternative notion being presented here, if the CS is a tone of 1000 cps and 1600 cps is the critical test GS, it will make a great difference whether the other GSs are (a) 1200 cps and 1400 cps or if the other GSs are (b) 1800 cps and 2000 cps. In the case of (a), the GS at 1600 cps will be three units from the CS; in the case of (b), 1600 cps will be one unit from the CS. If Ss allot their generalization responsiveness according to units of separation of GSs from the CS then it would be predicted that the 1600 cps stimulus would elicit more responsiveness in the (b) situation than in the (a) situation.

Further, it would be predicted that an important determinant of amount of response to any of the GSs would be their units separation from the CS. Thus, the 1200 cps GS in (a) should elicit about as much generalization as the 1600 cps GS in (b) since both are one unit of separation from the CS. Some empirical support for this interpretation of generalization phenomena is found in a comparison of studies by Hovland (1937) and Humphreys (1939). Hovland reports the generalization of a PGR response to tones 25, 50, and 75 jnds from the CS. Part of the Humphreys experiment repeated the Hovland procedure, confining itself to GSs that were 5, 15, and 25 jnds from the CS. The CS and 25 jnd tones were 1967 dv and 1000 dv, respectively. The two studies are compared in terms of the units hypothesis in Table 1. The

TABLE 1

Generalization stimuli in jnds from CS

Hovland	CS			25	50	75
Humphreys	CS	5	15	25		

units hypothesis would predict that the Humphreys 25 jnd tone would elicit as much response as the Hovland 75 jnd tone (both being three units from the CS). The generalization responsiveness in the two studies may be roughly compared in terms of relative generalization (response to GS/response to CS). The Humphreys 25 jnd GS/CS ratio was .72; the Hovland 75 jnd GS/CS ratio was .70. The 25 jnd Hovland GS (one unit of separation) elicited more relative generalization than the 25 jnd Humphreys GS (three units of separation). Humphreys termed this the "frame of reference" effect stating that the "generalized response may depend upon the setting in which stimuli are perceived." The writer has recently completed a number of studies testing the units hypothesis in SG in a number of continua, spatial, tactual and temporal and in terms of predictions regarding the summation of gradients (1959). An early study (1956) which replicated the Humphreys-Hovland comparison in the spatial continuum using the Brown, Bilodeau, and Baron (1951) apparatus lends strong support to the units interpretation.

This research on the units hypothesis has shown that this is an important variable in determining generalization behavior. However, it has been noted that the predictions of the units variable tend to break down at the extremes of the continuum being tested. An S trained to respond to 50 cps and tested at 20,000 cps will not behave the same as an S trained at 50 cps and tested at 100 cps despite the fact that the test stimulus is one unit of separation away in both cases.

REFERENCES

ANDREAS, B. G., Empirical gradients of generalization in a perceptual-motor task. *J. exp. Psychol.*, 1954, 48, 119-122.

ANREP, G. V., The irradiation of conditioned reflexes. *Proc. Roy. Soc., Ser. B*, 1923, 94, 404-425.

ARNHOFF, F. N., Ethnocentrism and stimulus generalization. *J. abnorm. soc. Psychol.*, 1956, 53, 138-139.

ARNHOFF, F. N., Ethnocentrism and stimulus generalization: A replication and further study. *J. abnorm. soc. Psychol.*, 1957, 55, 393-394.

ARNHOFF, F. N., & LOY, D. L., Relationship between two

measures of stimulus generalization: Influence of intelligence upon performance. *Psychol. Rep.*, 1957, 3, 465-470.

Bass, B., Gradients in response percentages as indices of non-spatial generalization. *J. exp. Psychol.*, 1958, 56, 278-281.

Bass, M. J., & Hull, C. L., The irradiation of a tactile conditioned reflex in man. *J. comp. Psychol.*, 1934, 17, 47-65.

Beach, F. A., Effects of testosterone propionate upon the copulatory behavior of sexually inexperienced male rats. *J. comp. Psychol.*, 1942, 33, 227-248.

Bender, L., & Schilder, P., Unconditioned reactions to pain in schizophrenia. *Amer. J. Psychiat.*, 1930, 10, 365-384.

Beritoff, J. S., On the fundamental nervous processes in the cortex of the cerebral hemispheres. I. The principle stages of the development of the individual reflex: Its generalization and differentiation. *Brain*, 1924, 47, 109-148.

Bilodeau, F. A., Brown, J. S., & Meryman, J. J., The summation of generalized reactive tendencies. *J. exp. Psychol.*, 1956, 51, 293-298.

Blackwell, H. R., & Schlosberg, H., Octave generalization, pitch discrimination and loudness thresholds in the white rat. *J. exp. Psychol.*, 1943, 33, 407-419.

Botwinick, J. Stimulus generalization of human voluntary responses: The relationship between amount of training and generalization of visual stimuli varied in the size dimensions. *Dissertation Abstr.*, 1953, 13, 1269-1270.

Bragiel, R. M., & Perkins, C. C., Jr., Conditioned stimulus intensity and response speed. *J. exp. Psychol.*, 1954, 47, 437-441.

Brown, J. S., The generalization of approach responses as a function of stimulus intensity and strength of motivation. *J. comp. Psychol.*, 1942, 33, 209-226.

Brown, J. S., Gradients of approach and avoidance responses and their relation to level of motivation. *J. comp. Physiol. Psychol.*, 1948, 41, 450-466.

Brown, J. S., Bilodeau, E. A., & Baron, M. R., Bidirectional gradients in the strength of a generalized voluntary response to stimuli on a visual spatial dimension. *J. exp. Psychol.*, 1951, 41, 52-61.

Brown, J. S., Clarke, F. R., & Stein, L., A new technique for studying spatial generalization with voluntary responses. *J. exp. Psychol.*, 1958, 55, 359-362.

Brush, F. R., Bush, R. R., Jenkins, W. O., & Whiting, J. W. M., Stimulus generalization after extinction and punishment: An experimental study of displacement. *J. abnorm. soc. Psychol.*, 1952, 47, 633-640.

Bush, R. R., & Mosteller, F., A model for stimulus generalization and discrimination. *Psychol. Rev.*, 1951, 58, 413-423.

Buss, A. H., A study of concept formation as a function of reinforcement and stimulus generalization. *J. exp. Psychol.*, 1950, 40, 494-503.

Buss, A. H., Stimulus generalization as a function of clinical anxiety and direction of generalization. *J. abnorm. soc. Psychol.*, 1955, 50, 271-273.

Buss, A. H., WEINER, M., & BUSS, E., Stimulus generalization as a function of verbal reinforcement combination. *J. exp. Psychol.*, 1954, 48, 433-436.

CAMERON, N., Perceptual organization and behavior pathology. In R. R. Blake & G. V. Ramsey (Eds.), *Perception, an approach to personality.* New York: Ronald, 1951.

CARSON, R. C., Intralist similarity and verbal rote learning performance of schizophrenic and cortically damaged patients. *J. abnorm. soc. Psychol.*, 1958, 57, 99-106.

CZEHURA, W. S., The generalization of temporal stimulus patterns on the time continuum. *J. comp. Psychol.*, 1943, 36, 76-90.

DENNY-BROWN, D., Theoretical deductions from the physiology of the cerebral cortex. *J. Neurol & Psychopath.*, 1932, 13, 52-67.

DUNN, W. L., Visual discrimination of schizophrenic subjects as a function of stimulus meaning. *J. Pers.*, 1954, 25, 48-64.

ERIKSEN, C. W., Some personality correlates of stimulus generalization under stress. *J. abnorm. soc. Psychol.*, 1954, 49, 561-565.

ESTES, W. K., Toward a statistical theory of learning. *Psychol. Rev.*, 1950, 57, 94-107.

FAGER, R. E., & KNOPF, I. J., Relationship of manifest anxiety to stimulus generalization. *J. abnorm. soc. Psychol.*, 1958, 57, 125-126.

FINK, J. B., & DAVIS, R. C., Generalization of a muscle action potential response to tonal duration. *J. exp. Psychol.*, 1951, 42, 403-408.

FINK, J. B., & PATTON, R. M., Decrement of a learned drinking response accompanying changes in several stimulus characteristics. *J. comp. physiol. Psychol.*, 1953, 46, 23-27.

FRICK, F. C., An analysis of an operant discrimination. *J. Psychol.*, 1948, 26, 93-123.

GARMEZY, N. Stimulus differentiation by schizophrenic and normal subjects under conditions of reward and punishment. *J. Pers.*, 1952, 20, 253-276.

GERWIRTZ, J. L., JONES, L. V., & WAERNERYD, K., Stimulus units and range of experienced stimuli as determinants of generalization discrimination gradients. *J. exp. Psychol.*, 1956, 52, 51-57.

Gibson, E. J., Sensory generalization with voluntary reactions. *J. exp. Psychol.*, 1939, 24, 237-253.

Gibson, E. J., A systematic application of the concepts of generalization and differentiation to verbal learning. *Psychol. Rev.*, 1940, 47, 196-229.

Goldstein, K., & Scheerer, M., Abstract and concrete behavior: An experimental study with special tests. *Psychol. Monogr.*, 1941, 53 (2, Whole No. 239).

Grandine, L., & Harlow, H. F., Generalization of the characteristics of a single learned stimulus by monkeys. *J. comp. physiol. Psychol.*, 1948, 41, 327-339.

Grant, D. A., & Dittmer, D. G., An experimental investigation of Pavlov's cortical irradiation hypothesis. *J. exp. Psychol.*, 1940, 26, 299-310.

Grant, D. A., & Schiller, J. J., Generalization of the conditioned galvanic skin response to visual stimuli, *J. exp. Psychol.*, 1953, 46, 309-313.

Green, E. J., A simplified model for stimulus discrimination. *Psychol. Rev.*, 1958, 65, 56-63.

Grice, G. R., & Saltz, E., The generalization of an instrumental response to stimuli varying in the size dimension. *J. exp. Psychol.*, 1950, 40, 702-708.

Gulliksen, H., Transfer of response in human subjects. *J. exp. Psychol.*, 1932, 15, 496-516.

Guttman, N., The pigeon and the spectrum and other perplexities. *Psychol. Rep.*, 1956, 2, 449-460.

Guttman, N., & Kalish, H. I., Discriminability and stimulus generalization. *J. exp. Psychol.*, 1956, 51, 79-88.

Hanson, H. M., Discrimination training effect on stimulus generalization gradient for spectrum stimuli. *Science*, 1957, 125, 888-889.

Hedlund, J. L., Construction and evaluation of an objective test of achievement imagery. Unpublished doctoral dissertation. State Univer. of Iowa, 1953.

Heyman, W., Certain relationships between stimulus intensity and stimulus generalization. *J. exp. Psychol.*, 1957, 53, 239-248.

Hilgard, E. R., Jones, L. V., & Kaplan, S. J., Conditioned discrimination as related to anxiety. *J. exp. Psychol.*, 1951, 42, 94-100.

Honig, W., Prediction of preference, transposition, and transposition reversals from stimulus generalization. Unpublished doctoral dissertation, Duke Univer., 1958.

Hovland, C. I., The effects of varying amounts of reinforcement upon the generalization of conditioned responses. *Psychol. Bull.*, 1935, 32, 731-732.

HOVLAND, C. I., The generalization of conditioned responses: I. The sensory generalization of conditioned responses with varying frequencies of tone. *J. gen. Psychol.*, 1937, 17, 125-148. (a)

HOVLAND, C. I., The generalization of conditioned responses: II. The sensory generalization of conditioned responses with varying intensities of tone. *J. genet. Psychol.*, 1937, 51, 279-291. (b)

HOVLAND, C. I., The generalization of conditioned responses: IV. The effects of varying amounts of reinforcement upon the degree of generalization of conditioned responses. *J. exp. Psychol.*, 1937, 21, 261-276. (c)

HULL, C. L., The problem of stimulus equivalence in behavior theory. *Psychol. Rev.*, 1939, 46, 9-30.

HULL, C. L., *Principles of behavior*. New York: Appleton-Century, 1943.

HULL, C. L., The problem of primary stimulus generalization. *Psychol. Rev.*, 1947, 54, 120-134.

HULL, C. L., Stimulus intensity dynamism (V) and stimulus generalization. *Psychol. Rev.*, 1949, 56, 67-76.

HULL, C. L., A primary social science law. *Sci. Mon.*, 1950, 17, 221-228. (a)

HULL, C. L., Behavior postulates and corollaries, 1949. *Psychol. Rev.*, 1950, 57, 173-180. (b)

HULL, C. L., *Essentials of behavior*. New Haven: Yale Univer. Press, 1951.

HULL, C. L., *A behavior system: An introduction to behavior theory concerning the individual organism*. New Haven: Yale Univer. Press, 1952.

HUMPHREYS, L. G., Generalization as a function of method of reinforcement. *J. exp. Psychol.*, 1939, 25, 361-372.

HUMPHREYS, L. G., The generalization of verbal expectations following two conditions of reinforcement. *Amer. Psychologist*, 1948, 3, 347.

JENKINS, H. M., & HARRISON, R. H., Auditory generalization in the pigeon. Final Report, *Air Force Contr. AF* 18(603)-85, 1958.

JENKINS, W. O., PASCAL, G. R., & WALKER, R. W., JR., Deprivation and generalization. *J. exp. Psychol.*, 1958, 56, 274-277.

JOHNSGARD, K. W., The role of contrast in stimulus intensity dynamism (V). *J. exp. Psychol.*, 1957, 53, 173-179.

JOHNSON, D. M., Generalization of a scale of values by the averaging of practice effects. *J. exp. Psychol.*, 1944, 34, 425-436.

KALISH, H. I., The relationship between discriminability and generalization: A reevaluation. *J. exp. Psychol.*, 1958, 55, 637-644.

Kalish, H. I., & Guttman, N., Stimulus generalization after equal training on two stimuli. *J. exp. Psychol.*, 1957, 53, 139-144.

Kling, J. W., Generalization of extinction of an instrumental response to stimuli varying in the size dimension. *J. exp. Psychol.*, 1952, 44, 339-346.

Lashley, K. S., & Wade, M., The Pavlovian theory of generalization. *Psychol. Rev.*, 1946, 53, 72-87.

Le Ny, J. F., Généralisation d'une attitude dans une epreuve de temps de reaction. *Année psychol.*, 1957, 57, 11-21. (a)

Le Ny, J. F., Généralisation d'une attitude dans une epreuve de temps de reaction. II. Cas d'une reaction discriminative. *Année psychol.*, 1957, 57, 329-337. (b)

Littman, R. A., Conditioned generalization of the galvanic skin response to tones. *J. exp. Psychol.*, 1949, 39, 868-882.

Loucks, R. B., An appraisal of Pavlov's systematization of behavior from the experimental standpoint. *J. comp. Psychol.*, 1933, 15, 1-47.

McClelland, D. C., Atkinson, J. W., Clarke, R. A., & Lowell, E. L., *The achievement motive.* New York: Appleton-Century, 1953.

Macerone, C., & Walton, A., Fecundity of male rabbits as determined by "dummy matings." *J. Agric. Sci.*, 1938, 28, 122-134.

McKinney, F., Quantitative and qualitative essential elements of transfer. *J. exp. Psychol.*, 1933, 16, 854-864.

Magaret, A., Generalization in successful therapy. *J. consult. Psychol.*, 1950, 14, 64-70.

Margolius, G., Stimulus generalization of an instrumental response as a function of the number of reinforced trials. *J. exp. Psychol.*, 1955, 49, 105-111.

Mednick, M. T., Mediated generalization and the incubation effect as a function of manifest anxiety. *J. abnorm. soc. Psychol.*, 1957, 55, 315-321.

Mednick, S. A., Distortions in the gradient of stimulus generalization related to cortical brain damage and schizophrenia. *J. abnorm. soc. Psychol.*, 1955, 51, 536-542.

Mednick, S. A., Generalization as a function of manifest anxiety and adaptation to psychological experiments. *J. consult. Psychol.*, 1957, 21, 491-494.

Mednick, S. A., A learning theory approach to research in schizophrenia. *Psychol. Bull.*, 1958, 55, 316-327. (a)

Mednick, S. A., Stimulus generalization as a function of level of achievement imagery. *Psychol. Rep.*, 1958, 4, 651-654. (b)

MEDNICK, S. A., Latency generalization gradients of a voluntary response. *Amer. J. Psychol.*, 1958, 71, 752-755. (c)

MEDNICK, S. A., Studies in stimulus generalization. Prog. Rep., NSF-Grant G-3855, 1959.

MEDNICK, S. A., & BRADBURN, N. M., On the definition of "space" in spatial generalization. *Amer. Psychologist*, 1956, 11, 439.

MEDNICK, S. A., & LEHTINEN, L. F., Stimulus generalization as a function of age in children. *J. exp. Psychol.*, 1957, 53, 180-183.

MEDNICK, S. A., & WILD, C., Stimulus generalization in brain damaged children. Final Rep., USPHS grant M-1519, 1958.

MILLER, N. E., Theory and experiment relating psychoanalytic displacement to stimulus-response generalization. *J. abnorm. soc. Psychol.*, 1948, 43, 155-178.

MILLER, W. C., & GREENE, J. E., Generalization of an avoidance response to varying intensities of sound. *J. comp. physiol. Psychol.*, 1954, 47, 136-139.

MONTGOMERY, K. C., Exploratory behavior as a function of "similarity" of stimulus situation. *J. comp. physiol. Psychol.*, 1953, 46, 129-133.

MOYLAN, J. J., Stimulus generalization in projective test (Rorschach) behavior. *J. Pers.*, 1959, 27, 18-37.

MURRAY, E. J., & MILLER, N. E., Displacement: Steeper gradient of generalization of avoidance than of approach with age of habit controlled. *J. exp. Psychol.*, 1952, 43, 222-226.

PAVLOV, I. P., *Conditioned reflexes.* Oxford: Oxford Univer. Press, 1927.

PERKINS, C. C., The relation between conditioned stimulus intensity and response strength. *J. exp. Psychol.*, 1953, 46, 225-231.

RABEN, M. W., The white rat's discrimination of differences in intensity of illumination measured by a running response. *J. comp. physiol. Psychol.*, 1949, 42, 254-272.

RAZRAN, G. H. S., Studies in configurational conditioning: V. Generalization and transposition. *J. genet. Psychol.*, 1940, 56, 3-11.

RAZRAN, G. H. S., Attitudinal determinants of conditioning and of generalization of conditioning. *J. exp. Psychol.*, 1949, 39, 820-829. (a)

RAZRAN, G. H. S., Stimulus generalization of conditioned responses. *Psychol. Bull.*, 1949, 46, 337-365. (b)

REISS, B. F., Genetic changes in semantic conditioning. *J. exp. Psychol.*, 1946, 36, 143-152.

RESTLE, F. A theory of discrimination learning. *Psychol. Rev.*, 1955, 62, 11-19.

RESTLE, F., & BEECROFT, R. S., Anxiety, stimulus generalization, and differential conditioning: A comparison of two theories. *Psychol. Rev.*, 1955, 62, 433-437.

ROSENBAUM, G., Temporal gradients of response strength with two levels of motivation. *J. exp. Psychol.*, 1951, 41, 261-267.

ROSENBAUM, G., Stimulus generalization as a function of level of experimentally induced anxiety. *J. exp. Psychol.*, 1953, 45, 35-43.

SCHILDER, P., The psychology of schizophrenia. *Psychoanal. Rev.*, 1939, 26, 380-398.

SCHLOSBERG, H., & SOLOMON, R. L., Latency of response in a choice discrimination. *J. exp. Psychol.*, 1943, 33, 22-39.

SHEPARD, R. N., Stimulus and response generalization: A stochastic model relating generalization to distance in psychological space. *Psychometrika*, 1957, 22, 325-345.

SHEPARD, R. N., Stimulus and response generalization: Deduction of the generalization gradient from a trace model. *Psychol. Rev.*, 1958, 65, 242-256. (a)

SHEPARD, R. N., Stimulus and response generalization: Tests of a model relating generalization to distance in psychological space. *J. exp. Psychol.*, 1958, 55, 509-523. (b)

SLATER-HAMMEL, A. T., Reaction time to light stimuli in the peripheral visual field. *Res. Quart.*, 1955, 26, 82-87.

SMITH, K. V., Learning and associative pathways of the human cerebral cortex. *Science*, 1951, 114, 117-120.

SPENCE, K. W., The nature of discrimination learning in animals. *Psychol. Rev.*, 1936, 43, 427-449.

SPENCE, K. W., The differential response in animals to stimuli varying within a single dimension. *Psychol. Rev.*, 1937, 44, 430-444.

SPENCE, K. W., The basis of solution by chimpanzees of the intermediate size problem. *J. exp. Psychol.*, 1942, 31, 257-271.

SPIKER, C. C., The effects of number of reinforcements on the strength of a generalized instrumental response. *Child Developm.*, 1956, 27, 37-44. (a)

SPIKER, C. C., The stimulus generalization gradient as a function of the intensity of stimulus lights. *Child Developm.*, 1956, 27, 85-98. (b)

WENAR, C. Reaction time as a function of manifest anxiety and stimulus intensity. *J. abnorm. soc. Psychol.*, 1953, 48, 129-134.

WICKENS, D. D., SCHRODER, H. M., & SNIDE, J. D., Primary stimulus generalization of the GSR under two conditions. *J. exp. Psychol.*, 1954, 47, 52-56.

WITKIN, H. A., LEWIS, H. B., HERTZMAN, M., MACHOVER, K., MEISSNER, P. B., & WAPNER, S., *Personality through perception*. New York: Harper, 1954.

WOLPE, J., Primary stimulus generalization: A neuro-physiological view. *Psychol. Rev.*, 1952, 59, 8-10.

WOODWORTH, R. S., *Experimental psychology*. New York: Holt, 1938.

YAMAGUCHI, H. G., Gradients of drive stimulus (S_D) intensity generalization. *J. exp. Psychol.*, 1952, 43, 298-304.

5

The Nature of the Effective Stimulus in Animal Discrimination Learning: Transposition Reconsidered*

Donald A. Riley

University of California

When an animal learns to discriminate between two stimuli lying on the same physical dimension, what is the nature of the effective stimulus with which the response is associated?

In 1937, Spence (13) presented a theory which assumed that the animal learns to approach the absolute properties of the positive stimulus and that independent of this, it learns not to approach the absolute properties of the negative stimulus. In those situations in which the animal learns to discriminate between two points on the same physical dimension, Spence defined the effective stimulus in conventional physical units—for example, the number of square centimeters in a size discrimination, or the number of foot candles in a brightness discrimination. Spence contrasted this absolute definition of the effective stimulus with Köhler's earlier assumption (7) that the animal responds to the relationship between the two stimuli, and learns to go to the larger or the brighter of the two stimuli. Spence made some additional assumptions that enabled him to predict the transposition of the learned response to pairs of test stimuli which differ from the training stimuli. In contrast to the relational theory,

* From *The Psychological Review*, 1958, 65, 1-7, and used here with the permission of the author and the American Psychological Association.

which made no quantitative predictions, Spence's theory predicted that transposition would decrease as the test stimuli became less and less similar to the training stimuli. This prediction has been confirmed in several experiments (1, 6, 9, 13).

This paper will present evidence that Spence's assumption that the animal responds to the absolute properties of the stimulus, defined in units such as absolute size or luminance, is untenable. This evidence also casts doubt on Spence's explanation of the decline in transposition. Two alternative reinterpretations of the facts of transposition will then be considered. Before presenting the new evidence, Spence's theory will be described, together with an example of the type of evidence supporting it.

Near and far transposition tests. The meaning of the terms "near transposition test" and "far transposition test" can be given schematically. Let letters A through J represent points on a physical continuum, such that the ratio of B to A is the same as C to B, and so on. If the S is originally trained to choose B in the presence of A and B, then a test with B and C is a near transposition test. A test with any other pair of adjacent stimuli (e.g., H and I) is a far transposition test. For example, if in original training the ratio of the magnitude of the positive to the negative stimulus is 2/1, then in the near transposition test, the ratio will be 4/2. In the far transposition test, the ratio might be 64/32, or 128/64. Although Spence and others have discussed other combinations of stimuli, in the interest of simplicity and brevity, the discussion here will be restricted to the case in which the test stimuli are of greater magnitude than the training stimuli.

The sample experiment which will now be described in this simplified form is one by Kendler (6). Two stimuli serving as cues to the presence or absence of reward were presented to the Ss (in this case, rats). These stimuli differed only in that one had a photometric value of .011 foot candle while the other had a value of .63 foot candle. Going to one of the stimuli (e.g., the brighter) was always followed by reward. Going to the other was followed by nonreward. After learning, the animal was tested with other pairs of stimuli. Different animals were

tested at different intensities, but in each test the ratio
between the two stimuli was the same as in original
training. In each test, the animals preferred the more
intense stimulus, but the magnitude of the preference
decreased as the intensity of the test pairs increased.[1]
That is, far transposition is weaker than near transposition. Similar results have been found with size as the
critical dimension (1, 9, 13).

   The absolute theory. Because Spence's theory is given
in detail in many references, it will be summarized here
only in very brief form. It assumes that if the animal is
regularly rewarded when it approaches one point on a
stimulus dimension, and is regularly nonrewarded when
it approaches another point on the same dimension, the
animal will develop corresponding approach (Excitatory)
and nonapproach (Inhibitory) tendencies. These E and I
tendencies will be elicited by other points on the dimension, but the intensity of the elicited tendency will
decline as the distance of the test point from the training
point increases. The shapes of the E and I gradients are
positively decelerated, and, in the simplest case, have the
same equation. The tendency to make an approach response to any point on the dimension will be a simple
function of the difference between the two opposing
tendencies. Since, at points above the training stimuli on
the stimulus continuum, the I generalization gradient will
fall more rapidly than the E gradient, transposition will
occur. As both curves fall, the greater E-minus-I value of
the more intense stimulus becomes relatively smaller, and
less transposition occurs.

   Limitations in the generality of the absolute theory.
While it is true that this absolute theory does account
for transposition, and for the drop in transposition in the
far test, some recent research, especially that of Lawrence
and his associates, appears to present findings incompati-

----

[1] The amount of transposition in Kendler's experiment did
not decline monotonically when the test stimuli were more
intense than the training stimuli. The animals transposed more
to the most remote stimuli than to those of intermediate
value. The reason for this is not clear, but one possibility is
that the voltage changes that were introduced changed the wave
length of the light. This in turn might influence brightness
discrimination.

ble with Spence's account of transposition. Baker and
Lawrence (2) found transposition with rats following
conventional training on a size-discrimination problem,
but did not find transposition when the training stimuli
were presented successively. Unfortunately, the two conditions differed in one respect other than simultaneity vs.
successiveness. The animals in the simultaneous condition
learned to criterion, and thus received almost 100% reinforcement toward the end of training. In contrast, the
animals in the successive condition had the same number of trials with the negative stimulus as with the positive stimulus throughout training, and consequently were
reinforced only 50% of the time. Baker and Lawrence
pointed out that in spite of this methodological flaw, the
results are not consistent with Spence's theory.

Another apparent contradiction of the absolute theory
is an experiment by Lawrence and DeRivera (10). Animals were trained in a discrimination problem in which,
on each trial, two doors showed the same stimulus
pattern. The bottom half of each door was always the
same medium gray (shade No. 4 in a set of seven shades).
The top half of each was either a shade of gray three
steps lighter (No. 1) than the bottom half, or a shade of
gray three steps darker (No. 7) than the bottom. The
animals were trained to jump to one door when the
upper parts were lighter than the lower, and to jump to
the other door when the upper parts were darker. After
training, the animals were given combinations that tested
between a relational interpretation of learning and an
absolute interpretation. For example, with No. 3 over
No. 1, the animal should jump to the side associated
with the lighter gray, according to the absolute hypothesis, because both cards are lighter than No. 4; but since
the relationship is dark over light, they should jump the
other way according to the relational hypothesis. The results predominantly supported the relational hypothesis.

Clearly, the results of Lawrence *et al.* appear to be in
contradiction to Spence's theory that the animal responds
to the cues in an independent fashion. As a possible solution of these apparent contradictions, Lawrence and De-
Rivera (10) and Hilgard (5) have suggested that under
some circumstances the animal responds relationally, and

that under other circumstances it responds absolutely. That is, perhaps it responds absolutely in a simple simultaneous discrimination situation, but not in others. It is possible, however, that *the decline in transposition in the far test* has not yet been adequately explained, and that an understanding of *this* phenomenon will resolve the apparent inconsistencies. Then, we will be in a better position to state testable alternatives concerning the nature of transposition.

A contrast interpretation of the drop in transposition. If, instead of defining each stimulus merely in terms of the patch alone, it is defined as a specific relationship between the value of the patch and the value of the surround, then the decline in transposition might result merely from the change in the relationship being responded to. Such a proposal is, of course, not new. In human perception, the effect of contrast on apparent brightness has been known for many years. Recently, Wallach (15) has shown that two test stimuli of radically different illumination will be judged approximately equal in brightness if the ratio of the test-stimulus intensity to surrounding intensity is the same for both stimuli. Similarly, Gibson (3) has shown that perceptual size constancy in humans depends on such factors as the texture gradient of the stimulus field surrounding the test stimulus. It is not unreasonable to assume that apes and rats might behave in a similar way.

An experimental test of the contrast hypothesis. The specific hypothesis to be tested is that after a brightness discrimination has been learned, there will be a drop in transposition on the far test only if the ratios of the test stimuli to their surround are changed.

The experiment was similar to Kendler's in that the rats were trained to discriminate brightness. All animals were trained in a modified Lashley jumping apparatus to jump to the more intense of two stimuli. The doors and the surrounding stimulation were illuminated from projectors hung near the top of the room. The different illuminations on the doors and the surround were determined solely by slides in the projectors, and by the size of openings in iris diaphragms on the projectors. During training, the brightnesses of the two doors and the surround, as measured by a Zeiss photometer, were in the ratio of 10/3/1, the surround having the value of 1. The surround had a reflected illumination of .05 foot candle.[2] During training, the rats were run 10 trials a day by the noncorrection method. Forced trials were used to break position habits. Following training to a criterion of 19/20 correct responses, all animals were tested under four different conditions. Each animal was tested on only one condition in a day, and on days between tests the animal was retrained to a criterion of 9/10 correct responses. Each test consisted of ten trials during which the animal was rewarded regardless of the correctness of its choice. The order of conditions was counterbalanced. The four conditions were: (a) near absolute—the two test patches were transposed one step up, and the surrounding stimulation was the same as in original training; (b) far absolute—the two test patches were made 5 steps brighter and the surrounding stimulation was the same as in original training; (c) near ratio—the same as (a) except that the illumination of the surround was increased so that the ratio of intensities of the test patches to the surround was the same as in original training; and (d) far ratio—the same as (b) except that the illumination of the surround was increased so that the ratio of the intensities of the test patches to the surround was the same as in original training. Sixteen hooded rats of the Long-Evans strain were used.

Predictions. For this experiment to offer a test between the absolute and the contrast hypotheses, it is essential that there be significantly less transposition on the far absolute condition than on the near absolute condition. If this requirement is met, then the absolute theory predicts a similar drop from the near ratio to the far ratio condition, for the only two parts of the stimulus situation that have been differentially reinforced are being changed, just as they are in the absolute conditions. On the other hand, the contrast hypothesis predicts a drop in transposition from the near to the far absolute condition but no

[2] I wish to thank J. Gulberg, Department of Zoology, University of California, for supervising the measurement of the physical stimuli, and Arnold Mechanic, who participated in the running of the experiment.

such drop in the ratio condition. If the ratio present in training is present in the test, then the animal should transpose, regardless of the absolute values of the stimuli.

Results. The main results are shown in Table 1. Their

TABLE 1

Mean number of responses to the brighter stimulus in ten choices

	Near Absolute	Far Absolute	Near Ratio	Far Ratio
Mean	9.25	6.94	9.19	9.69
SD	1.09	1.84	1.36	.54

meaning is unambiguous. The animals transpose almost perfectly in all except the far absolute condition. There were no effects of order. The only effect is a highly significant drop in transposition under the far absolute condition. A *t* test was run in which for each S the difference between near and far ratio was subtracted from the difference between near and far absolute. The *t* of 4.87 is significant at the .0002 level of confidence, for 15 degrees of freedom.

Interpretation of the results. It is clear, at least in the case of brightness discrimination, that the animal responds to the relationship between the test stimulus and the background. It is a change in this relationship rather than a change in the absolute value of the stimulus that causes the breakdown in transposition. While this experiment does not provide an explanation of transposition per se, it does show that the drop in transposition in the far test is not critical evidence for Spence's explanation of transposition. The most immediate effect of this finding is to force a reconsideration of possible interpretations of transposition. Two such possible interpretations that seem to this writer to be reasonable alternatives will be considered. Again, for simplicity, the discussion will use brightness discrimination as the example.

A reformulation of the E and I gradients hypothesis. If the effective stimulus is redefined as the ratio of the training or test patch to the surround, then it is possible to maintain the assumption that the animal responds separately to the two training stimuli. In this case, the appropriate description of the stimulus intensity dimension will also be expressed in such ratios. When an animal has been trained to approach one stimulus (defined in ratio terms) and not to approach the other, E and I tendencies will be reduced to the degree that test ratios change from training ratios. If these redefined generalization gradients are of the form postulated by Spence, this hypothesis can then account for transposition and for the decline in transposition with changing stimulus ratios.

Can this interpretation account for the findings of the other experiments that were critical of Spence's absolute hypothesis? Lawrence and DeRivera's experiment is somewhat complex for the present analysis, because relationships within the stimulus patch were changed in the tests, but the surrounding stimulation was always the same as in training. Nevertheless, their results at least do not appear inconsistent with this hypothesis. If the two parts of the stimulus patch are responded to in the way that the stimulus surround was responded to in the present experiment, then their animals learned to jump left when the ratio on the cards was in one direction and right when it was in the other direction. As the ratios were changed in the test conditions, the tendency to make the relational response decreased.

On the other hand, this reformulation of the absolute theory does not account for the failure of Baker and Lawrence to find transposition following successive training. Their experiment therefore seems critical, and should be repeated with the same pattern of reinforcements in the successive and simultaneous groups.

A reformulation of the relational hypothesis. Since the decline in transposition in the far test cannot be considered as evidence for an absolute definition of the stimulus, the question of the adequacy of Köhler's original relational hypothesis is reopened. In his discussion of transposition, Köhler merely described the animal as having learned to go to the larger or lighter part of the stimulus. This restricted theory is still inadequate, for the reason pointed out by Spence. It cannot account for the decline in transposition in the far test. Nor does it help Köhler's explanation to say that the figure-ground relationships determine the phenomenal brightness of the two test stimuli, and that the animal approaches the stimulus which is phenomenally brighter, for this still would not predict a breakdown in transposition in the far test. Another unworkable relational assumption is that the animal responds to the ratio between the two figure-ground ratios. This hypothesis would state that in the present experiment the animal responds to the relationship of 10/1 (the brighter) to 3/1 (the dimmer)—that is, to a relationship of 10/3 or 3.33. Now in the critical far-absolute test, the values are about 4,100/1 for the brighter stimulus and 1,230/1 for the dimmer. This of course reduces to 3.33 and perfect transposition is predicted. Since transposition is known to decline under these circumstances, this hypothesis is inadequate.

It seems clear that a workable relational hypothesis will be one that predicts perfect transposition as long as all stimulus values in the critical dimension are multiplied by the same factor. If the values in the original training are in the ratio of 10/3/1, then any test situation in which the ratio is the same must give perfect transposition.[3] To the extent that any of the three parts of the stimulus deviates from this, transposition will decline. One possible interpretation of such behavior would be that the animal approaches a stimulus that is defined by two intensity ratios, and does not approach one that is defined by two other intensity ratios. That is, the animal learns to approach a training stimulus which has an intensity that is a certain multiple of the intensity of the surround and a certain multiple of the intensity of the other training stimulus. Similarly, the animal learns not to approach a stimulus that has an intensity that is a certain multiple of the intensity of the surround and a certain fraction of the intensity of the other training stimulus. This hypothesis has no trouble in accounting for a decline in transposition in the far-absolute situation of the

[3] Although Köhler explicitly made this point when discussing the general problem of transposition (cf. 8, p. 218), he did not apply this principle either in the design or in the analysis of specific experiments. In discussing the experiments, only the changes in the test patches were considered.

present experiment. It is not so clear why there is no drop in transposition in the near-absolute situation, for here there is also a change in the ratios. One *ad hoc* interpretation is that, under the usual conditions of the transposition experiment, the near-absolute test is not a discriminably different relationship from the relationship present during training. There are a variety of reasons why this might be so. For example, since the difference between the training stimuli and the surround is substantial, a change of only one step may be relatively hard to detect. Further, twenty-four hours intervene between the last training trial and the first test trial. This increases the difficulty of discriminating between the two relationships.

This particular relational hypothesis is very similar to the reformulated absolute hypothesis. It differs only in that each critical stimulus is defined by two brightness gradients rather than just one. A direct test between these two hypotheses can be made in an experiment in which the stimulus area surrounding each stimulus patch may be independently varied. Then, following training identical to the present experiment, the ratio of test stimulus to surround could be kept constant, as in the ratio conditions of the present experiment, but the relationship between the two test stimuli could be changed from that of the training situation; e.g., the stimulus-surround value of the positive stimulus might be kept at 10/1, while the negative is changed from a training value of 3/1 to a test value of 30/10. As long as the stimulus-surround ratios are constant, the reformulated absolute hypothesis should predict that the animal would continue to approach the test stimulus that has the same ratio as the positive training stimulus, even though the relationship between the test stimuli is changed. This should be true regardless of the amount or direction of the change. The proposed relational hypothesis would predict breakdown in transposition as the ratio of the test stimuli to each other becomes more different from that of the training stimuli, even though the stimulus-surround ratios are the same as in original training.

There may be other relational hypotheses that would be consistent with the present facts. For example, Teas and Bitterman (14) have described conditions under which the rat appears to respond to the stimulus as a total configuration rather than responding selectively to different components of the stimulus. The only difficulty in applying this hypothesis to the present data is that this experiment was run under conditions that are probably closer to the condition in their study that elicited selective reactions from the rat.

Two further implications of the present experiment. It is worth noting that the present study has implications not only for transposition, but for the closely related problem of stimulus generalization along quantitative continua. It appears that there is a real possibility that if the relationships existing in original conditioning are present in generalization tests, stimulus generalization will be complete regardless of absolute stimulus values. Directly related to this point is an experiment by Perkins (12) that indicates that stimulus intensity dynamism is probably a contrast phenomenon.

The second point is more of a question than a direct implication of the present experiment. How much of transposition might be accounted for by subcortical or even retinal mediation rather than by cortical processes? Some time ago, Hebb (4) presented evidence that brightness discrimination is probably controlled subcortically. More recently, Motokowa (11) has presented evidence from retinal recordings of the frog indicating that action potentials are related to brightness contrast rather than intensity.

SUMMARY

Evidence has been presented that in animal discrimination learning, as in human perception, the effective stimulus to which the animal responds must be described as a relationship between parts of a stimulus complex. This finding allows a reinterpretation of Spence's explanation of the decline in transposition when test stimuli are remote from training stimuli. It also sets the conditions for a reinterpretation of transposition. Two alternatives are discussed.

REFERENCES

1. ALBERTS, E., & EHRENFREUND, D., Transposition in children as a function of age. *J. exp. Psychol.*, 1951, 41, 30-38.
2. BAKER, R. A., & LAWRENCE, D. H., The differential effects of simultaneous and successive stimuli presentation on transposition. *J. comp. physiol. Psychol.*, 1951, 44, 378-382.
3. GIBSON, J. J., *The perception of the visual world.* Boston: Houghton Mifflin, 1950.
4. HEBB, D. O., The innate organization of visual activity. III. Discrimination of brightness after removal of the striate cortex in the rat. *J. comp. Psychol.*, 1938, 25, 427-437.
5. HILGARD, E. R., *Theories of learning.* (2nd ed.) New York: Appleton-Century-Crofts, 1956.
6. KENDLER, T. S., An experimental investigation of transposition as a function of the difference between training and test stimuli. *J. exp. Psychol.*, 1950, 40, 552-562.
7. KÖHLER, W., Nachweis einfacher strukturfunktionen beim schimpansen und beim haushuhn: Über eine neue methode zur untersuchung des bunten farbensystems. *Abh. Preuss. Akad. Wissen,* 1918, Physikalisch-Mathematische Klass., No. 2, 1-101.
8. KÖHLER, W., *Gestalt psychology.* New York: Liveright, 1929.
9. KUENNE, M. R., Experimental investigation of the relation of language to transposition behavior in young children. *J. exp. Psychol.*, 1946, 36, 471-490.
10. LAWRENCE, D. H., & DeRIVERA, J., Evidence for relational discrimination. *J. comp. physiol. Psychol.*, 1954, 47, 465-471.
11. MOTOKAWA, K., Physiological induction in human retina as basis of color and brightness contrast. *J. Neurophysiol.*, 1949, 12, 475-488.
12. PERKINS, C. C., The relationshi between conditioned stimulus intensity and response strength. *J. exp. Psychol.*, 1953, 46, 225-231.
13. SPENCE, K. W., The differential response in animals to stimuli varying in a single dimension. *Psychol. Rev.*, 1937, 44, 430-444.
14. TEAS, D. C., & BITTERMAN, M. E., Perceptual organization in the rat. *Psychol. Rev.*, 1952, 59, 130-140.
15. WALLACH, H., Brightness constancy and the nature of achromatic colors. *J. exp. Psychol.*, 1948, 38, 310-324.

6

Partial Reinforcement: A Selective Review of the Literature Since 1950*

Donald J. Lewis[1]
Rutgers University

In May, 1950, Jenkins and Stanley published *Partial Reinforcement: A Review and Critique*, which is now a standard reference in the area. Its very excellence has probably inhibited other workers in the area from attempting another review of the literature. The partial reinforcement literature, however, is so large and has increased at such a rapid rate, that it is difficult now to maintain a perspective on the whole area. The present review is offered, with considerable trepidation, as an attempt to point out at least the major results and trends of the post-1950 research.

Even though the list of references is long, this review unfortunately is not exhaustive. Some studies are not included because they were believed by the writer to be insignificant, inconclusive, or badly conceived. Probably other studies, perhaps excellent ones, simply have been overlooked, although the writer has made a conscientious

* From *The Psychological Bulletin*, 1960, 57, 1-28, and used here with the permission of the author and the American Psychological Association. When this paper was originally published the author was at Louisiana State University.

[1] This report was supported by a grant from the National Science Foundation. The author wishes to express his appreciation to John W. Cotton of Northwestern University and D. W. Tyler of Louisiana State University who read the entire manuscript. Any inadequacies remaining are not to be attributed to them.

effort to read every study on partial reinforcement that has been published in major psychological and allied journals. Another large class of excluded studies are those which involve a free responding situation. This exclusion is purely arbitrary and does not mean that such studies are considered to be of less significance, nor that different principles necessarily will be required for their explanation. Only discrete trial studies are considered, primarily because these happen to be of major interest to the writer. A review of free responding studies is badly needed. A very few studies before 1950 are considered either because of their parametric design or their importance to theory.

This paper is organized around the major empirical variables that have been investigated in attempts to determine the effects of partial reinforcement on extinction. The aim in the data section has been to determine parametric relations between stimulus and response variables. Some studies whose primary purpose was to test a theoretical orientation do not allow such a determination, but they are considered to be valuable apart from their theory. Therefore, they, too, are cited in the data section. Without their theoretical context these studies may appear somewhat disjointed, but it is sometimes salutary to look at data only in relation to empirical variables. Other studies seem most important primarily for their contribution to theory and they are considered in the theory section. Some, of course, must be considered in both sections. Because this paper is concerned with extinction, acquisition phenomena are treated only incidentally. Perhaps a necessary introduction to this paper is a thorough reading of the Jenkins and Stanley (1950) paper. The issues and problems they discuss are not taken up again unless there is a clear need.

DATA

Percentage of reward. Following their review of the pertinent literature, Jenkins and Stanley (1950) arrived at an empirical generalization which stated: "All other things equal, resistance to extinction after partial reinforcement is greater than that after continuous reinforcement when behavior strength is measured in terms of single responses" (p. 222). Nine years and a great deal of research later this generalization still stands, perhaps more firmly than ever. Because this law of partial reinforcement seems so well established, there seems little point here in noting those studies involving only two percentages of reinforcement whose main point has been to demonstrate again the PRE (partial reinforcement effect). We will be primarily concerned in this section with studies that have attempted to determine a parametric law.

Grant and Schipper (1952) used an eyelid conditioning situation with a light CS and an airpuff UCS and counted the percentage of CRs in acquisition and extinction. The percentages of reinforcement used were 0%, 25%, 50%, 75%, and 100%. The results indicated that the percentage of CRs during acquisition was an increasing function of percentage of reinforcement with the greatest response strength for the highest percentage of reward. During extinction there was a rapid decrease in response strength for the 100% group, and less rapid for the others. The greatest resistance to extinction was for the 50% and 75% groups, falling off for both the 100% and 25% groups. The 0% group showed practically no conditioning and therefore no resistance to extinction. There was, then, a "hard core of resistance" to extinction in the region between, say, 40% and 80% reinforcement.

Duplicating in design the eyelid study discussed above, Grant, Hake, and Hornseth (1951) used a verbal conditioning situation. During acquisition, percentage of positive responses were again an increasing function of percentage of reinforcement, with each group emitting positive responses at about the same rate as it received reinforcements. In extinction, however, the 25% group gave the greatest resistance to extinction, yielding the hump of the ∩-shaped function toward the lower percentages.

Lewis and Duncan (1956b) used a "one-arm bandit" slot machine, modified so that payoffs could be controlled. Each payoff was worth 5¢ to the Ss, and the percentages used were 100%, 75%, 50%, 37.5%, 25%, 12.5%, and 0%. The total number of plays to quitting was found to be an inverse function of the percentage of reward with the 100% Ss quitting first and the 0% Ss quitting last. There was no evidence for a ∩-shaped function.

In another experiment, with 0%, 11%, 33%, 67%, and 100% reward, Lewis and Duncan (1957) asked their Ss to state for each trial of the 9-trial acquisition series their "expectation" of winning or not winning on the next trial. These expectancies were quantified on a scale from 1 to 6, with 1 representing a firm expectancy of not winning and 6 a firm expectancy of winning. The results showed that expectancies were a regular function of percentage of reinforcement both during acquisition and extinction, and that the expectancy of winning dropped off very rapidly during extinction for the 100% group. This was also the group that quit first. In this case there was a slight drop for the 0% group, suggesting a ∩-shaped function.

Using children from approximately five and one-half to six and one-half years of age in a partial reinforcement situation with plastic toys as reward, Lewis (1952) varied four percentages of reward—100%, 50%, 60%, and 0%—in a 10-trial acquisition series. He found no difference in resistance to extinction between the 50% and 60% groups and between the 100% and 0% groups, although the latter two groups quit significantly sooner than did the former, again a ∩-shaped function.

Five studies have been considered, each of which plotted at least four points along a percentage of reinforcement dimension. The wide variety of experimental situations used has undoubtedly helped to obscure a parametric function. Even so, a ∩-shaped function is found in four of the five studies. Grant and Schipper (1952), Grant, Hake, and Hornseth (1951), Lewis (1952), and Lewis and Duncan (1957) present evidence for such a ∩-shaped function with depressions at both the high and low percentages. Because a non-monotonic function usually means that at least two processes are operating, Grant and Schipper (1952) guessed as to what these two processes might be. The first process, they hypothesized, is a discriminative one. The higher the percentage of reinforcement, the more the acquisition series should "stand out" from the extinction series, and the less PRE should result. A discrimination process thus results in a decreasing function as a result of percentage of reinforcement. The second process is a learning one. With a response starting close to zero response strength, the greater the percentage of reward, for equal numbers of trials below some limit, the greater the response strength. Thus the learning process produces an increasing function, and the discrimination process should produce a trend in the opposite direction. The combination of these two results in a ∩-shaped function.

If Grant and Schipper are correct, the point of infection of the ∩ would need to vary with the degree of learning. The greater the degree of learning, the more the point of inflection should move toward the low end of the percentage scale. This is because with a greater degree of learning, the learning process should tend to drop out, leaving only the discrimination process in operation. Several percentages of reinforcement and numbers of acquisition trials need to be combined in the same experiment to verify this conjecture.

Pattern. Not only may reinforcement be given in different percentages, but within any percentage less than 100, the pattern may vary. Within 50% reinforcement, for example, the rewards may be given randomly, irregularly but not randomly, or regularly. And a large number of regular patterns are possible, depending on the length of the acquisition series. A systematic exploration of these variables is needed.

Grant, Riopelle, and Hake (1950) set up random (R), single alternation (SA), double alternation (DA), and 100% groups in an eyelid conditioning situation. At the end of acquisition the 100% and the R groups were about equal and superior to the DA and SA groups. During extinction the R group showed a very rapid decrement in response magnitude and ended below the other groups. This is one of the few studies reporting faster extinction following partial reinforcement. There is no ready explanation for this paradox.

Longnecker, Krauskopf, and Bitterman (1952) performed an experiment comparing SA and R groups, measuring the galvanic skin response (GSR). They found no statistically significant mean difference between R and SA at the end of acquisition, although the R group ap-

pears to have had a stronger response. Very interesting
was the saw-toothed acquisition curve for SA. Responses
were considerably stronger on reinforced trials than nonreinforced trials. During extinction the R group was
clearly and significantly more resistant to extinction than
the SA group.

Using a combination elevated runway and a jumping
platform with rats as Ss, Tyler, Wortz, and Bitterman
(1953) explored further the differences between SA and
R. Again, there were no differences at the end of acquisition, and again the SA group was significantly less resistant to extinction than the R. Also, the saw-toothed
acquisition function appeared for SA, developing about
the 60th trial. Faster runs were recorded after a nonreinforced trial. Earlier in acquisition just the opposite was
true; faster runs occurred after rewarded trials. A definite
patterning effect is thus discernible in these two studies,
not only in terms of resistance to extinction, but also in
terms of the acquisition function.

Hake and Grant (1951) and Hake, Grant, and Hornseth (1951) were concerned with the patterning effects
of *blocks* of reinforced and unreinforced trials. They varied factorially both the number of blocks (and therefore
the number of transitions from nonreinforced to reinforced trials) and the number of trials in blocks. This
procedure resulted in combining variables, since as the
number of transitions increased and as the number of
nonreinforced responses per block increased, the total
number of nonreinforced trials also increased. In one of
the studies (Hake & Grant, 1951) an eyelid conditioning
situation was used. No significant results were found.
This may be because of the combination of variables
mentioned above, or it may be that when working with
complete blocks of reinforced and nonreinforced trials, a
longer acquisition series is necessary. The acquisition
series used here was only 1, 3, and 5 transitions. In a
second experiment of identical design (Hake, Grant, &
Hornseth, 1951) but with a verbal conditioning situation, both the number of transitions and the number of
reinforced trials were significant variables. Three transitions resulted in greater resistance to extinction than

either 1 or 5, and the fewer the number of nonreinforced trials the greater the resistance to extinction.

Working with a modification of the Humphreys' board, Grosslight, Hall, and Murnin (1953) gave reinforcements in three different patterns. One group (RR) was reinforced on every trial, a second (RU) received reinforcements in a block always followed by a single block of nonreinforced trials, and the third (UR) had all the nonreinforced trials occurring as a block in the middle of a sequence of reinforced trials. After five acquisition sessions of this kind, an extinction session was given, and the number of "plus" responses determined for the three groups. The UR group was more resistant to extinction than the other two, and the RU group was more resistant to extinction than RR. A group, it seems, whose acquisition series ends with reinforcement is more resistant to extinction than a group whose acquisition series does not end with reinforcement. A similar finding was reported by Ishihara (1954).

Grosslight and Radlow (1955) obtained similar results with a response reversal situation and albino rats. Response reversal was significantly slower in the UR condition than in the RR and RU conditions. For this study, however, there was no difference between RR and RU. A likely explanation of this latter finding lies in the 24-hour interval separating the sessions in the animal study, whereas the interval was of the order of seconds or minutes for the human study. With a short interval between sessions, the RU group also has a reward closely following nonreinforcement, although not as closely as for the UR condition. For a second study (Grosslight & Radlow, 1957), with rats and a habit reversal problem, only one reinforced trial a session for three sessions was used in the RU and UR conditions. Again the UR was significantly slower to reverse, and there was no difference between RU and RR. Again there was a 24-hr. interval between sessions. Finally (Lewis & Duncan, 1956b), one study shows that irregular variations of patterns within a single percentage of reinforcement (25%) results in no difference in PRE.

It seems clear, reviewing the studies on patterning, that

SA results in less resistance to extinction than does R (Longnecker, Krauskopf, & Bitterman, 1952; Tyler, Wortz, & Bitterman, 1953). It also seems clear that blocks of nonreinforced trials which end a number of times with at least one reinforced trial are superior to continuous reinforcement and to those blocks which end in a nonreinforced trial (Grosslight & Radlow, 1957; Hake, Grant, & Hornseth, 1951). Little more is known about patterning because even the more obvious variables and their combinations have not been studied.

Secondary reinforcement. In the following discussion, S^n will represent a neutral stimulus serving as a discriminative stimulus which is presented before the response. And S^r will represent the stimulus used as a secondary reinforcer.[3] S^r is presented after the response whose strength it is hoped to strengthen or maintain. Primary reinforcement (S^R) is ordinarily necessary to make a stimulus serve as S^n or S^r, and S^R may be presented according to many different schedules. There are thus three variables, the S^n, the S^r, and the S^R, which may be manipulated somewhat independently, and as a result there are a number of different ways in which secondary reinforcement may be combined with partial reinforcement. Because each of these ways may bring about different results, the problem of the relationship of secondary reinforcement to partial reinforcement fractionates into the number of experimental designs by which the three may be combined.

Three principal experimental designs may be used during acquisition to vary the percentage of presentation of S^R and S^n. Design A-1: Primary reinforcement is given only part of the time and S^n is presented on every occasion. Design A-2: Whenever S^R is given, S^n is also presented, but when S^R is not given, neither is S^n. Design A-3: Primary reinforcement is presented on a certain percentage of trials and so is S^n, but the two percentages are varied independently so that S^R may coincide with S^n and it may not. These designs are represented in Table 1. Because the effects of "partial secondary reinforcement" can only be determined when compared to "continuous

---

[3] No position is implied on the issue of whether a stimulus must first serve as an S^D in order to serve as an S^r.

TABLE 1

Experimental	Reinforcer	
Design	S^R	S^n
A-1	partial	continuous
A-2	partial	partial, contingent on S^R
A-3	partial	partial, not contingent on S^R

secondary reinforcement," only those studies in which such a comparison is made will be cited in this section.

In addition to these general methods of combining primary and secondary reinforcement are two general methods of presenting S^r during extinction, or during the test trials. The S^r may be presented on every trial—Design E-1—or only on part of the trials—Design E-2. The studies available in this area will be classified according to the design used.

There seems to be only one study in which Design A-1 has been used. Peterson (1956) used a runway for acquisition, and a buzzer was presented on every trial just as the S entered a delay chamber. (Peterson was also interested in delay of reinforcement.) Tests for the effectiveness of S^r were given in a bar pressing device in which S had had no previous experience. Perhaps this procedure does not fit the usual paradigm for extinction, but as a test for the effectiveness of a secondary reinforcer it is certainly superior to ordinary extinction. Peterson found no difference between an S^r associated with 50% reinforcement and one associated with 100% reinforcement. There is also no evidence that any secondary reinforcement effects occurred with either percentage.

Notterman (1951) varied the number of nonreinforced trials in a runway with the number of reinforced trials held constant. He presented a light as S^n on each reinforced trial just as S entered the goal box. On nonreinforced trials S^n was not presented. Thus Notterman used Design A-2. Certain of his groups were then extinguished to the same level (although Notterman's argument for this is not as firm as would be desirable) in the absence of S^r. Then S^r was reintroduced for further trials but no primary reward was given. Response strength increased as a direct function of the number of orginally interspersed nonreinforced trials. The smaller the percentage of reinforcement, the greater the effectiveness of the S^r. The smallest percentage of reinforcement used was 33%.

No study has been reported using Design A-3. It is, however, reasonable to guess that if Design A-3 is combined with Design E-2, S^r will be most efficacious in maintaining a response or bringing one about anew.

Three designs for combining partial reinforcement with secondary reinforcement have been considered. For Design A-1, little can be said. Peterson (1956) found no clear evidence for secondary reinforcement even in a standard control group. Notterman (1951), with an A-2 design and a nice parametric study, found greater effectiveness for S^r with smaller percentages of reinforcement. Design A-3 is untried.

Successive acquisitions and extinctions. Perkins and Cacioppo (1950) gave one group of animals 16 acquisition trials, only 8 of which were reinforced, followed by 30 extinction trials. Seven days of this kind of training were given. A second group received the same succession of events except that all acquisition trials were reinforced. The results showed that the 50% Ss were more resistant to extinction throughout the extinction sequences, and the rate of extinction increased with successive extinctions.

Lauer and Estes (1955) used a jumping stand and gave three series, each of 14 acquisition and 8 extinction trials. For one group the first acquisition series was with 100% reinforcement, the second with 50%, and the third with 100% again. The other group started with 50% and alternated on successive acquisitions. They found that successive extinctions resulted in *less* extinction, both in rate and terminal level. Extinction rates were similar after 50% and 100%, except that there was a greater decrement on the first extinction day following 100% reinforcement.

Lauer and Estes (1955) pointed out that successive acquisitions and extinctions had a great deal in common with typical partial reinforcement in that nonreinforced trials (extinctions) follow reinforced trials (acquisitions). Razran (1955) has also made this point. The main difference between the two is in the length of the sequence of reinforced and nonreinforced trials, which actually makes successive acquisitions and extinctions identical to the patterning of partial reinforcement. Pursuing this comparison of successive acquisitions and extinctions to pattern of reinforcement, Lauer and Carterette (1957) gave one group successive acquisitions only (A-A) and another group received successive acquisitions and extinctions (A-E). Both groups received spaced trials. The A-A group was presumed to be analogous to 100% reinforcement and the A-E group was presumed to be analogous to 50% reinforcement. They found that the mean starting speed of the A-A group on all reacquisition series was *below* that of the A-E group, even though the former had had more reinforcements. This is a very interesting finding. Its typical partial reinforcement counterpart should show that the reinforced trial following a nonreinforced trial would be superior to a reinforced trial following another reinforced trial. Amsel (1958) presented data to indicate that this is what happens. Amsel interpreted his findings to indicate that nonreinforcement has a frustration-drive effect which serves to energize the behavior on the next trial. However, it is hard to see how the frustration-drive could persist over the 30-min. intertrial interval used by Lauer and Carterette (1957). It is just this effectiveness of partial reinforcement procedures on widely spaced trials that is most difficult to interpret.

The Perkins and Cacioppo study (1950) showed decreased resistance to extinction with successive extinctions, while both Lauer studies (Lauer & Estes, 1955; Lauer & Carterette, 1957) showed just the reverse. It is interesting to note that other successive acquisition and extinction studies (e.g., Bullock & Smith, 1953) report findings similar to Perkins and Cacioppo. The reason for the difference in results lies perhaps in the shortness of the extinction series in the two Lauer studies, 8 trials in one case and 12 in the other. The other studies in this area used a much longer extinction period.

In any case, the Lauer studies point the way to a considerable consolidation of partial reinforcement variables, in that successive acquisitions and extinctions can be considered as an aspect of the pattern and percentage of reinforcement. If any intertrial interval phenomena should turn out to be reliable, they should also show up as a function of the interval between the successive acquisition and extinction series.

Number of trials. Only a few studies have been concerned specifically with the relationship between partial reinforcement and the number of acquisition trials. A large number of studies (e.g., Jenkins and Stanley, 1950) however, have shown that acquisition responding is greater with 100% than with partial reinforcement. A study by Weinstock (1958) amplifies this statement so that it holds only for the early acquisition trials. Weinstock gave 109 acquisition trials and, for the later trials, the smaller percentage groups were performing better than the larger percentage groups, although there was no regular order. During acquisition, then, there is an interaction between percentage of reinforcement and number of trials.

Weinstock reports the usual PRE with relatively clear evidence that rate of decrement for the low percentage groups is less than that for the high percentage groups. In addition, the higher percentage groups achieve a different and lower asymptote than the lower percentage groups. Finally, Weinstock notes a significant increase in performance late in extinction for the 100% group. We are faced here with the anomalous situation that, at least for continuously rewarded groups, rewards depress response strength late in acquisition and nonrewards increase response strength late in extinction.

Lewis and Duncan (1956a, 1958a) in two studies combined different numbers of acquisition trials with different percentages of reinforcement. They found no interaction during extinction for the two variables, but the larger number of acquisition trials, in both cases, resulted in quicker extinction. Capaldi (1957, 1958) in two studies reports a very similar finding; the more acquisition trials, the *faster* the extinction. In his second study, Capaldi combined length of acquisition with pattern of reinforcement. Some Ss received rewards on every other trial, and

some received rewards randomly. The alternately rewarded, long acquisition group extinguished faster than
the alternately rewarded, short acquisition group, and
faster than either the short or long randomly rewarded
groups. There was no difference between the irregularly
rewarded groups as a function of the length of acquisition.

The Lewis and Duncan (1956a, 1958a) and Capaldi
(1958) studies differ on one point. Capaldi found decreased resistance to extinction after a long acquisition
series only for regular reinforcement. Lewis and Duncan,
however, found no exception for irregular reinforcement.
They stated that for a well-learned response the function
of acquisition trials, as far as resistance to extinction is
concerned, is to establish a stable stimulus pattern; the
more acquisition trials the stabler the pattern, and when
extinction begins, the stimulus change will be greater.
This should be true with regular and irregular reinforcement, although more acquisition trials would probably
be necessary with the latter. Capaldi may not have given
a sufficient number of acquisition trials to decrease resistance for his irregularly rewarded group. Also, he presents no evidence that his groups were equal at the end
of acquisition.

Spontaneous recovery. There is very little information
about spontaneous recovery as affected by any variable,
and certainly there is little known about the effect of
partial reinforcement on spontaneous recovery. Perkins
and Cacioppo (1950), whose study has been briefly described above, comment simply, "spontaneous recovery
was complete before each reconditioning trial." Notterman, Schoenfeld, and Bersh (1952) conditioned heart
rate by means of electric shock. The partial group showed
no evidence of extinction although the continuous group
did. No spontaneous recovery was possible for the partial
group, nor was any found for the continuous group.

Lewis (1956) with a straight alley found no differential
effect of partial reinforcement on spontaneous recovery;
spontaneous recovery occurred for both partial and continuous groups. Lauer and Estes (1955) found spontaneous recovery occurring from day to day following
100% reinforcement, but not following 50%. In fact,
there was a decrement in response between daily blocks

for the 50% group, but recovery seemed to occur within the daily blocks.

The empirical evidence is too meager and conflicting to warrant any firm conclusion about the effects of partial reinforcement on spontaneous recovery.

Punishment. In the avoidance conditioning situation, S can avoid getting punishment by an appropriate response. Thus, early in acquisition, S gets punished on some of the trials and not on others, a partial procedure. In the escape learning situation, S gets the punishment no matter what he does, and this is a continuous procedure. If, as is commonly conceived, shock offset is reinforcing, one would expect, from the principle of partial reinforcement, that extinction would be more prolonged after avoidance conditioning than after escape conditioning. Jones (1953), Logan (1951), and Sheffield and Temmer (1950) have shown this to be the case. Jones (1953) has also shown that an "intermittent escape" schedule, one that involves withholding punishment on some trials, results in greater resistance to extinction than orthodox escape. Wynne and Solomon (1955) have pointed out, in addition, that the avoidance *extinction* situation actually involves further learning of the instrumental response. They argue that two responses are learned during the acquisition series, one is the instrumental response and the other is a conditioned emotional response (CER). The CER has a longer latency than the instrumental response, and on most trials the instrumental response occurs before the CER can begin. The S is removed from the conditioned stimulus before the CER can be evoked. On some trials, however, the latency of the instrumental response is sufficiently long for the CER to occur, and thus the instrumental response serves to reduce the CER, and the instrumental response is reinforced. Because this type of reinforcement occurs on only some of the trials, the instrumental response is actually partially reinforced during extinction.

Intertrial interval. Sheffield (1949) reported evidence to indicate that the PRE could be obtained if the acquisition interval was massed (15 sec.) but not if it was spaced (15 min.), and gave an "aftereffects" interpretation of her results. Since her conclusion is based on a

presumed interaction between percentage of reinforcement and acquisition interval, the analysis of variance
was the appropriate statistical technique. Her analysis by
means of *t* was, however, suggestive of her conclusion.

Two attempts to replicate the Sheffield study have been
reported by Wilson, Weiss, and Amsel (1955). They
tried to manipulate the strength of the aftereffects of
rewarded trials by using dry food in one experiment and
water in the other; Sheffield had used wet mash. The results obtained by Wilson, Weiss, and Amsel were in
sharp disagreement with those of Sheffield. The 50% reinforcement conditions led to greater resistance to extinction independent of the acquisition interval. There was
no significant interval by reinforcement interaction either
by analysis of variance or analysis of covariance. Lewis
(1956) also replicated Sheffield's experiment except that
he used a 2 min. distributed interval. He obtained essentially the same results as those of Wilson, Weiss and
Amsel. Again the PRE was obtained whether or not the
acquisition trials were distributed or massed.

With an eyelid conditioning apparatus, Grant, Schipper, and Ross (1952) used a $2 \times 2 \times 2$ factorial design
similar to that of Sheffield except that the intertrial intervals were 10 sec. or 40 sec. The extinction results were
quite complex in that there was a triple interaction among
the three variables of the experiment. The authors interpreted this interaction to mean that the superiority of the
50% groups during extinction was increased when there
was a change in the distribution of trials from acquisition
to extinction.

The Sheffield design was also used by Grant, Hornseth, and Hake (1950) in a light-guessing experiment
using a Humphreys' board (Humphreys, 1939). The intertrial intervals were 5 sec. and 45 sec. Again the PRE
was obtained independent of the acquisition interval.
Tyler (1956) in a discrimination situation found the
PRE after a 15 min. acquisition interval, and Weinstock
(1954, 1958) in two studies found the PRE after a 24-hr.
interval between acquisition trials. The only study not
showing the PRE after spaced acquisition trials was that
of Rubin (1953), but it is impossible to separate the
effects of the intervals from possible other effects such as

those of secondary reinforcement, and little can be concluded from this study.

The conclusion seems to be rather firm that the PRE obtains whatever the spacing of the acquisition trials.

Drive. There are only two papers directly relevant to the effects of different drive levels on partial reinforcement. One by Lewis and Cotton (1957) is essentially negative. Using 1, 6, and 22 hr. of food deprivation with 50 and 100% reinforcement for each drive level, they found that the interaction between the two variables did not attain significance.

The other study relevant to this variable is that of Linton and Miller (1951). Two groups of hungry rats received acquisition training with either 100% or 50% reinforcement. Each of these two groups was subdivided into two groups during extinction, one of each pair being extinguished while satiated, the other under the acquisition drive. Although appropriate for a factorial analysis of variance, the data were analyzed by *t* tests. The results indicated that the group partially reinforced and extinguished under the same drive as used during acquisition was more resistant to extinction than the other three, which were not different from each other. In part, the results were interpreted in terms of drive-stimulus generalization. Another part of the explanation had to do with the absence of a frustration drive for the partial-satiation group. It was believed that the absence of the frustration drive for the satiation group prevented the PRE from appearing.

Because a motivational interpretation of the PRE is not uncommon (Amsel, 1958) more studies are needed combining drive with different schedules of reinforcement.

Discrimination. In one sense, all studies using a choice situation and the noncorrection method involve partial reinforcement, because an incorrect trial is never reinforced. As the number of correct trials increases, so does the percentage of reinforcement. Lewis and Cotton (1958) have pointed out the complexity of the T maze as far as partial reinforcement is concerned. The two arms and the stem of the T maze each have a *different* percentage of reward obtaining. The correct arm is rewarded 100% of the time. The incorrect arm is rewarded 0%, and stem is rewarded at varying percentages, low during the early trials and almost 100% as the response is learned. Discrimination situations have thus afforded a difficult arena for the study of partial reinforcement. But because choice situations are so commonly used and because partial reinforcement is such an effective variable, studies are needed to tease out the effect of the different percentages of reward in the different sections of the apparatus. At a minimum, extinction running speeds should be determined separately for the stem and two arms of the T maze. It might also be desirable to duplicate in a runway the pattern of reinforcement usually obtained in the stem of a T.

Some information about partial reinforcement is available from response reversal studies, even though response reversal does not qualify as an orthodox extinction operation.

Wike (1953) showed that a response acquired under conditions of partial reinforcement is more resistant to reversal training than a continuously reinforced response. This finding has been confirmed by Grosslight and Radlow (1955), Grosslight, Hall, and Scott (1954), and Kendler and Lockman (1958), but not by Buss (1952).

Babb (1956) has shown that an irrelevant stimulus associated with reward 70% of the time facilitates later performance when the irrelevant stimulus becomes relevant. When the irrelevant stimulus is associated with reward 50% of the time, it has no effect on later learning. When associated with reward 30% of the time, later learning is inhibited by this previously irrelevant stimulus.

In general, partial reinforcement retards later response reversal.

Generalization and complex stimuli. In a study investigating the gradient of primary stimulus generalization to tones, Wickens, Schroder, and Snide (1954) established conditioned galvanic reactions to one of three tones, each of which was separated by 25 jnd's. For one group, in addition to the tones, a click was randomly presented 12 times without reinforcement.

During test trials a gradient of generalization was found for the group without clicks, but no gradient was discovered in the group with clicks. The failure to obtain a gradient for the click group seemed attributable to a generally high resistance to extinction.

Other evidence is available (Brown 1947) to indicate that the generalization gradient is very broad on the first test trials, becoming sharper with further test trials. Because the test trials are usually nonreinforced, generalization, and of course discrimination, is at least a by-product of extinction. A variable which increases resistance to extinction should, then, decrease any generalization gradient. From this, one would conclude that partial reinforcement should increase the amount of generalization, which is indicated by the Wickens, Schroder, and Snide (1954) study. Further evidence on this important problem is needed from other experimental situations.

The experimenters later reasoned that "if a complex stimulus is presented along with reinforcement and an element of the complex is presented at some other time without reinforcement, then this latter action increases the resistance to extinction of the complex stimulus itself" (Wickens & Snide, 1955, p. 257).

An experiment (Wickens & Snide, 1955) was undertaken to test this hypothesis directly. The general procedure consisted of employing as the CS a light and a tone which came on simultaneously. Two groups were conditioned and extinguished to this stimulus complex. For the experimental group one or the other aspect (the light alone or tone alone) of the total complex was occasionally presented during the training without reinforcement. According to the hypothesis, the experimental group should show greater resistance to extinction than the control. This hypothesis was supported by the data.

Magnitude of reward. Lewis and Duncan (1956b) combined different magnitudes of reward with partial reinforcement using a modified slot machine. Their rewards were 1, 10, 25, and 50 cents for each rewarded acquisition play. There was no significant interaction between amount of reward and the five different percentages of reward used in this situation. Hulse (1958), however, with an enclosed alley and magnitudes of .08 gm and 1.0 gm pellets, found a larger PRE with the larger sized pellet. The two experiments differ so greatly that it is almost futile to guess at the crucial difference. One possibility, however, lies in the intertrial interval which Hulse believes important for reward-percentage interactions. Hulse used a 24-hr. interval and Lewis and Duncan used a massed trial situation. Also, there may again be a difference between a *performance* situation like Lewis and Duncan's and essentially a *learning* one like Hulse's.

Confinement. In addition to magnitude Hulse also varied the length of the goal box confinement. He found that the PRE was less if there was a *change* in confinement from acquisition to extinction. Different extinction confinements had no effect, confirming a previous study by Hulse and Stanley (1956). Acquisition confinements were not effective by themselves either.

Variable delay of reward. Crum, Brown, and Bitterman (1951), in testing one of the theoretical notions of Sheffield (1949), introduced a new and interesting variable into the partial reinforcement literature. For one group of Ss, reward was given immediately. For a second group, reward was given immediately on half of the trials and it was delayed for 30 sec. on the other half. The trials on which reward was delayed were irregularly interspersed among the others. They found the typical PRE for the variable delayed group. Confirmation was soon made available by Scott and Wike (1956). Logan, Beier, and Kincaid (1956) showed that the PRE occurred when delays were variably 0 and 30 sec., but not when they were 0 and 9 sec. Kintsch and Wike (1957) used a T maze and gave one group immediate reward on the correct trials, another group 10-sec. delays on half of the correct trials, and a third group 30 sec. delays on half of the correct trials. The results were essentially the same as those of Logan, Beier, and Kincaid (1956); and PRE appeared with 30 sec. variable delay, but not with 10 seconds. Feher (1956), however, had found increased resistance to extinction with constant acquisition delays of 10 seconds.

Wike and McNamara (1957) used an alley runway, and varied percentage of delay. One group was delayed on 25% of the trials, a second group was delayed on 50% of the trials, and a third group was delayed on 75% of the trials. All delays were 30 seconds. On the other trials Ss received reward immediately. The 25% group extinguished faster than the other two, which were not significantly different. Apparently, reward must be delayed on more than 25% of the trials for the PRE to occur. It would be interesting to know the shape of the function between 25% and 50%.

Peterson (1956) combined partial delay with partial reinforcement in an interesting experiment. One group was reinforced on every trial with no delay. Another also had 100% reinforcement with delays on various trials of 0, 10, 20, and 30 sec. A third group had 50% reinforcement with delays of 0, 10, 20, and 30 sec. on the reinforced trials. A final group had 50% reinforcement with no delay on the reinforced trials. The 50% group with delay was most resistant to extinction. The 100% group with delay and the 50% group without delay were about equal and next most resistant to extinction. Least resistant to extinction was the 100% no delay group.

In conclusion, it seems that partial delays of 30 sec. result in increased resistance to extinction, but partial delays of 10 sec. or less do not. The delays must occur on more than 25% of the trials, and when partial reinforcement is combined with partial delay, resistance to extinction is the greatest.

Situations. Having established an empirical phenomenon in one experimental situation we take some practical, and sometimes theoretical, interest in determining the variety of situations in which the phenomenon holds. In this section an attempt will be made to review quickly some of the different experimental situations in which the PRE has been explored.

Lewis (1952) used children in a button pushing situation. The rewards were plastic cowboys and, in a 10-trial acquisition series, were given 100%, 60%, 50%, and 0% of the time. There was no difference in PRE between the 50% and 60% groups, nor between the 100% and 0% groups, but the former two groups were superior to the latter two. Fattu, Mech, and Auble (1955) with a similar situation measured the number of responses to extinction after 100%, 50%, and 25% reinforcement. The 25% group was considerably the most resistant to extinction, followed by the 50% and 100%

groups in that order. Fattu, Auble, and Mech (1955) were not able to repeat their results although the same trend was apparent.

Goss and Rabaiola (1952) had Ss learn one of three nonsense syllables to a color stimulus. The correct response was reinforced with a buzzer 100%, 75%, and 50% of the time for the different groups. The speed of attainment of a criterion of learning was an increasing function of the percentage of reward. After the criterion was reached the reward conditions were switched. Half of each acquisition group was given 0% reward, and the reward percentage was halved for the other. The mean number of correct responses decreased faster for the 50% and 0% group than for the 100% to 0% group. This runs counter to the usual PRE. Also, Goss and Rabaiola report an increase in correct responses after about eight trials of no reward.

Hirsch (1957) presented his Ss with a series of words to which they were to respond with a number. The correct number was one less than the number of letters in the words. He reinforced his Ss either 100% or 67% of the time for the correct responses. All reinforcement was omitted after a criterion was attained. Again there was no significant PRE. Perhaps, if more of a "persistence" measure of extinction had been used in these two studies, the typical PRE would have occurred.

Kanfer (1954) and Spivok and Papajohn (1957) varied percentage of reinforcement in an autokinetic situation. A restricted class of S's verbal statements about movement was selected for reinforcement. Kanfer rewarded these responses at 100%, 67%, 50%, and 0% for different groups, bringing all but the 0% group to the same criterion of performance. The reward was removed. The typical PRE was found in that the greater number of "critical" responses was found in the partial group. The S's awareness of the reinforcement was not an essential condition for the PRE. Kanfer also pointed out that the rate of extinction may be as important as the total number of responses emitted. Spivok and Papajohn (1957) compared 100% reinforcement with a variable interval schedule, finding greater PRE for the latter.

Finally, Lewis and Cotton (1958) found the PRE in

a **T** maze with a correct turn response measure. Their animals had partial reinforcement administered by being placed in the goal by hand with food present on 50% of the placements. However, both the 50% and 100% groups were worse than a control group that did not receive nonresponse reinforcement.

THEORY

In 1950, discussing the various theories of partial reinforcement, Jenkins and Stanley (1950) ennumerated five essentially different theories. These were: (*a*) response unit, (*b*) aftereffects, (*c*) discrimination, (*d*) secondary reinforcement, and (*e*) expectancy. All of these remain today as viable entries in the partial reinforcement sweepstakes although the response-unit hypothesis is rarely used for discrete trial phenomena, and the expectancy hypothesis has been much battered of late and seems to have no articulate supporter remaining. In addition, there are two new entries since 1950. These are: (*a*) a competing response theory of Weinstock (1954), and one by Hulse and Stanley (1956), and (*b*) a mediating response theory, espoused by Amsel (1958), Kendler, Pliskoff, and D'Amato (1957) and Logan, Beier, and Kincaid (1956) among others.

Aftereffects. One of the first, and probably still as good as any, statements of the aftereffects theory is that of Sheffield (1949). She pointed out that the aftereffects of reinforcement are quite different from the aftereffects of nonreinforcement. When reinforcement occurs, S would have a food taste in the mouth, perhaps food particles, and still other stimuli associated with eating. After a nonreinforced trial the aftereffects would include frustration, searching, etc. Obviously the stimuli following nonreinforcement would be very different from those following reinforcement. If the stimulus aftereffects of nonreinforcement are still present on the next trial, and the next trial results in reinforcement, then the instrumental running response would be conditioned to the aftereffects of nonreinforcement, and the S would actually learn to respond to the stimuli of nonreinforcement. Since the extinction stimuli are those of nonreinforcement, S has learned to respond during extinction. Those Ss who are rewarded on every trial never have the opportunity to respond to nonreinforcement cues and thus have not learned to respond to extinction stimuli.

But this is only the learning factor of the aftereffects theory as Sheffield describes it. There is also a primary generalization factor. For the continuously reinforced Ss, the advent of extinction introduces new stimuli for the first time, those from nonreinforcement. With the introduction of new stimuli there will be a response decrement due to primary stimulus generalization. For the partially reinforced Ss there would be no new stimuli introduced with extinction, since nonreinforcement had occurred repeatedly during the acquisition.

To demonstrate the adequacy of her reasoning, Sheffield ran 50% and 100% groups, factorially combined with massed and distributed acquisition trials. With massed trials the aftereffects of nonreinforced trials should still be present at the initiation of the succeeding trial, as the theory requires. With distributed trials this would not be the case. Her results probably confirmed her theory for the PRE seemed to appear, as tested by t, only after massed trials and 50% reinforcement.

Following some implications of Sheffield's hypothesis, Grosslight and Radlow (1955) and Grosslight, Hall, and Murnin (1953) found that several series of trials in which a single nonreinforcement is followed by reinforcement would result in the PRE, if the nonreinforcement were followed by a reinforcement. The authors interpret their results in terms of a Sheffieldian aftereffects theory, in that the aftereffects of the nonreinforced trials are presumed to be conditioned to the instrumental response because they are followed by a reinforcement, but it should be noted that a discrimination hypothesis would handle the results equally well.

Linton and Miller (1951) found no PRE when extinction, after partial reinforcement under normal deprivation conditions, was carried out under conditions of drive satiation and with the reward present on each trial. They reasoned that this was because there were very different aftereffects occurring during satiated "extinction" and that the instrumental response had not been conditioned during acquisition to these aftereffects.

As noted in the section on intertrial interval, Wilson, Weiss, and Amsel (1955) repeated Sheffield's study twice, with minor variations and without her results. In one case the variation was such as to enhance the aftereffects. In the other, the variation served to reduce the aftereffects, but in neither case was the massed acquisition-partially reinforced group more resistant to extinction. Lewis (1956) also repeated Sheffield's study using a 2-min., instead of a 15-min. spaced interval. The graph of his results appeared to be Sheffieldian, but the appropriate statistical analysis showed no significant effect.

Continuing the attack on the aftereffects hypotheses Tyler (1956) found the PRE in a discrimination situation even after a 15-min. acquisition interval and, even more devastating, Weinstock, on two occasions (1954, 1958) has found the PRE even when acquisition trials were spaced 24 hours apart. This suggests that long range aftereffects are more important than previously believed.

Tyler, Wortz, and Bitterman (1953) reasoned that if Sheffield were right, a simple pattern—alternating reinforcement with nonreinforcement—should give a greater PRE than a random pattern, because alternation maximizes the number of times nonreinforcement follows reinforcement. Their results showed just the opposite; alternation resulted in quicker extinction than did the random pattern.

Another ingenious attack on the aftereffects theory was performed by Crum, Brown, and Bitterman (1951). If the reward were delayed after each trial, they argued, the aftereffects for the succeeding trial would always be those of reinforcement. They compared a group which received delay of reward on some of its trials and immediate reward on others with a group that received immediate reward on all trials. The partial delay group showed the PRE very nicely. Peterson (1956), Logan, Beier, and Kincaid (1956), and Wike (1953), have confirmed the results of Crum, Brown, and Bitterman.

Feher (1956) performed some interesting variations on the delay of reward. She compared delays given before the reward with delays given after the reward. For the latter, Ss were simply left in the goal box for a specified period of time. She found that both delay groups extinguished slower than groups without delay. And the delay-before-reward group extinguished slower than the delay-after-reward group, again counter to an aftereffects notion.

Katz (1957) ran three groups of animals in a test of the aftereffects notion. The acquisition trials were given in two quite different runways. One trial was given on the first runway, followed immediately by a trial on the second runway. One group (P-C) was given partial reinforcement on the first runway and continuous reinforcement on the second. A second group (C-P) was given just the reverse: continuous reinforcement on the first and partial on the second. The final group (C-C) was given continuous reinforcement on both runways. For the P-C group, all nonreinforced trials occurring in the first runway were followed by reinforced trials in the second runway. For the C-P group there was no similar opportunity for conditioning the aftereffects of nonreinforcement. All extinction trials were given in the second runway. The results showed that the C-P was slowest to extinguish, followed by the P-C group, and the C-C group extinguished most rapidly. This would indicate that other factors than aftereffects are most important in bringing about the PRE.

The only conclusion that can be drawn from these experiments is that, at best, Sheffieldian aftereffects are not important contributors to the PRE, and they probably have no effect whatsoever.

Discrimination. The discrimination theory, which was apparently first advanced by Mowrer and Jones (1945), has had the advantage of being less specifically stated than the aftereffects theory, and the longevity of a theory is apparently inversely related to the specificity with which it can be stated and tested. In general the discrimination theory states that resistance to extinction is a function of the similarity of the acquisition stimuli to the extinction stimuli. The more similar the stimulus conditions are in the two situations, the greater the resistance to extinction. The problem then becomes one of stating and demonstrating the variables of which similarity may be said to be a function. Once lawful relationships are obtained between similarity variables and behavior, any controversy over whether discrimination theory is a perceptual one, or refers to something going on in the rat's mind, is superfluous. The major task for discrimination theorists, then, is one of stating specifically what variables determine similarity.

Probably the most vigorous supporters of the discrimination hypothesis have been the Texas group, although their research has been aimed more at disproving the aftereffects theory than it has at giving support to a discrimination theory. Longnecker, Krauskopf, and Bitterman (1952) and Tyler, Wortz, and Bitterman (1953) showed that a simple alternating pattern of reinforcement and nonreinforcement resulted in quicker extinction than a random pattern. Since this was contrary to an aftereffects theory, they argued, there must be some serial patterning that occurs, enabling Ss to discriminate the acquisition series and to stop responding quickly when it ceases.

Bitterman, Fedderson, and Tyler (1953) and Elam, Tyler, and Bitterman (1954) gave rewards in one end box and nonrewards in a very different one. One group was extinguished with the rewarded end box present and another group was extinguished with the nonrewarded box. Presumably, the stimulus situations from acquisition to extinction would be more similar when the nonrewarded end box was present because these stimuli had always in the past accompanied nonrewards. Using the rewarded end box during extinction would bring about a stimulus change because these stimuli had always accompanied rewards. The predicted results occurred, and were interpreted according to the discrimination theory. The authors tended to speak as if the discrimination were perceptual in some fashion, but, of course, all they could do was to relate behavior to stimuli, in this case stimulus change. There is no need to introduce an intervening perceptual process to handle this data.

Monkeys were given their choice, by Elam and Tyler (1958), between two stimuli, A and B. For one group, the A stimulus was rewarded 60% of the time and the

B stimulus was rewarded 40% of the time. For the second group, the A stimulus was also rewarded 60% of the time but the B stimulus was rewarded 0% of the time. During extinction, the A stimulus was rewarded 0% of the time and the B stimulus was rewarded 100% of the time for both groups. Results showed that during acquisition, A was much more preferred by the second group, but during extinction, A extinguished much more rapidly for the second group. Elam and Tyler attribute the much faster extinction of A for the second group to the greater stimulus change from acquisition to extinction occurring for this group than the other.

Goodnow and Pettigrew (1956) presented a somewhat similar problem to four groups of human Ss. The apparatus was a "two-armed bandit." One group received reward for a LR (left-right) pattern of responses, the second received reward for an LL pattern, a third was given an LLR pattern, and the fourth was given a random pattern. After an acquisition series of trials, all groups were given a random pattern for a while and then all groups were switched to a final LR pattern. Both the initial LR and LL groups learned the final pattern faster than the random group. (Many of the LLR group did not learn the initial pattern.) Goodnow and Pettigrew concluded that the final pattern was made more discriminable because of the stability of the initial response pattern. Also, there was less of a stimulus change for the two initially systematic groups than for the initially random group.

McClelland and McGown (1953) gave one group of animals irregular reinforcement in various parts of a circular shaped apparatus. Another group always found the reinforcement in the same place. Results showed that the inconsistently rewarded group was more resistant to extinction. The authors concluded: "Omission of reinforcement changes the cue pattern less if the original cue pattern is complex or variable, than if it is simple and invariant."

Sheffield and Temmer (1950) have shown that the superior resistance to extinction of avoidance learning to escape learning can be given a partial reinforcement interpretation. Jones (1953) found that an "intermittent

escape" group, one that was not punished on every trial
but still could not learn to avoid, was more resistant to
extinction than an orthodox escape group. Also a "limited
avoidance" group extinguished slower than the escape
group. "Limited avoidance" referred to a condition in
which the S was placed on an initially uncharged grid,
but the current would be turned on before S could get
off the grid. The faster S moved the less shock he would
take, and in this sense it was an avoidance condition, but
even so, S would always get the punishment. The "limited avoidance" group was also more resistant to extinction than the pure escape group. The acquisition
conditions, according to Jones, were more like the extinction conditions for the "intermittent escape" and the
"limited avoidance" conditions than they were for the
escape conditions.

In several studies Lewis and Duncan (1956a, 1956b,
1957, 1958a, 1958b) found that 0% reinforcement
showed more resistance to extinction than 100% reinforcement, and more than most other percentages of
reinforcement. Their situation, a "one-armed bandit,"
differed from most others in that no learning was involved in the performance of the lever pulling response.
All Ss, on coming into the experimental room, already
knew how to pull a lever. The experimenters argued,
therefore, that the acquisition series served primarily to
set the extinction series apart, and that 0% acquisition
was most like the extinction series. In one of these studies (1958a) they found, contrary to most previous results, that extinction was quicker after a long acquisition
series. Again they attributed this to the pure performance
situation in which a relatively long acquisition series
would serve to make the initial stimulus situation more
stable.

Somewhat similar results have been reported by Capaldi (1957, 1958).

Brand, Woods, and Sakoda (1957) in a two alternative
situation varied both the difference in percentage of reinforcement and the difference in the ratio of reinforcement. The difference, for example, between 57% and
25% is 50%, and the ratio is three to one. The difference
between 100% and 50% is also 50%, but now the ratio

is two to one. They found that extinction is quicker when the percentage difference is great (a finding in a line with a discrimination hypothesis), but that the ratios had practically no effect.

Fehrer (1956), who found that delay of reinforcement leads to increased resistance to extinction, also interprets her study according to a discrimination theory in that having a delay come before a reward affords an experience—that of no reward—much like the initial experience during extinction.

All of the studies that have been reviewed in this section so far present evidence that has been interpreted as favorable to discrimination theory. There are two recent studies, however, that present a considerable hurdle for discrimination theory to jump. Marx (1958) gave two groups of animals acquisition training in a runway with food pellets presented in the end box in a glass cup. During extinction one group was presented with the empty cup on every trial, and one group was presented with the empty cup on only half of the trials; on the other half the food cup was absent. There was a greater stimulus change for the group that had the cup on only half of the trials, yet this group extinguished slowest. In a more elaborate experiment, Brown and Bass (1958) varied the stimulus conditions—different alleys—in both acquisition and extinction. They found that variable extinction conditions resulted in increased resistance to extinction. In both of these experiments, stimulus change increased resistance to extinction instead of decreasing it as the discrimination hypothesis would seem to demand, but, it should be noted, only 100% reinforcement was used in both studies.

In addition, Brown and Bass found that irregular stimulus conditions during acquisition had no effect on resistance to extinction. This seems to run counter to previous evidence (MacKintosh, 1955), but Brown and Bass have the better designed study in that theirs was a factorial combination of variables in both acquisition and extinction. MacKintosh extinguished all Ss under constant conditions, making it impossible, as Brown and Bass point out, to distinguish between learning condition irregularities and the change from irregular acquisition to constant extinction. Both the Brown and Bass and the Marx study are consistent with much previous evidence (e.g., Glazer, 1958) indicating that stimulus novelty and change increases performance. It seems, then, that one must at least conclude that stimulus change during extinction must be weighed more heavily in increasing resistance to extinction than constancy of stimulus conditions from acquisition to extinction. In any case, the studies of Brown and Bass (1958) and Marx (1958), complicate the task of discrimination theorists.

Secondary reinforcement. Denny (1946) is usually given credit for the formal introduction of the secondary reinforcement hypothesis into the area of partial reinforcement. He pointed out that on reinforcement trials the stimuli of the goal box are associated with primary reinforcement and therefore should acquire secondary reinforcing power. On nonreinforced trials and during extinction, secondary reinforcement should be taking place which would retard extinction.

The attack on the secondary reinforcement hypothesis began with Bitterman, Feddersen, and Tyler (1953) and Elam, Tyler, and Bitterman (1954). They found that rats extinguished in the goal box in which they had received their reinforced trials—the nonreinforced trials were given in a very different goal box—showed less PRE than those extinguished in the goal box which was present for nonreinforced trials. According to a Hullian (1943) secondary reinforcement hypothesis, the results should have been just the opposite. The stimuli associated with primary reward and present during extinction should have prolonged extinction performance. In only slightly different situations Notterman (1951) and Freides (1957) have duplicated the significant aspects of these studies. They found no difference between the two relevant groups, but this still does not support a secondary reinforcement interpretation.

Mason (1957) has reported an interesting experiment. His animals learned two discriminations. In one, the positive stimulus was rewarded 100% of the time; in the other it was rewarded 50% of the time. On the test trials both positive stimuli were presented and the S's preference on successive trials constituted the response measure. Most Ss chose the stimulus that had been rewarded 100% of the time, even when twice as many total trials had been given to the 50% rewarded stimuli, so that the total number of primary rewards in the two situations was the same, but the 50% group would have had secondary reinforcement in addition. These results were interpreted as opposed to a secondary reinforcement hypothesis.

The results of Fehrer (1956) can also be interpreted as opposed to a secondary reinforcement interpretation of partial reinforcement. Two of her groups involved goal box delays. One was given a 30-sec. delay before a 10-sec. eating period, and one was given a 10-sec. eating period followed by a 30-sec. delay. Another group was allowed to eat for a full 40-sec. in the goal box. The goal box stimuli had a longer association with primary reward for the latter group and should have resulted in slower extinction than the other two. Just the opposite happened; both delay groups extinguished slower than the none-delay group.

Hulse and Stanley (1956) reported, but only at the .10 level of significance, that the PRE occurred only when the S^r was present on every training trial.

The evidence, at this point, seems quite conclusive that secondary reinforcement is not the sole explanation of the PRE, but that it can be exceptionally efficacious was indicated by Zimmerman (1957), who used a free responding situation. He suggested that when an S^n is irregularly associated with reinforcement, it loses none of its S^n function and maintains its S^r function over a considerable time. It is most effective as an S^r when presented irregularly again. Zimmerman's study is based on very few animals, and needs to be replicated before it can be accepted with absolute confidence, but it seems probable that a stimulus, when irregularly associated with reinforcement and then used irregularly as an S^r, can have very powerful reinforcing value. At this point, however, it becomes difficult to distinguish between a discrimination hypothesis and a secondary reinforcement one. It seems likely, in fact, that they are basically the same.

Competing response. Weinstock (1954) has presented an "habituation" theory which states essentially that nonreinforced responses "habituate" by some unspecified process and drop out. For a group of partially rewarded Ss, competing responses are made during acquisition on the nonreinforced trials, and these competing responses drop out. Thus when extinction begins, the competing responses have already habituated and the instrumental response continues strongly. No habituation of the competing responses occurs during acquisition for the continuously reinforced group, and their onset during extinction results in a rapid decrease in the instrumental response.

The only experiments aimed directly at testing this notion—although Tyler (1956) has pointed out that Weinstock's theory does not explain why random reinforcement results in a greater PRE than alternating reinforcement—are those of Stanley and Clayton (1955) and Hulse (1958). Stanley and Clayton assumed that if Ss were delayed in the goal box, more competing responses would occur and thus habituate. They gave immediate reinforcement and a 30-sec. delay to two groups during acquisition and broke these two down factorially to immediate goal box removal and a 30-sec. delay during extinction. The acquisition delay group was not more resistant to extinction than the immediately rewarded group. These results are opposed to Weinstock's habituation theory, if habituation is a function of time in the goal box, but they are also opposed to the results of Fehrer (1956) who found that 30-sec. delays, both before and after the reinforcement, retarded extinction.

In another study, Hulse and Stanley (1956) presented a theory somewhat similar to that of Weinstock (1954). They also argued that competing responses occur during the nonreinforced acquisition trials, but for them the competing responses do not "habituate." The Ss learn to do something other than eat during these trials. When extinction starts, the partially reinforced Ss do the "something else" that they learned during acquisition and are quickly removed from the stimuli which evoke eating, and thus the conditioned eating response is protected from rapid extinction. At this point Hulse and Stanley follow the notion of Sheffield, Roby, and Campbell (1954), that the faster extinction of conditioned eating

leads to a faster loss of the instrumental response. This is
because the conditioned eating response works backward
over the maze stimuli and constitutes an important part
of the stimulus situation leading to the instrumental
response.

Hulse and Stanley's theory appears to be more specific
than Weinstock's because it does not contain such a
vague term as "habituation" playing an important role.
Also Hulse and Stanley indicate how the goal box competing response can affect behavior occurring at the beginning of the apparatus. But this notion, too, runs into
difficulty when Freides' (1957) data are considered. He
found that behavior in the goal box (approaching food)
could extinguish while a runaway response remained
strong.

Mediational responses. It should be noted that the
theory of Hulse and Stanley (1956) involved a mediating
conditioned eating response and could very properly be
considered in this section also.

Wilson, Weiss, and Amsel (1955) and Amsel (1958)
have argued for a mediating frustration response as an
explanation of the PRE. During partial reinforcement an
emotional response develops on the unreinforced trials.
The emotional response works backward over the maze
stimuli and is evoked by the stimuli of the start box. The
emotional response has stimulus properties, as do all responses, and these stimuli become conditioned to the instrumental response. Since the emotional response does
not get conditioned during acquisition to the instrumental response for the 100% Ss, they show a sharp response decrement during extinction.

Essentially the same idea is presented by Kendler,
Pliskoff, D'Amato, and Katz (1957), except that no
special properties, such as emotionality, are ascribed to
the mediating response. Lewis and Duncan (1958b) also
used a mediating response to interpret their data and
show how some language behavior is related to it.

Logan, Beier, and Kincaid (1956) maintain that resistance to extinction is a direct function of the degree
to which the mediating response persists beyond the time
at which reinforcement usually occurs. "Postreinforce-
ment time cues" do not occur during 100% acquisition

because reinforcement is given every time as soon as S enters the goal box. They do, however, occur during extinction, evoking the mediating response and quick extinction results. With longer delays of reinforcement during acquisition such as occur in a varied delay procedure, the occurrence of mediating responses to post-reinforcement time cues will be increased because the mediating response is eventually reinforced after the delay. Thus the mediating response continues over a longer time for the partial delay Ss, and gets rewarded for being prolonged. It will occur over a longer period during extinction also. Because the mediating response lasts longer, and is conditioned, presumably, to the instrumental response, the instrumental response will also last longer. Logan, Beier, and Kincaid (1956) are not entirely clear on this point, however.

Expectancy. Expectancy "theory" was brought into partial reinforcement by Humphreys (1939). He considered that his early partial reinforcement studies were contrary to a drive reduction point of view, but that the data could be handled nicely by a concept of expectancy. Basically, he argued that partial reinforcement resulted in an expectancy of irregular reinforcement and that continuous reinforcement resulted in an expectancy of regular reinforcement. He further stated that it was easier to change from a regular expectancy of one kind (that rewards occur on every trial) to a regular expectancy of another kind (that rewards do not occur on any trial), than it was to change from an irregular expectancy (that rewards occur on only some of the trials) to a regular expectancy.

Lewis and Duncan (1957) attempted to test Humphreys' notion by having their Ss state, before each trial, the confidence they held that they would win or lose on the next trial. They found no evidence in their data for Humphreys' notion that those with irregular expectancies of winning would continue longer during extinction than those with regular expectancies. Insofar as Humphreys meant some over-all kind of expectancy, these data are not pertinent since they are trial-by-trial expectancies.

The two-light Humphreys board has been a standard apparatus for studying expectancies—"yes" and "no" statements—for a number of years. Recently several studies have appeared with this device which have used a shift in stimulus presentation probabilities. In order to respond to the postshift probabilities, presumably the responses to the preshift probabilities must extinguish. Thus this situation seems to afford a means, at least indirectly, of studying expectancies during extinction.

Parducci (1957), with a two-choice betting game, gave separate groups three preshift probabilities—15%, 50%, and 70%. Then all groups were shifted to 70%. He found more complete adjustments to the postshift probability when the magnitude of the shift was greatest. He interpreted his results according to a discrimination theory and counter to Humphreys' regularity of expectancy analysis. He also concluded, although the evidence is not very clear on this point, that the expected *permanence* of shift was more important than the magnitude of shift.

Goodnow and her colleagues (Goodnow, 1955; Goodnow & Pettigrew, 1955; Goodnow & Pettigrew, 1956; Goodnow & Postman, 1955) in a number of studies have hypothesized that guesses would be more likely to approach 100% to the most probable light if the situation were a "chance" one than if it were a "problem solving" one. James and Rotter (1958) also hypothesized that the "chance" and "skill" situations would make a difference to resistance to extinction. They gave one set of instructions to indicate that the task involved chance only, and one set to indicate that the task was skill only. Instructions were combined factorially with 50 and 100% reinforcement. Their hypothesis was confirmed. With skill instructions, the 100% group took longer to extinguish than the 50% group. With chance instructions, just the reverse was true. James and Rotter interpret their results as the effects of symbolic processes of some kind, whereas Goodnow and Postman (1955), in a slightly different situation, maintain that "awareness" is not a necessary part of such probability discriminations.

Perhaps every study cited in this report could be reinterpreted according to an expectancy notion, and that is the main weakness of such a point of view. There seems to be no way of disproving it. Certainly not much recent research has been oriented around expectancies, and this concept is apparently moribund as an explanation of the PRE.

CONCLUSION

The writer began this review of the literature on partial reinforcement in the hope of arriving at some explanation of the PRE. Unfortunately, he is at least as far away from an explanation now as when he started. Conflicts and contradictions in data contribute their share of confusion, but probably more important has been the absence of the right kind of data. In the data section of this paper an attempt was made to discover parametric laws. Except in very few instances, this was impossible. Not many experimenters seem to be interested in how one variable relates to another along the major range of both variables. Most experimenters are interested in "theory" testing. As a result, we have a large number of two or three group experiments, using a widely different array of apparatus, sometimes combined in factorial designs, telling us that our theoretical notions are largely inadequate, but not telling us a great deal more. To determine a parametric law probably at least five points are needed along each dimension. With fewer than five points, the task of stating the law—describing it by an equation—is relatively trivial. With five or more points, and a small number of constants, the dimension can be described with some precision, assuming the data are reliable and that a dimension is actually present. Certainly curve fitting can be an arbitrary procedure, and certainly it is not all there is to theory, but, also certainly, a theory ought to be about something, and parametric data make a wonderful subject matter. But this is just saying, in a more elaborate way, "more research is needed."

The writer feels no desire at present to carry cudgels for any of the "theories" now available, nor does he have a theory of his own to contribute that he has any confidence in, nor does he think it sporting to take further "pot shots" at the existing theories. The writer remains almost as empty of an understanding of partial reinforcement now as when he began to review the literature, but he still considers the problems in the area to be fascinating.

BIBLIOGRAPHY

Amsel, A., The role of frustrative nonreward in noncontinuous reward situations. *Psychol. Bull.*, 1958, 55, 102-119.

Babb, H., Proportional reinforcement of irrelevant stimuli and transfer value. *J. comp. physiol. Psychol.*, 1956, 49, 586-589.

Bijou, S. W., Patterns of reinforcement and resistance to extinction in young children. *Child Develop.*, 1957, 28, 47-54.

Bijou, S. W., Operant extinction after fixed intertrial schedules with young children. *J. exp. Anal. behav.*, 1958, 1, 25-30.

Bitterman, M. E., Fedderson, W. E., & Tyler, D. W., Secondary reinforcement and the discrimination hypothesis. *Amer. J. Psychol.*, 1953, 66, 456-464.

Brady, J. V., Extinction of a conditioned "fear" response as a function of reinforcement schedules for competing response. *J. Psychol.*, 1955, 40, 25-34.

Brand, H., Woods, A. J., & Sakoda, J. M., Effects of a random versus pattern instructural act in a contingent partial reinforcement situation. *Psychol. Rep.*, 1957, 3, 473-479.

Brown, J. S., The generalization of approach responses as a function of stimulus intensity and the strength of motivation. *J. comp. physiol. Psychol.*, 1947, 37, 92-98.

Brown, J. S., & Bass, B., The acquisition and extinction of an instrumental response under constant and variable stimulus conditions. *J. comp. physiol. Psychol.*, 1958, 51, 499-504.

Bullock, D. H., & Smith, W. C., An effect of repeated conditioning-extinction upon operant strength. *J. exp. Psychol.*, 1953, 46, 349-352.

Buss, A. H., Some determinants of rigidity in discrimination-reversal learning. *J. exp. Psychol.*, 1952, 44, 222-227.

Capaldi, E. J., The effect of different amounts of alternating partial reinforcement on resistance to extinction. *Amer. J. Psychol.*, 1957, 70, 451-452.

Capaldi, E. J., The effect of different amounts of training on the resistance to extinction of different patterns of partially reinforced responses. *J. comp. physiol. Psychol.*, 1958, 51, 367-371.

Clayton, F. L., Secondary reinforcement as a function of reinforcement scheduling. *Psychol. Rep.*, 1956, 2, 377-380.

Cowles, J. T., Food-tokens as incentives for learning by chimpanzees. *Comp. Psychol. Monogr.*, 1937, 14, 1-96.

CRUM, J., BROWN, W. L., & BITTERMAN, M. E., The effect of partial and delayed reinforcement on resistance to extinction. *Amer. J. Psychol.*, 1951, 64, 228-237.

DENNY, M. R., The role of secondary reinforcement in a partial reinforcement learning situation. *J. exp. Psychol.*, 1946, 36, 373-389.

DENNY, M. W., WELLS, R. H., & MAATCH, J. L., Resistance to extinction as a function of the discrimination habit established during fixed-ratio reinforcement. *J. exp. Psychol.*, 1957, 53, 451-456.

ELAM, C. B., & TYLER, D. W., The discrimination hypothesis and cue reversal. *Amer. J. Psychol.*, 1958, 71, 583-586.

ELAM, C. B., TYLER, D. W., & BITTERMAN, M. E., A further study of secondary reinforcement and the discrimination hypothesis. *J. comp. physiol. Psychol.*, 1954, 47, 381-384.

FATTU, N., AUBLE, D., & MECH, E. V., Partial reinforcement related to "free" responding in extinction with preschool children. *J. exp. Educ.*, 1955, 23, 365-368.

FATTU, N., MECH, E. V., & AUBLE, D., Partial reinforcement in a bar pressing situation with pre-school children. *J. genet. Psychol.*, 1955, 87, 251-255.

FEHRER, ELIZABETH, Effects of reinforcement and of pre- and post-reinforcement delays on learning and extinction. *J. exp. Psychol.*, 1956, 52, 167-176.

FREIDES, D., Goal-box cues and pattern of reinforcement. *J. exp. Psychol.*, 1957, 53, 361-371.

GLANZER, M., Curiosity, exploratory drive, and stimulus satiation. *Psychol Bull.*, 1958, 55, 302-315.

GOODNOW, JACQUELINE J., Determinants of choice-distributions in two choice situations. *Amer. J. Psychol.*, 1955, 68, 106-116.

GOODNOW, JACQUELINE J., & PETTIGREW, T. F., Effects of prior patterns of experience upon strategies and learning sets. *J. exp. Psychol.*, 1955, 49, 381-389.

GOODNOW, JACQUELINE J., & PETTIGREW, T. F., Some sources of difficulty in solving simple problems. *J. exp. Psychol.*, 1956, 51, 385-392.

GOODNOW, JACQUELINE J., & POSTMAN, L., Probability learning in a problem-solving situation. *J. exp. Psychol.*, 1955, 49, 16-22.

GORMEZANO, I., & GRANT, D. A., Progressive ambiguity in the attainment of concepts on the Wisconsin card sorting test. *J. exp. Psychol.*, 1958, 55, 621-627.

GOSS, A. E., & RABIOLA, E. J., Response strength in a modified Thorndikian multiple-choice situation as a function of varying proportions of reinforcement. *J. exp. Psychol.*, 1952, 43, 106-114.

GRANT, D. A., HAKE, H. W., & HORNSETH, J. P., Acquisition and extinction of a verbal conditioned response with differing percentages of reinforcement. *J. exp. Psychol.*, 1951, 42, 1-5.

GRANT, D. A., HAKE, H. W., RIOPELLE, A. J., & KOSTLAN, A., Effect of repeated pretesting with conditioned stimulus upon extinction of the conditioned eyelid response to light. *Amer. J. Psychol.*, 1951, 14, 247-251.

GRANT, D. A., HORNSETH, J. P., & HAKE, H. W., The influence of the intertrial interval on the Humphreys' "random reinforcement effect" during the extinction of a verbal response. *J. exp. Psychol.*, 1950, 40, 609-612.

GRANT, D. A., RIOPELLE, A. J., & HAKE, H. W., Resistance to extinction and the pattern of reinforcement. I. Alternation of reinforcement and the conditioned eyelid response. *J. exp. Psychol.*, 1950, 40, 53-60.

GRANT, D. A., & SCHIPPER, L. M., The acquisition and extinction of conditioned eyelid responses as a function of the percentage of fixed-ratio random reinforcement. *J. exp. Psychol.*, 1952, 43, 313-320.

GRANT, D. A., SCHIPPER, L. M., & ROSS, B. M., Effect of intertrial interval during acquisition on extinction of the conditioned eyelid responses following partial reinforcement. *J. exp. Psychol.*, 1952, 44, 203-210.

GROSSLIGHT, J. H., HALL, J. F., & MURNIN, J., Patterning effect in partial reinforcement. *J. exp. Psychol.*, 1953, 46, 103-106.

GROSSLIGHT, J. H., HALL, J. F., & SCOTT, W. F., Reinforcement schedules in habit reversal—a confirmation. *J. exp. Psychol.*, 1954, 48, 173-174.

GROSSLIGHT, J. H., & RADLOW, R., Patterning effect of the nonreinforcement-reinforcement sequence in a discrimination situation. *J. comp. physiol. Psychol.*, 1955, 49, 543-547.

GROSSLIGHT, J. H., & RADLOW, R., Patterning effect of the nonreinforcement-reinforcement sequence involving a single nonreinforced trial. *J. comp. physiol. Psychol.*, 1957, 50, 23-25.

HAKE, H. W., & GRANT, D. A., Resistance to extinction and the pattern of reinforcement: II. Effect of successive alternation of blocks of reinforced and unreinforced trials upon the conditioned eyelid response to light. *J. exp. Psychol.*, 1951, 41, 216-220.

HAKE, H. W., GRANT, D. A., & HORNSETH, J. P., Resistance to extinction and the pattern of reinforcement: III. The effect of trial patterning in verbal conditioning. *J. exp. Psychol.*, 1951, 41, 221-225.

HIRSCH, J., Learning without awareness and extinction follow-

ing awareness as a function of reinforcement. *J. exp. Psychol.*,
1957, 54, 218-224.

HULL, C. L., *Principles of behavior.* New York: Appleton-
Century, 1943.

HULSE, S. H., JR., Amount and percentage of reinforcement and
duration of goal confinement in conditioning and extinction.
J. exp. Psychol., 1958, 56, 48-57.

HULSE, S. H., JR., & STANLEY, W. C., Extinction by omission
of food as related to partial and secondary reinforcement.
J. exp. Psychol., 1956, 52, 221-227.

HUMPHREYS, L. G., Acquisition and extinction of verbal expectation in a situation analogous to conditioning. *J. exp. Psychol.*, 1939, 25, 294-301.

ISHIHARA, S., An experimental investigation of partial reinforcement. *Jap. J. Psychol.*, 1954, 25, 9-100.

JAMES, W. H., & ROTTER, J. B., Partial and 100% reinforcement under conditions of chance and skill. *J. exp. Psychol.*,
1958, 55, 394-403.

JENKINS, W. O., & RIGBY, M. K., Partial (periodic) versus
continuous reinforcement in resistance to extinction. *J. comp.
physiol. Psychol.*, 1950, 43, 30-40.

JENKINS, W. O., & STANLEY, J. C., JR., Partial reinforcement:
A review and critique. *Psychol. Bull.*, 1950, 47, 193-234.

JONES, M. B., An experimental study of extinction. *Psychol.
Monogr.*, 1953., 67, (19, Whole No. 369).

KANFER, F. H., The effect of partial reinforcement on acquisition and extinction of a class of verbal responses. *J. exp.
Psychol.*, 1954, 48, 424-432.

KATZ, S., Stimulus aftereffects and the partial reinforcement
extinction effect. *J. exp. Psychol.*, 1957, 53, 167-172.

KENDLER, H. H., & LACHMAN, R., Habit reversal as a function
of schedule of reinforcement and drive strength. *J. exp. Psychol.*, 1958, 55, 584-591.

KENDLER, H., PLISKOFF, S., D'AMATO, M., & KATZ, S., Non-
reinforcements vs. reinforcements as variables in the partial
reinforcement effects. *J. exp. Psychol.*, 1957, 53, 269-276.

KINTSCH, W., & WIKE, E. L., Habit reversal as a function of
length of partial delay of reinforcement. *Psychol. Rep.*, 1957,
3, 11-14.

LAUER, D. W., & CARTERETTE, T. S., Changes in response
measures over repeated acquisitions and extinctions of a running habit. *J. comp. physiol. Psychol.*, 1957, 50, 334-338.

LAUER, D. W., & ESTES, W. K., Successive acquisitions and
extinctions of a jumping habit in relation to schedule of
reinforcement. *J. comp. physiol. Psychol.*, 1955, 48, 8-13.

LEWIS, D. J., Partial reinforcement in a gambling situation.
J. exp. Psychol., 1952, 43, 447-450.

LEWIS, D. J., Acquisition, extinction, and spontaneous recovery as a function of percentage of reinforcement and intertrial intervals. *J. exp. Psychol.*, 1956, 51, 45-53.

LEWIS, D. J., & COTTON, J. W., Learning and performance as a function of drive strength during acquisition and extinction. *J. comp. Psychol.*, 1957, 50, 189-194.

LEWIS, D. J., & COTTON, J. W., Partial reinforcement and non-response acquisition. *J. comp. physiol. Psychol.*, 1958, 51, 251-254.

LEWIS, D. J., & DUNCAN, C. P., The effect of partial reinforcement and length of acquisition-series upon resistance to extinction of a motor and a verbal response. *Amer. J. Psychol.*, 1956, 69, 644-646. (a)

LEWIS, D. J., & DUNCAN, C. P., Effect of different percentages of money reward on extinction of a lever-pulling response. *J. exp. Psychol.*, 1956, 52, 23-27. (b)

LEWIS, D. J., & DUNCAN, C. P., Expectation and resistance to extinction of a lever-pulling response as a function of percentage of reinforcement and amount of reward. *J. exp. Psychol.*, 1957, 54, 115-120.

LEWIS, D. J., & DUNCAN, C. P., Expectation and resistance to extinction of a lever-pulling response as a function of percentage of reinforcement and number of acquisition trials. *J. exp. Psychol.*, 1958, 55, 121-128. (a)

LEWIS, D. J., & DUNCAN, C. P., Vicarious experience and partial reinforcement. *J. abnorm. soc. Psychol.*, 1958, 57, 321-326. (b)

LINTON, H. B., & MILLER, N. E., The effect of partial reinforcement on behavior during satiation. *J. comp. physiol. Psychol.*, 1951, 44, 142-148.

LOGAN, F. A., A comparison of avoidance and non-avoidance eyelid conditioning. *J. exp. Psychol.*, 1951, 42, 390-393.

LOGAN, F. A., BEIER, E. M., & ELLIS, R. A., Effect of varied reinforcement on speed of locomotion. *J. exp., Psychol.*, 1955, 49, 260-266.

LOGAN, F. A., BEIER, E. M., & KINCAID, W. D., Extinction following partial and varied reinforcement. *J. exp. Psychol.*, 1956, 52, 65-70.

LONGNECKER, E. D., KRAUSKOPF, J., & BITTERMAN, M. E., Extinction following alternating and random partial reinforcement. *Amer. J. Psychol.*, 1952, 65, 580-587.

McCLELLAND, D. C., & McGOWN, D. R., The effect of variable food reinforcement on the strength of a secondary reward. *J. comp. physiol. Psychol.*, 1953, 46, 80-86.

MACKINTOSH, I., The resistance to extinction of responses acquired under irregular conditions of learning. *J. comp. physiol. Psychol.*, 1955, 48, 363-370.

McNamara, H. J., & Wike, E. L., The effects of irregular learning conditions upon rate and permanence of learning. *J. comp. physiol. Psychol.*, 1958, 51, 363-366.

Marx, M. H., Resistance to extinction as a function of continuous or intermittent presentation of a training cue. *J. exp. Psychol.*, 1958, 56, 251-255.

Mason, D. J., The relation of secondary reinforcement to partial reinforcement. *J. comp. physiol. Psychol.*, 1957, 50, 264-268.

Mowrer, O. H., & Jones, H. M., Habit strength as a function of the pattern of reinforcement. *J. exp. Psychol.*, 1945, 43, 293-311.

Notterman, J. M., A study of some relations among aperiodic reinforcement, discrimination training, and secondary reinforcement. *J. exp. Psychol.*, 1951, 41, 161-169.

Notterman, J. M., Schoenfeld, W. N., & Bersh, P. J., Partial reinforcement and conditioned heart rate response in human subjects. *Science*, 1952, 115, 77-79.

Parducci, A., Alternative measures for the discrimination of shift in reinforcement-ratio. *Amer. J. Psychol.*, 1957, 70, 194-202.

Perkins, C. C., Jr., & Cacioppo, A. J., The effect of intermittent reinforcement on the change in extinction rate following successive reconditionings. *J. exp. Psychol.*, 1950, 40, 794-801.

Peterson, L. P., Variable delayed reinforcement. *J. comp. physiol. Psychol.*, 1956, 49, 232-234.

Prokasy, W. F., Jr., The acquisition of observing responses in the absence of differential external reinforcement. *J. comp. physiol. Psychol.*, 1956, 49, 131-134.

Razran, G., Partial reinforcement of salivary CRs in adult human subjects: Preliminary study. *Psychol. Rep.*, 1955, 1, 409-416.

Reynolds, W. F., Acquisition and extinction of the conditioned eyelid response following partial and continuous reinforcement. *J. exp. Psychol.*, 1958, 55, 335-341.

Rubin, L. S., A demonstration of superior resistance to extinction following continuous reinforcement as compared with partial reinforcement. *J. comp. physiol. Psychol.*, 1953, 46, 28-32.

Saltzman, I. J., Maze learning in the absence of primary reinforcement: A study of secondary reinforcement. *J. comp. physiol. Psychol.*, 1949, 42, 161-173.

Scott, E. D., & Wike, E. L., The effect of partially delayed reinforcement and trial distribution on the extinction of an instrumental response. *Amer. J. Psychol.*, 1956, 69, 264-268.

Sheffield, F. D., Roby, T. B., & Campbell, B. A., Drive reduction versus consummatory behavior as determinants of reinforcement. *J. comp. physiol. Psychol.*, 1954, 47, 349-354.

SHEFFIELD, F. D., & TEMMER, H. W., Relative resistance to extinction of escape training and avoidance training. *J. exp. Psychol.*, 1950, 40, 287-298.

SHEFFIELD, VIRGINIA, F., Extinction as a function of partial reinforcement and distribution of practice. *J. exp. Psychol.*, 1949, 39, 511-526.

SPIVOK, M., & PAPAJOHN, J., The effect of the schedule of reinforcement on operant conditioning of a verbal response in the autokinetic situation. *J. abnorm. soc. Psychol.*, 1957, 54, 213-217.

STANLEY, W. C., & CLAYTON, F. L., An experimental test of Weinstock's hypothesis concerning the effect of partial reinforcement and extinction. *Psychol. Rep.*, 1955, 1, 421-424.

STEVENSON, H. W., & PIROJNIKOFF, L. A., Discrimination learning as a function of pretraining reinforcement schedules. *J. exp. Psychol.*, 1958, 56, 41-44.

TYLER, D. W., Extinction following partial reinforcement with control of stimulus-generalization and secondary reinforcement. *Amer. J. Psychol.*, 1956, 69, 359-368.

TYLER, D. W., WORTZ, E. C., & BITTERMAN, M. E., The effect of random and alternating partial reinforcement on resistance to extinction in the rat. *Amer. J. Psychol.*, 1953, 66, 57-65.

WEINSTOCK, S., Resistance to extinction of a running response following partial reinforcement under widely spaced trials. *J. comp. physiol. Psychol.*, 1954, 47, 318-322.

WEINSTOCK, S., Acquisition and extinction of partially reinforced running response at a 24-hr. intertrial interval. *J. exp. Psychol.*, 1958, 56, 151-158.

WICKENS, D. D., SCHRODER, H. M., & SNIDE, J. D., Primary stimulus generalization of the GSR under two conditions. *J. exp. Psychol.*, 1954, 47, 52-56.

WICKENS, D. D., & SNIDE, J. P., The influence of a component of a complex stimulus on resistance to extinction of the complex itself. *J. exp. Psychol.*, 1955, 49, 257-259.

WIKE, E. L., Extinction of a partially and continuously reinforced response with and without a rewarded alternative. *J. exp. Psychol.*, 1953, 46, 255-256.

WIKE, E. L., & MCNAMARA, H. J., The effects of percentage of partially delayed reinforcement on the acquisition and extinction of an instrumental response. *J. comp. physiol. Psychol.*, 1957, 50, 348-351.

WILSON, M. P., Periodic reinforcement interval and number of periodic reinforcements as parameters of response strength. *J. comp. physiol. Psychol.*, 1954, 47, 51-56.

WILSON, W., WEISS, E. J., & AMSEL, A., Two tests of the Sheffield hypothesis concerning resistance to extinction, partial reinforcement and distribution of practice. *J. exp. Psychol.*, 1955, 50, 51-60.

WYNNE, L. E., & SOLOMON, R. L., Traumatic avoidance learning: Acquisition and extinction in dogs deprived of normal peripheral autonomic function. *Genet. psychol. Monogr.*, 1955, 52, 241-284.

ZIMMERMAN, DONALD W., Durable secondary reinforcement: Method and theory. *Psychol. Rev.*, 1957, 64, 373-383.

7

Secondary Reinforcement: A Review of Recent Experimentation*

Jerome L. Meyers[1]
University of Massachusetts

In the past decade, psychology has witnessed two important research trends in the area of secondary reinforcement. Whereas the bulk of previous research[2] was concerned with demonstrating the existence of secondary reinforcement, recent experimentation has centered about (a) the question of defining secondary reinforcement and, in particular, exploring alternative explanations of the data and (b) the investigation of parameters which effect various measures of secondary reinforcement. Some experimenters have been concerned with differentiating between the role of the originally neutral stimulus as a cue and as a reinforcer (9, 30, 33, 43). Others have been interested in testing the applicability of a discrimination hypothesis (3, 25). Much experimentation has dealt with the effects of such variables as drive (7, 13, 14, 20, 27, 36, 38, 40, 41, 42), frequency of pairing of the neutral and primary reinforcing stimuli (2, 19, 27), reinforcement schedules (5, 10, 11, 24, 25, 29, 30), and amount of reinforcement (6, 21, 23).

This paper is a review of recent experimentation dealing with the problems outlined above. An attempt has

* From *The Psychological Bulletin*, 1958, 55, 284-301, and used here with the permission of the author and the American Psychological Association.

[1] The author wishes to thank N. A. Myers for her helpful comments on the manuscript.

[2] See Miller's review of the literature (28).

been made to integrate and evaluate the results of a number of experiments, to point out areas of agreement and disagreement among experiments, and to suggest the directions future research should take.

A DISCRIMINATIVE STIMULUS HYPOTHESIS

A study of Schoenfeld, Antonitis, and Bersh (37) has been instrumental in redefining a secondary reinforcer and in focusing attention upon the possible equivalence of secondary reinforcers and discriminative stimuli. Two groups of rats were given food pellet reinforcements for bar pressing responses. For the experimental group a light of one-second duration went on at the onset of eating, rather than simultaneous with bar pressing and prior to eating as is usual in secondary reinforcement experiments. No light stimulus was presented to the control group. The measure of secondary reinforcement was the rate of bar pressing during extinction trials when the light alone was presented. The lack of a significant difference between the rates of the two groups led the authors to conclude that the neutral stimulus must precede the primary reinforcer if secondary reinforcement is to occur.

To explain their results, Schoenfeld, et al. put forth the hypothesis that the efficacy of the originally neutral stimulus during extinction trials is dependent upon its serving as a discriminative stimulus during training. A discriminative stimulus is one whose presence is a cue for a particular response, and whose absence is a cue for not responding. If, for example, bar pressing in the presence of light is rewarded while bar pressing in the absence of light is not rewarded, light becomes a discriminative stimulus. Since in the experiment under discussion (in which secondary reinforcement was not obtained) the conditions for the light becoming a discriminative stimulus did not hold, the authors concluded that the neutral stimulus must be established as a discriminative stimulus if it is to function as a secondary reinforcer.

Dinsmoor (9) designed an experiment to further investigate the relationship between secondary reinforcers and discriminative stimuli. He gave his animals extensive discrimination training in the Skinner box. They were then divided into three groups, each of which was extinguished under one of three conditions. One group was extinguished with the discriminative stimulus, a light, continuously present except during three-second intervals following each bar press. The difference between the extinction response rate of this group and the extinction response rate of a control group was a measure of the role of the discriminative stimulus. A second group had to press the bar to evoke the discriminative stimulus for three seconds. Here, the difference between the extinction response rate of this group and that of the control group was a measure of secondary reinforcement. The control group was extinguished in the complete absence of the discriminative stimulus. The cumulative response curves for the first two groups virtually coincided and were consistently higher than that of the control group. Dinsmoor pointed out that the secondary reinforcer is a stimulus whose presence is contingent upon the response, while the discriminative stimulus is presented without regard to the subject's pattern of response. He concluded that the distinction between the reinforcing and discriminative functions of a stimulus can only be made in terms of this difference in temporal schedules for presenting the stimulus.

An experiment by Ratner (33) appears to present a challenge to the discriminative stimulus hypothesis. A group of rats was trained to approach a water dipper at the sound of a click. After this training, water was removed and a bar was inserted into the apparatus and, for half of the animals, a click followed each bar press. Both goal approaching and bar pressing responses were counted. A significant difference in the number of presses for the click and noclick groups was obtained, but there was little difference in the number of goal approaching responses or in the number of bar presses followed by goal approaching responses. Ratner concluded that, despite the acquisition of secondary reinforcing properties, the click was not a discriminative stimulus for goal approaching during extinction trials.

Ratner's brief reports of his study did not permit an extensive presentation of the training procedure, but his statement that the rats were trained to run to a dipper at the sound of a click strongly implies that at that point in the experiment the click was a discriminative stimulus for goal approaching. Therefore, we must conclude that the click lost its discriminative property while becoming a reinforcer for a new response, bar pressing. The results suggest that a stimulus may be reinforcing, although lacking discriminative properties. It cannot be concluded, however, that discrimination training is not a necessary condition for the establishment of secondary reinforcers. In view of its implications for Schoenfeld's hypothesis (37) in particular, and for secondary reinforcement theories in general, the study certainly merits replication.

A recent experiment by Wyckoff, Sidowski, and Chambliss (43) casts doubt not only upon the discriminative stimulus hypothesis, but upon the general concept of secondary reinforcement as well. Wyckoff et al. point out that if the bar and the reinforcement magazine are close together, any stimulus which has become a discriminative stimulus for goal approaching will tend to keep the subject in the vicinity of the bar, thus increasing the probability that the bar will be pressed. In the apparatus used by Wyckoff et al. the bar was placed at the opposite end of the box from the reinforcement magazine. The rats were initially trained to approach and lick a dipper at the sound of a buzzer. During the subsequent test session, the buzzer was presented to the experimental group after each bar press, and to the control group after each 10-second interval of nonbar pressing. Despite the fact that the buzzer was firmly established as a discriminative stimulus, and despite the fact that the situation was designed so that one group would be reinforced for bar pressing and the other group for not bar pressing, no difference was obtained in rate of bar pressing.

These results are highly suggestive. It is possible that discrimination training is necessary to establish a secondary reinforcer for two reasons: (a) The discriminative stimulus keeps the animal in the vicinity of the bar, and (b) the discriminative stimulus keeps the animal active, again increasing the probability of the appropriate response. As Wyckoff points out, other studies involving other apparatuses and procedures have yielded secondary reinforcement effects. However, the data gathered in a large number of Skinner box studies are now open to serious doubt, and it is evident that these experiments should be repeated with the apparatus modifications employed by Wyckoff et al.

The paucity of experimental evidence prevents any meaningful evaluation of the discriminative stimulus hypothesis, at present. Certainly, it cannot be concluded that discrimination training is a necessary requirement for establishing a secondary reinforcer, particularly when the secondary reinforcer is defined in terms of learning a new response rather than in terms of resistance to extinction. If discrimination training is necessary, it is still not clear whether the originally neutral stimulus must retain its discriminative properties during the test session if it is to serve as a secondary reinforcer. Ratner's results suggest a negative answer to this, but for conclusive evidence more experiments utilizing measures of goal approaching behavior, such as number and latency of responses, are required. Finally, in light of Wyckoff's results, the possibility should be considered that the apparent role of discrimination training in establishing secondary reinforcers is, at least in part, a function of the apparatus design. This will require further experimental verification.

A DISCRIMINATION HYPOTHESIS

Two studies by Bitterman and his associates (3, 12) have led to the formulation of a discrimination hypothesis of secondary reinforcement. Both experiments involved the same basic design, the major difference being in the length of intertrial intervals employed. Rats were required to run the length of a runway and then jump to a goal box. On rewarded trials the interior of the goal box was black and on nonrewarded trials it was white. On extinction runs, half of the animals ran to the black interior while the other half ran to the previously nonrewarded white interior. A secondary reinforcement approach must lead to a prediction of shorter running times for the first group. However, in both experiments, the group tested in the presence of the previously nonrewarded color was superior. Conditioning and extinction are similar for this group in that in both phases of the experiment they are consistently not rewarded when a particular color is present. On the basis of these results, it was suggested that a secondary reinforcement principle is not sufficient to explain resistance to extinction, and that resistance to extinction is a function of the similarity between conditions of training and extinction. A number of the experiments in the next section should facilitate an evaluation of the discrimination hypothesis and an understanding of its implications for research in this area.

SCHEDULES OF REINFORCEMENT

Dinsmoor, Kish, and Keller (11) gave two groups of rats discrimination training in a Skinner box, then presented the discriminative stimulus, a light, to one group after each response in the dark, and to the second group periodically, that is, only after the first response in each five minute dark period. Rate of responding was higher in the regular reinforcement group in the early sessions, but the periodic reinforcement group showed a higher response rate by the fourth session. The authors concluded that regular and periodic reinforcement do not produce different total effects. The generality of this conclusion must remain in question. It is possible that the use of other procedures to establish the light as a secondary reinforcer, or the use of periods other than five minutes in duration might yield different results, presumably an advantage for the periodic technique. In any event, it would be of interest to investigate the effects of other schedules of secondary reinforcement.

Dinsmoor (10) has also explored the effects of periodic schedules of primary reinforcement upon the establishment of secondary reinforcers. One group of rats was given discrimination training and its response rate was then measured in alternate light and dark periods, with food withheld. A second group was given the same training but the prevalent test condition was darkness, each bar press being followed by three seconds of light. Food reward was presented periodically to both these groups in the presence of light during training. A third group was regularly reinforced for responses in the presence of light and was tested in the same manner as the first group. The periodic reinforcement groups showed greater response rates during the test session than did the regular reinforcement group. The secondary reinforcement group, which was "rewarded" by the three-second light, showed a cumulative response curve similar to that of the periodic reinforcement group tested in alternate light and dark phases. The results thus substantiate the hypothesis of a functional relation between secondary reinforcers and discriminative stimuli and suggest the importance of schedules of primary reinforcers in the establishment of secondary reinforcers.

Clayton (5) has recently investigated the effects of regular and intermittent reinforcement, both primary and secondary, upon the strength of secondary reinforcement. Her rats were reinforced for bar pressing in the presence of light according to one of three schedules: 150 regular reinforcements, 150 reinforcements given over 250 trials (a trial being defined as the presentation of a light which goes off when the response is made), and 100 reinforcements given over 150 trials. Each of these groups was then extinguished in one of two ways: presentation of the light after each bar press or presentation of the light after 60% of the bar presses. No significant effects were obtained. Comparison of the six experimental groups with a control group which was extinguished in the absence of light showed significantly more responses for the experimental groups. The absence of effects due to reinforcement schedule is somewhat disturbing since it is reasonable to expect that (a) intermittent primary reinforcement should increase resistance to extinction and (b) if the light is a reinforcing stimulus, its intermittent presentation during extinction sessions should increase resistance to extinction. Nor are Clayton's results on primary reinforcement scheduling in accordance with expectations based on the Dinsmoor (10) study of the effects of primary periodic reinforcement. It is possible that two days of discrimination training are not sufficient to establish differences between continuous and intermittent reinforcement groups, and that the rats extinguished too rapidly for the intermittent secondary reinforcement to have any appreciable effect upon response rate.

Saltzman (35) trained rats on a runway, rewarding half the rats in a white goal box, the other half in a black goal box. He then tested the rats in a U maze, forcing them to choose between a white and black goal box, with no food reward present in either box. Groups given alternate rewarded and nonrewarded trials in the runway learned the maze problem as well as groups working for food, and made significantly fewer errors than secondary reinforcement groups given only rewarded runway trials. It appears that partial reinforcement during training is more effective than continuous reinforcement in establishing secondary reinforcers. This conclusion is supported by Notterman's (30) finding that secondary reinforcement is a monotonically increasing function of the number of unrewarded trials given during training.

McClelland and McGown (24) designed an experiment to approximate the variable training which occurs in the nonlaboratory situation, in an attempt to establish less transient secondary reinforcement effects than generally have been shown. One group of rats (the specific-reinforcement group) was required to enter a circular goal alley, and turn left. Food was always found in the same place, a fixed distance to the left of the entry, and in front of a barrier (thus preventing a rat from approaching the food from the right). A second group (the general-reinforcement group) was rewarded in four different parts of the alley in a random order. Since no barrier was present they were permitted both right and left turns from the entry. Furthermore, on half the trials these rats found the pellets on the floor of the alley, while on the other half of the trials, the rats were required to stop in the "correct" section, before a food pellet was awarded to them. To test the secondary reinforcement value of the goal alley, a T maze was placed at the entrance, and the rats were placed at one end of the horizontal bar and given the choice of running straight ahead or turning into the vertical bar and into the alley. During this test, the general-reinforcement group showed quicker entry into the goal alley, and less learning errors than the specific-reinforcement group. At the end of 25 trials, the general-reinforcement group showed no decrement in speed of entering the alley. These results suggest that increasing variability in the conditions present during training hinders the extinction of a secondary reinforcer.

Melching (25) varied the percentage of neutral stimulus presentations during Skinner box conditioning sessions. His rats were trained in one of three ways; either a buzzer always sounded following a bar press, or the buzzer sounded following 50% of the bar presses, or the buzzer never sounded. All bar presses were followed by food pellet delivery. Each of these groups was then extinguished in one of two ways; either with the buzzer following each bar press or without the buzzer presented at all. Melching found an overall significant difference in number of extinction bar presses between the groups. Since he unfortunately does not report the training or extinction conditions main effects or the interaction effect of the two, this overall significant F is difficult to interpret. However, t tests between all possible pairs of conditions yield one interesting comparison. No significant difference was found between the two groups conditioned with the buzzer following 50% of the bar presses. Secondary reinforcement theory would lead to a prediction of high extinction response rate for the group extinguished with the buzzer present. Melching accounts for these results in terms of a stimulus generalization hypothesis. For example, he suggests that stimulus generalization from 50% buzzer-during-conditioning to 100% buzzer-during-extinction was equivalent to stimulus generalization from 50% buzzer-during-conditioning to 0% buzzer-during-extinction. This would account for the lack of a difference in the extinction rates of the two groups. The results of other comparisons between groups are accounted for in a similar manner. Stimulus generalization hypothesis appears to be another label for Bitterman's discrimination hypothesis (3, 12).

Myers (29) varied the percentage of candy reward (100%, 50%), the percentage of token reward during training (100%, 50%), and the percentage of token reward during extinction (100%, 0%). The subjects were 3-6 year-old children, and the measure of extinction was the rate of button pressing during extinction. Partial reinforcement on candy and on token led to more extinction responses than continuous reinforcement, and, contrary to Melching's (25) results, all four groups receiving the token during extinction made significantly more responses than those not receiving the token during extinction.

These investigations of reinforcement procedures merit attention for two reasons. Until it is experimentally demonstrated that conditions can be found under which secondary reinforcement appears to be effective for more than 45 minutes in a Skinner box or 15 trials in a U maze, there is reason to doubt that much of human learning is motivated by secondary reinforcers. The Saltzman (35) and McClelland (24) studies are thus highly significant as indicators of ways in which more potent secondary reinforcers can be established. Myers' Ss, particularly the group receiving 50% token and 50% candy reinforcement, and the token during extinction, also showed little decline in response rate by the end of the extinction sessions. There is a need for further investigation of the effects of the percentage of primary and secondary reinforcement during training, the percentage of secondary reinforcement during extinction, and the schedule of presentation of both primary and secondary reinforcers.

The experiments reviewed in this section are also of interest because of their relationship to Bitterman's discrimination hypothesis. The Saltzman (35) and Myers (29) studies indicate that secondary reinforcement is something more than a result of the discriminability of test and training sessions. A discrimination theory would predict that a group running to a white goal box on both rewarded and nonrewarded trials during training would show greater learning in the U maze than a group running to a white goal box on rewarded trials and a black goal box on nonrewarded trials. The former group undergoes nonrewarded "white" trials in both training and test sessions, and should thus be less able to discriminate. Saltzman, however, found a difference in the opposite direction. A discrimination hypothesis leads to the prediction that Myers (29) should obtain results similar to those obtained by Melching (25). In Melching's terms, all those groups undergoing changes of equal magnitude in stimulus complex from conditioning to extinction should respond at about the same rate during extinction. However, all of Myers' groups receiving the token during extinction gave significantly more responses than those not receiving the token.

If certain experiments do not appear to support the discrimination hypothesis, there are still many results which are most simply described in discrimination terms. The Bitterman studies (3, 11) fall in this category. One of the first secondary reinforcement studies, that of Bugelski (4), is also simply explained by a discrimination hypothesis. Two groups of rats receive a click and food following each bar press. One group is extinguished with the click, the other without. There is no need to postulate a secondary reinforcer; extinction is more similar to conditioning for the "click" group.

McClelland and McGown (24) have related their results to a discrimination viewpoint. They argue that the stimulus complex for the general-reinforcement group is proportionately less changed by the absence of food during the test than is the stimulus complex for the specific reinforcement group. This greater similarity (for the general-reinforcement group) of training and test sessions would then account for the superior performance of the general-reinforcement group.

Myers (29), on the basis of differences between token-during-extinction and no-token-during-extinction groups, has suggested a modification of the discrimination hypothesis. She is able to explain her significant main effects, and in fact the observed rank ordering of her eight experimental groups, by assuming (a) that the token, through pairing with candy, has acquired secondary reinforcement properties and (b) that differences between per cent reinforcement in extinction and in conditioning are also of importance. Myers' view can be stated in the equation:

$$X = AY + BZ + C \qquad [1]$$

while the Bitterman-Melching approach may be expressed as

$$X = A|\,Y\,| + BZ + C \qquad [2]$$

where

> $X =$ total number of extinction responses
> $Y =$ the difference between percentage of secondary reinforcement in conditioning and extinction
> $Z =$ the difference between percentage of primary reinforcement in conditioning and extinction
> $|Y|$ is an absolute value

A and B are slope constants

and C is the slope intercept constant, presumably to be identified with free operant level. Both Myers and Melching are concerned with differences between the stimulus complex in conditioning and extinction. The former also assumes a secondary reinforcement factor which leads her to take the direction of differences into account.

Research dealing with ability of subjects to discriminate changes in the stimulus complex would seem to be a prerequisite to a reliable evaluation of the discrimination hypothesis. For example, it is quite possible that changes from 50% (during conditioning) to 100% (during extinction) buzzer or token presentation are not as readily discriminable as changes from 50% to 0%. Before we can adequately make quantitative predictions about extinction performance on the basis of either Equation [1] or [2], it may be necessary to scale subjective differences in percentage presentation, and to then restate our equations in terms of the subjective differences between conditioning and extinction.

At the present time it appears that some form of a discrimination hypothesis, possibly one which leaves room for the concept of secondary reinforcement, is promising. The approach has broad generality, being applicable to both Skinner box (4, 25) and runway (24) experiments, as well as to studies in which resistance to extinction (3, 4, 11, 25) is measured and studies in which the learning of a new response (24) is measured. The hypothesis takes into account the experimental conditions during both training and test sessions and facilitates predictions

about learning or resistance to extinction in light of these
conditions.

FREQUENCY OF PRIMARY REINFORCEMENT

It is reasonable to hypothesize that the effectiveness of
secondary reinforcement is a function of the frequency
of pairing of the primary reinforcer and the neutral
stimulus during training. This hypothesis has been investigated in a number of studies. Bersh (2), using a light
as the neutral stimulus, and bar press rate during extinction as the measure of secondary reinforcement, varied
the number of paired presentations of food and light over
a range of six points extending from 0 to 120. The only
significant differences in extinction rates were between
the 0 and 120 reinforcement groups and between the 20
and 120 reinforcement groups. A plot of the median
number of responses as a function of frequency of primary reinforcements yielded a negatively accelerated
curve which appeared to have reached its asymptote, suggesting that increased frequency of reinforcement would
have had little further effect. The results of this experiment might discourage the hypothesis that frequency
of reinforcement is an important parameter in the secondary reinforcement field. However, the lack of significant differences between the controls (no pairings of
primary reinforcer and neutral stimulus) and all groups
except the most extreme (120 pairings) would suggest
that Bersh's procedure was not an optimal one for establishing and measuring secondary reinforcement.

Corroboration of Bersh's results and additional information as well have come from an experiment by Miles
(27). He also used a Skinner box and measured bar press
rate during extinction, but he introduced a number of
methodological innovations. The range of frequency of
reinforcement covered six points from 0 to 160 reinforcements. A combination of light and click was paired
with each food pellet presented. Extinction was carried
on to a criterion rather than for a definite time interval.
Perhaps the most important aspect of the design was the
use of six nonsecondary reinforcement groups, conditioned in exactly the same way as the secondary reinforce-

ment groups but extinguished without the light-click combination present. Plotting number of extinction responses as a function of frequency of reinforcement led to the finding that the secondary reinforcement groups showed greater resistance to extinction than the nonsecondary reinforcement groups at all data points, and that both curves were negatively accelerated and appeared to approach somewhat different asymptotes at about the same rate. Miles computed the ratio of nonsecondary reinforcement rate of responding to secondary reinforcement rate for each of the six data points. A plot of the six ratios against frequency of reinforcement revealed no marked deviation from a straight line. Miles therefore concluded that the presence of secondary reinforcement leads to the same proportionate increase in extinction response rate throughout the parameter.

Hall (19) tested T maze learning (white against black goal boxes) after the subjects had either 25, 50, or 75 reinforced runs on a straightaway to a goal box which was always either black or white for any one rat. The number of correct runs increased linearly with increased frequency of primary reinforcement, the 25 and 75 reinforcement groups being significantly different. Extrapolation to zero reinforcements suggests that the response-frequency of reinforcement function is negatively accelerated as both Bersh (2) and Miles (27) found.

Further research is required to more precisely determine the shape of the performance-frequency of reinforcement function. Well-controlled and extensive experiments, utilizing the learning of a new response as a measure of secondary reinforcement, would also be welcome. Considering the lack of adequate controls and the limited range of values explored, the Hall (19) experiment can only be considered a first step in that direction.

TEMPORAL INTERVALS

Bersh (2) varied the duration of a light presented prior to the dispensing of a food pellet. During test sessions, a bar was inserted into the box, and each bar press was followed by one second of light. The 10 second duration group (10 seconds was the longest interval used) made significantly fewer responses than the others. The shape of the response-duration function is interesting in that response rate was greatest for the one second group, rather than for the .5 second group, which had the shortest delay between onset of light and of food. Although Bersh offers no reason for this, a discrimination viewpoint suggests an explanation of his data. Since all groups received the light for one second during test sessions, there is greatest similarity between training and test sessions for the one second training group. This, of course, assumes a rather fine temporal discrimination on the part of the rat. The test of this explanation would be an experiment in which duration of the light during test sessions is varied. A discrimination hypothesis leads to the prediction of a shift in the maxima point of the response-duration function with changes in the duration of the light during test sessions.

Jenkins (22) has also explored the role of the temporal interval between neutral and primary reinforcing stimulus presentation. His study differed from that of Bersh in two major respects. The test of secondary reinforcement was resistance to extinction of a bar-pressing response rather than learning, and the neutral stimulus, a buzzer, did not remain on during the interval preceding food presentation. Jenkins found that rate of response during extinction decreased monotonically as the interval between buzzer and food onset increased.

It appears that the interval between the onset of the neutral and the onset of the primary reinforcing stimulus does affect secondary reinforcement. Only subsequent research will reveal whether differences in the functions obtained by Bersh and Jenkins can be related to procedural differences.

AMOUNT OF PRIMARY REINFORCEMENT

The effect of varying the amount of primary reinforcement upon the strength of secondary reinforcement has been investigated by Lawson (23), D'Amato (6), and Hopkins (21). In the first of two experiments, Lawson used resistance to extinction of a runway response as a measure of secondary reinforcement. The secondary reinforcer was the end box in which food had been found previously. Although secondary reinforcement groups differed significantly from controls, there was no evidence of differential secondary reinforcement effects resulting from different amounts of reward during training. In a second experiment, an end box which had held food rewards during runway training was placed in one arm of a U maze. Again, no evidence was provided for significant effects of amount of primary reinforcement.

D'Amato provided for an apparently more sensitive measure of secondary reinforcement. Instead of comparing high and low reward groups, he gave all Ss experience with high reward in one goal box, and with low reward in another. The test consisted of 15 choices between the two goal boxes (no food present) in a T maze. D'Amato found significant preferences for that goal box which had previously held the larger reward. D'Amato has suggested that the difference between his experimental results and those of Lawson may be due to the fact that all of Lawson's Ss encountered one goal box in which they had never before been rewarded. It seems more parsimonious to assume that the effect of amount of reward is so slight, that it can only be detected when the S is forced to choose between secondary reinforcers previously associated with different sized rewards.

Hopkins found no significant difference in single unit T maze learning for secondary reinforcement among five groups who differed in amount of primary reward received during training on a discrimination problem. Again, it is possible that the design, which was similar to Lawson's, did not permit a precise evaluation of the effects of amount of reward.

It appears that certain refinements of experimental design are necessary for the establishment of differential primary reinforcement effects. The D'Amato technique merits further application to determine whether differential effects can be shown consistently when each S chooses between high and low reward-associated secondary reinforces. Investigators in this area might consider the problem of using D'Amato's design to investigate a wide range of amounts of reward, thereby establishing the shape of the function relating amount of reward and performance. The use of a multiple choice apparatus may be necessary for an efficient design.

THE ROLE OF DRIVE

Deprivation Schedules

Hall (20) investigated the relation between strength of drive during training and strength of secondary reinforcement during test sessions. Training consisted of learning a runway response to a particular goal box under either 6 or 22 hours' water deprivation. The rats then had to choose between the previously rewarded goal box and a previously unrewarded goal box in a U maze. Both groups were under 22-hour deprivation during this test of secondary reinforcement. There was no significant difference between the two groups in performance in the U maze.

Certain aspects of Hall's study deserve comment. No information is provided on the running times of the two groups during the training sessions. The absence of differences during the test sessions might have clearer implications if Hall had provided information about the effect of deprivation upon performance in the runway phase of the experiment. Data from other sources do not clarify the situation, since there is some disagreement in the literature regarding the effects of drive upon performance (8, 15, 26). Secondly, the investigation of only two points along the parameter leaves us with a rather incomplete picture of the relation between drive state during training and strength of secondary reinforcement. Finally, an evaluation of the strength of the secondary reinforcer used would have been facilitated if a control group had been run (possibly one which received a food reward in the U maze).

In a number of studies, drive state at the time of the secondary reinforcement test has been varied. Miles (27) conditioned rats in a Skinner box under 24 hours deprivation pairing each reinforcement with a light and a click. This stimulus complex was then presented during extinction sessions to six groups who had been deprived of food for either 0, 2½, 5, 10, 20 or 40 hours. The secondary rein-

forcement groups were superior to comparably deprived
control groups (in which light and click were absent during extinction). The response functions for both experimental and control groups were negatively accelerated,
the distance between the curves increasing with hours of
deprivation.

The Miles study is the only thorough parametric study
of drive. However, Estes (13), Schlosberg and Pratt (36),
Wike and Casey (42), and Seward and Levy (38) have
all been concerned with the effect of satiation at the
time of the test of secondary reinforcement strength.

Estes measured the learning of a bar press response in
two groups of rats, one deprived of food for 23 hours and
the other deprived for 6 hours. Both groups were "rewarded" only by the sound of the reinforcer, which had
been previously associated with the presentation of water.
The 6-hour group responded less than the 23-hour group,
its rate being lower than it had previously been in an
unrewarded free operant situation. Also, the 6-hour
group did not differ significantly from a control group
which had not had any secondary reinforcement training.
It was concluded (a) that animals could be motivated
by a secondary reinforcer when primary motivating conditions differed between training and test sessions and
(b) that some type of strong primary motivation is necessary if the animal is to work for the secondary reinforcer.

Schlosberg and Pratt (36) used the sight and aroma of
inaccessible food as a secondary reinforcer. Rats who
were run in a single unit T maze while hungry learned to
select the correct arm. Errors increased markedly whenever
the rats were run while satiated.

Wike and Casey (42) rewarded the runway performance of satiated rats with food pellets. These animals
performed better than controls who received nothing.
There is a decided difference between the results of the
Schlosberg and Pratt study, in which the subjects only
saw and smelled the food, and the Wike and Casey
study, in which the subjects were permitted to manipulate
the food as well. It is conceivable that the Wike and
Casey experiment involved a manipulatory drive, and
that secondary reinforcement was not an effective factor.
This view could be explored by running a satiated group

which would find manipulable, inedible objects in the end-box.

The results of a study by Seward and Levy (38) are somewhat equivocal. The rats' preferences for either end-box position in a single unit T maze was determined. During the 9 days of training, half of the subjects received reinforcement (food and water) in the preferred end-box (Group P), half in the nonpreferred end-box (Group N). The animals were then run while satiated for 7 days. There was a significant difference in favor of Group P, in the proportion of choices of the originally preferred position. This difference did not increase over test days, indicating that while satiated rats can be motivated by secondary reinforcers, this motivation does not lead to improved learning over time.

Both resistance to extinction (27) and learning (13, 36, 38, 42) measures yield the conclusion that secondary reinforcement strength increases with increased drive state. There is still too little evidence to permit us to decide whether or not secondary reinforcement is effective with satiated subjects. Estes (13) and Schlosberg and Pratt (36) have obtained negative results, while Wike and Casey (42) and Seward and Levy (38) have offered evidence to suggest that satiated subjects are influenced by secondary reinforcers. There appears to be a need for extensive, well-controlled research which will permit the statement of those experimental conditions under which satiated animals are motivated by secondary reinforcers.

Generalization of Drive

In a number of experiments, subjects have been tested for secondary reinforcement under motivating conditions other than those present during training. It has been previously pointed out that Estes (13) has shown that secondary reinforcers motivate behavior in the presence of a drive other than that present during training. Estes (14) also found transfer effects in two other experiments. However, the experimental group responded at a lower rate than a group learning under the original motivating conditions.

D'Amato (7) trained thirsty rats in a runway, rewarding them with water in a white cup in the goal box. They were then tested, while hungry, in a T maze, the correct response consisting of a turn to the former goal box. The correct turn was made significantly more often than chance expectancy, thus supporting the hypothesis that secondary reinforcement can be effective under motivating conditions other than those prevalent during training. Similar results were obtained in a second experiment, in which the rats were trained while hungry, and run in the T maze while thirsty.

Wike and Casey (41) found that thirsty, food-satiated rats ran faster to an end-box containing food pellets than did similarly motivated rats who ran to an empty end-box. This again suggests that secondary reinforcers are effective in the absence of the relevant drive. However, as in the previously considered study by these authors (42), there can be no assurance that the reinforcing factor was not the manipulability of the pellets.

In the first of two experiments, Reid and Slivinske (34) measured resistance to extinction of a bar pressing response which was consistently followed by a click. Two groups of rats had been trained to discriminate between food and water on the basis of a relevant drive. They were then deprived of food, and trained to bar press for food pellets, which were accompanied by a click. Half of these animals were then tested while hungry, the other half while thirsty. Another group of rats had no discrimination training, but were also trained to bar press for food pellets, and were also subdivided into two extinction groups. Assuming that generalization is a failure to discriminate, the authors predicted (a) that of the two hungry groups, the one with discrimination training would show greater resistance to extinction and (b) that of the two thirsty groups, the one without discrimination training would respond at a higher rate. In regard to the first hypothesis, no significant results were obtained. In regard to the second hypothesis, significant results, opposite to the predictions, were obtained. The authors concluded that secondary reinforcement, as they measured it, does not generalize from one drive to another.

It is apparent that the strength of secondary reinforcement is greatest when measured under those drive conditions which were present during training. There is agreement, however, that secondary reinforcers are effective in the presence of an irrelevant drive, when the measure of their effectiveness is the learning of a new response. Reid and Slivinske, attempting to account for their failure to show transfer of secondary reinforcement have emphasized that they were measuring resistance to extinction. It is true that operational differences exist between the Estes studies on the one hand and the Reid and Slivinske study on the other. There is no obvious reason, however, for suspecting that the learning of a new response would occur in the presence of a different drive state, while the maintenance of an old one would not. It indeed appears quite reasonable to expect the reverse. It should also be noted that Webb (40) has shown that an irrelevant drive can be effective in maintaining a higher response rate during extinction.

The results of this area are further confounded by two factors, the difficulty of ensuring satiation, and the difficulty of equating drives. Estes (14) has pointed out that since thirst reduces food-intake, thirsty rats feeding ad libitum on food may not completely reduce their hunger. Osgood (31, p. 435) has suggested the use of drives other than thirst and hunger as a possible way of circumventing this difficulty. The second difficulty is more amenable to investigation. It might prove interesting to hold one drive constant during training and vary the extent of the irrelevant drive during test sessions, and to hold the irrelevant drive constant during the test, and vary the relevant drive during training.

CONCLUSIONS

The secondary reinforcement literature yields few conclusions which can be substantiated by a number of experiments, and which are not contradicted by other experiments. There is no consistent picture of the effects of schedules of reinforcement, amount of primary reinforcement, satiation or irrelevant drives. Both the discrimination hypothesis and the discriminative stimulus hypothesis must deal with experimental results which do not appear to be easily reconciled to these particular ap-

proaches. It is apparent that we have made only a
tentative start towards an understanding of secondary reinforcement and the variables which affect its strength.
There are a number of problems which future investigators might well consider.

Methodology

A number of writers have pointed out that two types
of measures have been used in secondary reinforcement
experiments, i.e. either resistance to extinction or learning of a new response. Reid and Slivinske (34) have suggested that different phenomena are involved and that
the results of resistance to extinction studies may best be
explained in terms of a discriminative stimulus hypothesis. Certainly the field is ripe for a systematic comparison of these two sets of operations. Can consistent
differences be shown, over a number of parameters, when
other variables (e.g. the neutral stimulus, the apparatus,
the number of training trials) are held constant? A research program dealing with this point might do much to
yield a clear definition of secondary reinforcement, and
of the operations necessary to establish it.

The measurement technique is only one of a number
of variables which could account for the inconsistency of
results in this area. Comparison of results is difficult when
there is little standardization of apparatus, criterion, and
controls. T mazes, runways, Skinner Boxes, and jumping
stands have all been used. Subjects have been run for
various numbers of trials, or for various periods of time,
or until various periods of time have elapsed since the last
response. Many of the studies are inadequately controlled
in the sense that no comparison group (either a nonsecondary reinforcement group, or a primary reinforcement
group) was run. The experimenter has the responsibility
of indicating how powerful, or how slight, the effects of
secondary reinforcement were at any level of the parameter under investigation. Saltzman's (35) use of a primary
reinforcement group demonstrates that a powerful secondary reinforcement situation can be established in the
laboratory. Miles' (27) investigations of drive and habit
strength parameters permit comparison between secondary and nonsecondary reinforcement groups at all points

on the parameters, and, in this respect, should serve as a model for future investigations. Unfortunately, there are a number of studies reviewed in this paper which lack such comparison groups.

The techniques used in data analysis have generally been unsophisticated. The t test has been used repeatedly in situations requiring the use of analysis of variance followed either by "post-mortem" tests (39) or, with ordered variables, orthogonal polynomials (18). Experiments in this area invariably involve measures taken over time or trials, and often over a number of points of a parameter. In many of these studies, information about the shape and rate of change of such functions could be obtained by the proper use of trend analysis techniques (1, 18). It is time that psychologists realized that the formulation of behavioral laws necessitates information about more than the differences in location of groups.

What is a Neutral Stimulus?

One of the most surprising aspects of research in this area is that little attention has been paid to the neutral stimulus . . . what it is and how it is related to the primary reinforcer in the learning situation. Experimenters have used buzzers, tones, clicks, and lights of various intensities as well as white and black end boxes as neutral stimuli. It is doubtful that these are all equally "neutral." It is quite possible that the particular stimulus chosen for pairing with the primary reinforcer is an important variable. There are recent studies (17, 32), for example, indicating that light functions as a reinforcer for rats, and that its effectiveness is related to its intensity. It would certainly be worthwhile to vary the intensity of the "neutral" stimulus, to ascertain whether any general relation exists between intensity and secondary reinforcement strength. The results of a study by Fink and Patton (16) are also suggestive. Rats learned a drinking response in the presence of a complex of light, sound, and touch. The removal of any of these caused a decrement in amount consumed, but the size of the decrement was a function of which component was removed. The concept of a "neutral" stimulus therefore appears to be an unprofitable one. However, there are many stimuli whose reinforcer capacities change after pairing with a primary reinforcer. The extent of such increments in reinforcement capacity as they relate to the physical properties of the stimulus seems worthy of systematic investigation.

A distinction may be made between two techniques for establishing secondary reinforcers. The stimulus to be conditioned may be presented with, or immediately before, the primary reinforcer as in classical conditioning and as in the bulk of the studies reported here. On the other hand, the subject could be required to manipulate the stimulus in order to obtain the primary reinforcer, as in operant conditioning and as in Myers' (29) study with school children. In both situations the reinforcement capacity of some stimulus has been increased, but the training operations differ. One may ask whether either situation is generally more effective when other variables are held constant, and if so, whether this difference in effect is due to differences in proprioceptive feedback, the utilitarian aspect of the token, the period of time for which the stimulus is available on each trial, or some other factor. Here again is a problem which has received scant attention, but which might reveal information about those factors which facilitate the establishment of effective secondary reinforcers.

This paper has emphasized the evaluation of experimental conditions which may affect strength of secondary reinforcement and has ignored the role of secondary reinforcement as an explanatory concept in learning theory. Since the concept of secondary reinforcement has been widely regarded as a panacea for the reinforcement theorist's ills, and has therefore assumed a vital role in certain learning theories, this failure to relate the data to theory may perturb some. The author feels that secondary reinforcement is inadequately defined and inadequately demonstrated, that there is much disagreement about its relation to a number of variables, and that there are many gaps in our knowledge. Thus the use of secondary reinforcement as a foundation for any theory seems premature. The need, at this time, is for further and better research, rather than for more theory or defense of theory.

REFERENCES

1. ALEXANDER, H., A general test for trend. *Psychol. Bull.*, 1946, 43, 533-557.
2. BERSH, P. J., The influence of two variables upon the establishment of a secondary reinforcer for operant responses. *J. exp. Psychol.*, 1951, 41, 62-73.
3. BITTERMAN, M. E., FEDDERSEN, W. E., & TYLER, D. W., Secondary reinforcement and the discrimination hypothesis. *Amer. J. Psychol.*, 1953, 66, 456-464.
4. BUGELSKI, R., Extinction with and without sub-goal reinforcement. *J. comp. Psychol.*, 1938, 26, 121-134.
5. CLAYTON, F. L., Secondary reinforcement as a function of reinforcement scheduling. *Psychol. Reports*, 1956, 2, 377-380.
6. D'AMATO, M. R., Secondary reinforcement and magnitude of primary reinforcement. *J. comp. physiol. Psychol.*, 1955, 48, 378-380.
7. D'AMATO, M. R., Transfer of secondary reinforcement across the hunger and thirst drives. *J. exp. Psychol.*, 1955, 49, 352-356.
8. DEVALOIS, R. L., The relation of different levels and kinds of motivation to variability of behavior. *J. exp. Psychol.*, 1954, 47, 392-398.
9. DINSMOOR, J. A., A quantitative comparison of the discriminative and reinforcing functions of a stimulus. *J. exp. Psychol.*, 1950, 40, 458-472.
10. DINSMOOR, J. A., Resistance to extinction following periodic reinforcement in the presence of a discriminative stimulus. *J. comp. physiol. Psychol.*, 1952, 45, 31-35.
11. DINSMOOR, J. A., KISH, G. B., & KELLER, F. S., A comparison of the effectiveness of regular and periodic secondary reinforcement. *J. gen. Psychol.*, 1953, 48, 57-66.
12. ELAM, C. B., TYLER, T. W., & BITTERMAN, M. E., A further study of secondary reinforcement and the discrimination hypothesis. *J. comp. physiol. Psychol.*, 1954, 47, 381-384.
13. ESTES, W. K., A study of motivating conditions necessary for secondary reinforcement. *J. exp. Psychol.*, 1949, 39, 306-310.
14. ESTES, W. K., Generalization of secondary reinforcement from the primary drive. *J. comp. physiol. Psychol.*, 1949, 42, 286-295.
15. FINAN, J. L., Quantitative studies in motivation. I. Strength

of conditioning rats under varying degrees of hunger. *J. comp. Psychol.*, 1940, 29, 119-134.

16. FINK, J. B., & PATTON, R. M., Decrement of a learned drinking response. *J. comp. physiol. Psychol.*, 1953, 46, 23-27.

17. FORGAYS, D. G., & LEVIN, H., Learning as a function of sensory stimulation of various intensities. *Amer. Psychol.*, 1957, 12, 411.

18. GRANT, D. A., Analysis-of-variance tests in the analysis and comparison of curves. *Psychol. Bull.*, 1956, 53, 141-154.

19. HALL, J. F., Studies in secondary reinforcement: I. Secondary reinforcement as a function of the frequency of primary reinforcement. *J. comp. physiol. Psychol.*, 1951, 44, 246-251.

20. HALL, J. F., Studies in secondary reinforcement: II. Secondary reinforcement as a function of the strength of drive during primary reinforcement. *J. comp. physiol. Psychol.*, 1951, 44, 462-466.

21. HOPKINS, C. O., Effectiveness of secondary reinforcing stimuli as a function of the quantity and quality of food reinforcement. *J. exp. Psychol.*, 1955, 50, 339-342.

22. JENKINS, W. O., A temporal gradient of derived reinforcement. *Amer. J. Psychol.*, 1950, 63, 237-243.

23. LAWSON, R., Amount of primary reward and strength of secondary reward. *J. exp. Psychol.*, 1953, 46, 183-187.

24. McCLELLAND, D. C., & McGOWN, D. R., The effect of variable food reinforcement on the strength of a secondary reward. *J. comp. physiol. Psychol.*, 1953, 46, 80-86.

25. MELCHING, W. H., The acquired reward value of an intermittently presented neutral stimulus. *J. comp. physiol. Psychol.*, 1954, 47, 370-373.

26. MEYER, D. R., Food deprivation and discrimination reversal learning of monkeys, *J. exp. Psychol.*, 1951, 41, 10-16.

27. MILES, R. C., The relative effectiveness of secondary reinforcers throughout deprivation and habit strength parameters. *J. comp. physiol. Psychol.*, 1956, 49, 126-130.

28. MILLER, N. E., Learnable drives and rewards. In S. S. Stevens (Ed.), *Handbook of Experimental Psychology.* New York: Wiley, 1951. Pp. 435-472.

29. MYERS, N. A., Extinction of an operant response in children following partial and regular primary and secondary reinforcement procedures. Unpublished doctoral dissertation, Univer. of Wisconsin, 1957.

30. NOTTERMAN, J. M., A study of some relations among aperiodic reinforcement, discrimination training, and secondary reinforcement. *J. exp. Psychol.*, 1951, 41, 161-169.

31. Osgood, C. E., *Method and theory in experiment psychology*. New York: Oxford Univer. Press, 1953.

32. Premack, D., Collier, G., & Roberts, C. L., Frequency of light-contingent bar pressing as a function of the amount of deprivation for light. *Amer. Psychologist*, 1957, 12, 411.

33. Ratner, S. C., Reinforcing and discriminative properties of the click in a Skinner box. *Psychol. Reports*, 1956, 2, 332.

34. Reid, L. S., & Slivinske, A. J., A test for generalized secondary reinforcement during extinction under a different drive. *J. comp. physiol. Psychol.*, 1954, 47, 306-310.

35. Saltzman, I. J., Maze learning in the absence of primary reinforcement: a study of secondary reinforcement. *J. comp. physiol. Psychol.*, 1949, 42, 161-173.

36. Schlosberg, H., & Pratt, C. H., The secondary reward value of food for hungry and satiated rats. *J. comp. physiol. Psychol.*, 1956, 49, 149-152.

37. Schoenfeld, W. N., Antonitis, J. J., & Bersh, P. J., A preliminary study of training conditions necessary for secondary reinforcement. *J. exp. Psychol.*, 1950, 40, 40-45.

38. Seward, J. P., & Levy, N., Choice-point behavior as a function of secondary reinforcement with relevant drives satiated. *J. comp. physiol. Psychol.*, 1953, 46, 334-338.

39. Stanley, J. C., Additional "post-mortem" tests of experimental comparisons. *Psychol. Bull.*, 1957, 54, 128-130.

40. Webb, W. B., The role of an irrelevant drive in response evocation in the white rat. *Amer. Psychologist*, 1947, 2, 303.

41. Wike, E. L., & Casey, A., The secondary reinforcing value of food for thirsty animals. *J. comp. physiol. Psychol.*, 1954, 47, 240-243.

42. Wike, E. L., & Casey, A., The secondary reward value of food for satiated animals. *J. comp. physiol. Psychol.*, 1954, 47, 441-443.

43. Wyckoff, L. B., Sidowski, J., & Chambliss, D., An experimental study of the relationship between secondary reinforcing and cue effects of a stimulus. *J. comp. physiol. Psychol.*, 1958, 51, 103-109.

8

Learning Theory and the New "Mental Chemistry"*

W. K. ESTES[1]

Stanford University

Hovering in the background of our scientific enterprises is a question which we, as investigators, can afford neither to raise very often nor to overlook entirely. Namely, do we have good reason to believe that the general methods and working assumptions underlying our research can be counted on to lead in the long run to satisfactory interpretations of our phenomena? In the psychology of learning, there has been a division of labor, with the experimentalists doing the overlooking, and each theorist having his turn at bringing up this question along with his answer. The answer is, of course, in each instance that the particular theorist's tactics point down the high road while those of the opposition lead into dark and forbidding *culs-de-sac*.

* From *The Psychological Review*, 1960, 67, 207-223, and used here with the permission of the author and the American Psychological Association. When this paper was originally published the author was at Indiana University.

[1] This paper comprises, in substance, the writer's Presidential Address to the Division of Experimental Psychology, American Psychological Association, 1959. Several indebtednesses deserve acknowledgment: an unrestricted grant from the Ford Foundation supported portions of the experimental work; periods of relative freedom from academic routine in stimulating surroundings were made possible by the Department of Psychology, Northwestern University and the Institute for Mathematical Studies in Social Sciences, Stanford University during the spring and summer, respectively, of 1959 while the paper was in preparation.

For my own part, although my hands are not entirely clean in the matter of theorizing, I had been content until very recently to go along with the single-minded "learning experimentalist," assuming that the Lord will look after those who remember their control groups and mind their Ps and Fs. The incident which jarred me out of this comfortable way of life began as a simple (in fact, as will be seen, unusually simple) bit of experimentation with no philosophical overtones. The original purpose of the experimentation was to provide more cogent empirical support than had hitherto been available for one of the central concepts of learning theory.

Several recent reviewers (e.g., Deese, 1958; Estes, 1956; Kendler, 1959; Restle, 1959) have noted that despite the popular stereotype of "learning theory" as virtually synonymous with "controversy," there has steadily, although unobtrusively, accumulated a body of concepts and assumptions which command relatively wide agreement and which contribute motivation and direction to a great part of the research being done in the field of learning. At the center of this core of communality one finds a concept which represents the distillation of centuries of theorizing about learning, not to speak of 70-odd years of experimentation and the tradition of functionalism and, later, behaviorism: the concept of associative strength. In the "mental mechanics" and "mental chemistry" of pre-experimental associationism, this concept was verbalized in terms of the strength of associations between ideas; with Thorndike, it became strength of stimulus-response bonds; with Hull, the basic quantitative constructs of habit strength and excitatory potential. And it is in terms of this concept that contemporary learning theorists express the basic distinction between learning and performance, as well as their fundamental postulates relating the growth of habits to the number of training trials ("reinforcements").

There is little disagreement even in the precise quantitative form of these postulates, perhaps because our standards of acceptability come directly from the observed forms of empirical curves relating probabilities of learned responses, as well as measures of resistance to extinction or forgetting, to the number of training trials. Thus in a whole array of contemporary theories we find exactly the same equations expressing the effect of a reinforced training trial upon associative strength (cf. Restle, 1959). In Hull's system, this equation is

$$\Delta H = k(M - H)$$

where ΔH represents the change in habit strength (H) on any reinforced trial, M is the maximum value of habit strength, and k is a constant. Spence's (1955) revision of Hull's theory is based on the same postulate, although there is some question as to whether the H in the equation should be replaced by E, representing excitatory potential (Spence, 1955, 1958). Similarly, in statistical learning theory (Estes, 1959) the corresponding assumption has been expressed in the form

$$\Delta p = \theta(1 - p)$$

where Δp represents the change in the proportion of stimulus elements connected to a given response, and θ is a constant (the proportion of stimulus elements sampled on the trial). In the stochastic model of Bush and Mosteller (1955), the same linear function is assumed, "strength" being simply identified with response probability. For application to learning theorists, a well-known quotation may aptly be reversed to read, "In strength there is union." And with respect to the experimental literature, it seems fair to say that the assumptions that associative strength increases with reinforcement, decreases during retention intervals, and generalizes to new stimuli are the cornerstones of most contemporary treatments of conditioning and elementary verbal learning.

Areas of substantial agreement concerning either facts or interpretations, let alone both, are rare enough in the field of learning so that one might think we would do well to treasure the one we have located and carefully avoid doing anything to disturb it. This I (along with most of my fellow theorists and experimentalists) was happy to do, until my hand was forced by some purely experimental developments. The first of these was the, by now well-known, work of Kimble and his associates (1955, 1956; Dufort & Kimble, 1958) who, working with an eyelid conditioning situation, tried the novel procedure of omitting the CS on a substantial block of trials during an acquisition series. The rather surprising result of this variation was that the course of acquisition was virtually unaffected. Their interpretation was that only the first few reinforcements are actually effective in modifying the strength of associations between CS and CR, the rest of the "conditioning curve" actually reflecting some nonassociative process. The second development was contributed by Rock (1957), who found no retardation in the speed of paired-associate learning when he introduced the device of replacing missed items with new ones at the end of every trial. Rock interpreted his findings as indicating that associations form on an all-or-none basis and that it is only associative strength in the sense of resistance to forgetting that grows as a function of number of reinforcements.

It seemed curious that both of these deviations from the usual experimental paradigms had yielded results which are in some respects sharply at variance with the generally accepted conception of the acquisition process. Of course these findings might turn out to have special explanations that would leave the established conception undisturbed. But then again, they might not. In the case of the Kimble, Mann, and Dufort (1955) study, counterexplanations and counterexperiments have already begun to pour into the literature (see, e.g., Goodrich, Ross, & Wagner, 1957) with the result so far of complicating matters still further rather than of clearing anything up. One might argue that concepts and assumptions which have been supported by a large accumulation of experimental findings cannot be seriously threatened by one or two apparently negative results. But this argument is weakened by the observation that all of the empirical support for the conceptualization of learning in terms of associative strength is quite indirect in character.

The basic concepts and assumptions of learning theory are universally supposed to refer to states and processes of the individual organism. Yet the existing evidence for the assumption that associative strength is an increasing function of number of reinforcements comes from performance curves representing average response measures over groups of learners, or from measures of resistance to extinction or retention scores averaged over groups of learners having different values of the independent variable. Even the few bits of negative evidence are indirect, depending on performance curves obtained under deviations from the usual experimental paradigms but still representing changes in average scores over series of trials for groups of subjects (Ss). It would seem that if our basic conceptions are sound, it should be possible to cut through the web of group performance curves and obtain more direct and compelling evidence for the existence of the assumed states and processes in individual organisms. This, in any event, is what I set out to accomplish for the concept of associative strength in a series of experiments now to be reported.

ON THE DEFINITIONS OF "REINFORCEMENT," "TEST TRIAL," AND "LEARNING"

In standard human learning situations, "learning" is almost universally defined and measured in terms of a change in the probability, or frequency, with which a given stimulating situation evokes a response (or instances of a response class) that has been designated as "correct" by the experimenter. With one reservation, to be noted below, I shall follow this usage. But the situation is quite different with "reinforcement," the same term being used in at least two quite different senses by different investigators and thus promoting no end of confusion. My own habitual usage is the "neutral definition" (Hilgard, 1956, p. 409) which identifies reinforcement empirically with the operation that is supplied by the experimenter in order to produce learning, as defined above, in any given situation. In a paired-associate situation, the reinforcing operation is the paired presentation of the stimulus and response members of an item; in classical conditioning it is the paired presentation of CS and US; in verbal conditioning, the reinforcing operation for a given predictive response (e.g., predicting that the left light will appear) is the occurrence of the corresponding event (appearance of the left light)—in each case without regard to whether the S correctly anticipated the response member of the paired-associate item, gave a CR prior to occurrence of the US, or correctly predicted the event on the trial in question. The only property that different types of reinforcing operations are assumed to share is their common quantitative effect on the conditional probabilities of the possible alternative responses to the stimulating situation in which reinforcement occurs.

A narrower definition, favored especially by writers associated with a drive-reduction interpretation of reinforcement, would limit the term reinforcement to an operation that follows and is contingent upon the occurrence of the reinforced response on any trial. In this usage, reinforcement in paired-associate learning occurs only when the S has made a correct response in anticipation of the paired stimulus-response presentation, and reinforcement in verbal conditioning occurs only on trials when the S correctly predicts the trial outcome. Whether, according to this view, reinforcement occurs on only those trials of a classical conditioning experiment on which a CR occurs prior to the US depends upon theoretical decisions as to whether the CR and UR are "the same response" and whether reinforcement occurs at the onset or the termination of the US.

The primary advantage I see in the "neutral definition" is that it can be applied in an objective and consistent manner independently of one's position on systematic or theoretical issues. Learning certainly may occur prior to the first correct anticipation in a paired-associate experiment, prior to the first correct prediction in verbal conditioning, prior to the first CR in classical conditioning. The present usage permits us to speak, for example, about changes in probability of a response as a function of reinforcements on trials preceding its first occurrence, on the one hand, and changes as a function of reinforcements on trials including and following its first occurrence, on the other, without changing our definition of reinforcement.

It should be emphasized that the neutral definition does not beg such questions as whether presentation of a US following a CR constitutes the same reinforcing operation as presentation of a US on a trial when the

CR did not occur; these two procedures represent instances of the same reinforcing operation if and only if they produce the same change in the probability of evocation of the CR by the CS. However, it seems strategic to avoid issues of this sort when, as in the present investigation, we are concerned with the nature of the changes in response tendencies during learning rather than with the conditions giving rise to these changes. Consequently, in the experiments to be reported, we have attempted so far as possible to avoid the customary confounding of reinforcement with antecedent response. In paired-associate situations, for example, we have deviated from the usual anticipation procedure by separating the reinforcement (paired-presentation of stimulus and response members of an item) from the test for learning (presentation of the stimulus member alone) so that an item may receive more than one reinforcement before the first test trial or may receive repeated test trials without intervening reinforcement.

For purposes of measuring retention, it would be ideal if one could give test trials on which no learning at all occurred. Indeed, so long as "learning" is conceived solely in terms of the definition given above (increase in probability of the "correct" response to a given stimulus), this goal is not too difficult to approximate. It seems intuitively clear, and can be demonstrated empirically (Estes, Hopkins, & Crothers, 1960), that no systematic increase in probability of correct responses to, say, paired-associate items will occur over a series of trials on which the stimulus members are presented alone and the S's responses receive no reward or informational feedback from the experimenter. We cannot, however, rule out the possibility that on these trials there might be learning in the sense of an increase in probability of whatever responses, correct or incorrect, actually occur. In fact, there is evidence that such learning does occur, but at a relatively low rate compared to the learning that occurs on reinforced trials (Estes et al., 1960). Consequently, in the analyses to follow, I shall assume that unreinforced trials can be treated, without serious error, simply as "neutral" test trials when primary interest is in measuring the effects of preceding reinforced trials.

UNITARY ASSOCIATION VS. HABIT HIERARCHY

If the stimulus-response relation established by reinforcement were a unitary, all-or-none connection of some
sort, then the learning of a new response to a stimulus
would automatically displace a previously associated response. Contrariwise, in every variant of the concept of
associative strength, it is assumed that a number of different responses may simultaneously be associated with
the same stimulus, the relative strengths of association
depending primarily upon preceding frequencies of reinforcement of the different responses in the presence of
the stimulus. This latter assumption has been embodied
in Hull's "habit family hierarchy."

To spell out the question at issue in experimental
terms, let us suppose that first Response A and subsequently Response B have been reinforced in the presence
of a given stimulus (or stimulus complex—the nature of
the stimulation does not matter so long as it is the same
on each trial) for each member of a group of Ss and that
a test trial now reveals an observed probability (relative
frequency) of .5 for each response. Does this mean that
for each S both Response A and Response B now have
approximately equal habit strengths and therefore equal
probabilities of evocation by the given stimulus? Such is
the interpretation required by the conception of associative strength (habit strength, excitatory potential, proportion of conditioned elements, or whatever) as well as
by any of the contemporary models formulated in terms
of continuously variable response probabilities for individual Ss. Stated in these concrete terms, however, it
does not seem that the assumption need depend for support only on extremely indirect evidence, as has hitherto
been the case. To test these implications of the strength
concept quite directly, we apparently need only rein-
force two different responses to the same stimulus for an
individual S, and then, by means of a series of unreinforced test trials, give the two responses an opportunity
to exhibit their relative strengths—if such exist. The predictions under test would be straightforward. On the hypothesis of associative strength, or habit family hierarchy,

we expect individual Ss to shift back and forth between the two previously reinforced responses over a series of tests. On the hypothesis of a unitary, all-or-none association between stimulus and response, we expect that an individual S who makes Response A, say, on the first test trial with a given stimulus will not shift to B on subsequent tests.

A paired-associate learning situation offered a number of convenient features for an empirical realization of the hypothetical experiment just described. The stimuli and reinforcements are readily controllable; and, by embedding a stimulus to which two different responses are to be reinforced in a conventional list, one can make S's task appear little different from familiar learning situations. For each of 20 Ss, the procedures were replicated with six eight-item lists, all made up on the same principles.[2] The stimuli were all consonant syllables and the responses one-syllable words. Half of the items in each list had single correct responses; examples are:

STIMULUS	RESPONSE
HTX	wish
JFR	sped

These were simply "ballast" and will not be considered further. The other half of the items had two correct responses for each stimulus; examples are:

STIMULUS	RESPONSES
DGR	thaw, weep
BCG	pink, rule

The two correct responses to each stimulus were reinforced equally often for each S. By "reinforcement," in this context, we mean simply a paired presentation of stimulus and correct response to S; by "test," a presentation of the stimulus member of an item alone. In half of the replications, there were exactly two reinforcements preceding the test trials, one on each response; in the remaining replications, there were four reinforcements, two on each response, prior to the test trials. Following the

[2] This experiment was conducted at Indiana University with the assistance of E. J. Crothers.

reinforcements, a series of unreinforced test trials was given, the order of the stimuli being randomized anew for each test.

The critical data for our purposes are the proportions of cases in which the response given on the first test trial to a given stimulus was repeated on the second test. According to an interpretation in terms of associative strength, or habit family hierarchy, repetitions (AA or BB) and shifts (AB or BA) should have occurred with roughly equal frequencies.[3] According to the notion of a unitary association, AA and BB should have each occurred about half of the time and the shifts AB and BA not at all. The results were as follows: Following two reinforcements, there were 85% repetitions and 15% shifts on the first test trials, the percentages being based on all items that had correct responses on both tests. Following four reinforcements, these values were 89% for repetitions and only 11% for shifts. On later pairs of tests, the frequencies of AB and BA shifts were even smaller. Thus the results do not offer very impressive support for the assumption that a habit hierarchy exists in the individual S following the reinforcement of two different responses to the same stimulus. On the other hand, the data appear quite harmonious with an assumption of unitary association, since the proportions of AB and BA shifts appear small enough to be attributable to minor uncontrolled factors such, for example, as fluctuations in context (background stimulation, stimulus traces from preceding items) from one trial to the next.[4]

[3] The response given on the first test trial was the more recently reinforced response in approximately 60% of cases. Thus more instances of AA than BB would be expected; nevertheless the proportions of repetitions and shifts expected on the associative strength hypothesis are nearly equal (.52:.48).

[4] It should be noted that these results cast doubt on the concept of habit hierarchy only as applied to response probabilities in the presence of a stimulus situation that has been manipulated as a unit over the series of reinforced and test trials. M. S. Schoeffler (personal communication) and, in another unpublished study, Crothers and I have obtained positive evidence for the existence of a habit hierarchy associated with a compound stimulus, components of which have been separately correlated with reinforcements during the training trials. The results with compounding provide a control for the present experiment. If

Although the present experiment failed to produce the anticipated direct support for the concept of associative strength, a "strength theorist," particularly one working within the framework of Hull's system, may not be too disturbed. With the benefit of an ad hoc assumption concerning the range of "behavioral oscillation," the model of Hull and Spence can be made to yield the prediction that, of two responses reinforced to the same stimulus, one or the other will dominate on test trials, thereby preventing shifts from one to the other on the part of individual Ss. In order to obtain a more decisive test of the strength conception, we evidently require an even simpler experiment in which only one response is ever reinforced.

With the hope of forestalling an indefinite regress through a series of progressively more refined experiments, suppose we ask what is the minimum set of operations and observations actually needed in order to demonstrate learning. Normally there must be a pretest in order to determine the initial probability of the to-be-learned behavior in the test situation; in practice the experimenter often has a priori information about initial response probabilities which makes the pretest dispensable. There must be a presentation of some reinforcing operation, and afterward a test to assess the change in performance produced by the reinforcement. If the function of response occurrences and nonoccurrences is to be determined, there will have to be a second test trial. And there we have it. Controlled comparisons relative to effects of the principal events occurring during an acquisition series can, in principle, be accomplished in an experiment running to about a trial and a half. By usual standards, this constitutes what can only be called a "miniature experiment." However, miniature experiments appeared to be what the tactical situation called for, and therefore miniature experiments are what we set out to run.

---

the very high proportions of repetitions reported above were attributable to learning that occurred on the first test trial, or to some nonassociative variable, then a similar excess of repetitions should have occurred over successive tests with stimulus compounds; however, no such excess was observed either in Schoeffler's study of compounding or in ours.

CONCEPTIONS OF THE ACQUISITION PROCESS:
ASSOCIATIVE STRENGTH VS. ALL-OR-NONE
MODELS

In the first of these experiments,[5] we used a paired-associate situation with consonant syllables as stimuli and numbers as responses. Forty-eight Ss were run with an eight-item list, yielding 384 observations on the first test trial. The principal portion of the experiment consisted simply in presenting each S once with each stimulus-response pair and then testing with each stimulus alone (in a new random order). Before proceeding to the results, let us examine the outcome expected on the basis of the notion of learning as a change in associative strength. In Figure 1 the situation is schematized in terms of a single item. The four squares at the left represent four hypothetical Ss, the emptiness of the squares indicating that all start the experiment with zero probabilities of making the correct response. Now we give a single reinforcement (paired presentation of the stimulus and correct response), the result of which is to raise the probability of the correct response (C) to, say, .25. The upper arrow leads to the theoretical state of affairs after this reinforcement, according to an interpretation based on the conception of associative strength. The strength of the association is increased for all of the Ss; and, neglecting for the moment possible individual differences, the probability of the correct response is now .25 for each individual, the one at the upper right who happened to make a correct response on the test, and the three who did not.

Suppose now that the interpretation based on the concept of strength were completely wrong and that stimulus-response associations really formed on an all-or-none basis. Then the state of affairs after the reinforcement should be as shown in the lower part of the figure. Again the probability of a correct response increases from zero to .25, but the .25 now refers only to the group, not to

---

[5] This experiment was conducted at Indiana University with the assistance of B. L. Hopkins; for a full report of the method and results see Estes et al. (1960).

any individual S. One S has formed the association (darkened square), and three have been unaffected by the reinforcement (empty squares).

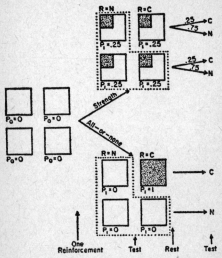

Fig. 1. *Schema representing effects of a single reinforcement according to incremental (upper branch) vs. all-or-none (lower branch) theories. Squares represent Ss, with the proportion of darkened area in each indicating the probability of the correct response (C) for the given individual.*

To distinguish empirically between these two logically possible outcomes, we need only add the remaining half-trial to our trial-and-a-half, i.e., give another test without intervening reinforcement. Now, if the upper branch of the diagram is essentially correct, all Ss should have equal probabilities of making the correct response on the second test trial, regardless of what they did on the first test. But if the lower branch is correct, correct responses on the second test should come only from Ss who made correct responses on the first test. None should come from Ss who made incorrect responses (N) on the first test, for these Ss would not have profited at all from the learning trial.

There might be some attenuation of the expected proportions of correct responses on Test 2 by Ss making correct responses on Test 1 if there is any forgetting in this situation, but the proportions of correct following incorrect provide a critical comparison. If the all-or-none view is correct, then this proportion should be zero, or at least no greater than could be achieved by sheer guessing. But if any version of the strength conception is correct, then the proportion of correct following incorrect responses should be greater than chance. In order to make the outcomes that can be tolerated by the two interpretations sharply different, we need only choose our experimental materials and conditions so that the overall proportions correct on both first and second tests are well above chance. It can be seen in Figure 2 that this has been achieved, for approximately 50% of the items were correct on the first test and nearly 40% on the second. Considering the critical lower branch of the diagram, leading from an incorrect response on the first test to a correct response on the second, we see that the results lean strongly in the direction prescribed by an all-or-none conception, for the 9% of correct following incorrect responses is less than the 12½% that could be achieved even by rather unintelligent guessing with an eight-item list if the reinforcement had no effect at all on these items. The difference between this value and the 71% of correct following correct responses is so large that a statistical test would be an empty formality.

A possible defense that might be advanced by a "strength theorist" is the hypothesis that the 51% of cases with incorrect responses on the first test simply represent preponderantly slower learners or more difficult items than the 49% of cases with correct responses. If so, then a control condition in which a second reinforcement is given between the first and second tests should yield a percentage of correct responses on Test 2 following incorrect on Test 1 that is much smaller than the percentage correct on Test 1. This control was run (with the same 48 Ss but different items), and the result is shown in Figure 3. The effect of the first reinforcement on the

full set of Ss and items was to raise the probability of a
correct response from near zero to .40; the effect of the
second reinforcement on cases having incorrect responses

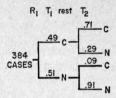

Fig. 2. *Results of miniature experiment on acquisition of
paired-associates. Empirical values are proportions of
instance in which correct (C) and incorrect (N)
responses on first test trial after a single reinforcement
(paired presentation of stimulus and response members)
were followed by C and N responses on a second test
trial.*

on the first test was to raise the probability of a correct
response from near zero to .46. Thus there seems to be
no support forthcoming for the hypothesis of a large dif-

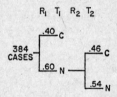

Fig. 3. *Proportion correct on test after a second reinforcement
for cases not having correct responses on first test
compared with proportion correct on first test for the
full set of Ss and items. The Ss and situation are the
same as those represented in Figure 2.*

ference in learning rate between cases which did and
cases which did not have correct responses on the first
test.

Although it would be nice to claim credit for rare prescience in predicting the outcome of this little experiment, the fact is that the result came as a distinct jar to my preconceptions. In designing the study, our idea was not to undermine the strongly entrenched concept of associative strength, but to support it by showing that the results of Rock's experiments, apparently calling for an all-or-none interpretation, must be attributed to some artifact concealed in his ingenious but somewhat complex procedures. Thus when Hopkins and I examined the data from our initial group of 24 Ss and found the pattern shown in Figures 2 and 3, our first reaction was to replicate the whole thing with another group. But when the two replications turned out to agree in every essential respect, we were left with no obvious course but to begin digesting an unanticipated and not entirely palatable conclusion. The most cleanly controlled comparisons we had managed to devise yielded no evidence that repeated reinforcements in this situation have any function other than to give repeated opportunities for the discontinuous formation of a learned association between observed stimuli and responses.

Still, it is well known that theoretical doctrines do not yield readily to negative evidence. One whose theories are based on a concept of strength will lose little ground if he can make a stand on the claim that all-or-none acquisition is simply a peculiarity of the paired-associate experiment and not characteristic of human learning in general. To evaluate this possible defense of the strength concept, we clearly shall have to turn to some different situation that is quite different in the response mechanism and reinforcing operations from paired-associate learning. Eyelid conditioning meets these specifications, and it is convenient for our purposes since a colleague, I. Gormezano, has kindly made available his data from an intensive period of data collecting in the Wisconsin conditioning laboratory. Gormezano trained a sufficiently large group, approximately 170 Ss, under identical conditions so that the first few acquisition trials can be treated as one of our miniature experiments and analyzed in much the same way as the paired-associate study.

The situation obtaining over the first couple of trials

is schematized in Figure 4. In the diagram, T_1 is the first CS presentation, prior to the first reinforcement, and we shall consider only Ss who made no CR on this test. Thus the initial probability of a CR is taken to be zero. Sup-

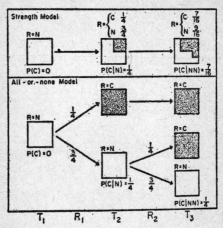

Fig. 4. *Schema for first two trials of eyelid conditioning experiment showing changes in CR probability (proportion of darkened area in squares representing Ss) prescribed by incremental vs. all-or-none theories.*

pose now that the effect of the first reinforcement is to raise the probability of a CR to .25. According to the strength conception, shown in the upper panel, each S has his strength of conditioning increased by the same amount by this reinforcement and now has probability .25 of making a CR. Then the second reinforcement increases the conditioned strength for each S again; and, regardless of whether or not a particular S happened to make a CR on T_2, he now has a higher probability ($7/16$ if we apply the linear function mentioned earlier).[6] Ac-

[6] For this example, the parameter θ in the function $\Delta p = \theta (1 - p)$ is equal to $1/4$ and after the first experiment p is also equal to $1/4$. Therefore we have
$$\Delta p = 1/4 (1 - 1/4) = 3/16$$
and for the new probability after the second reinforcement,
$$p + \Delta p = 1/4 + 3/16 = 7/16$$

cording to an all-or-none conception, the situation after the first reinforcement, shown in the lower panel, is that for ¼ of the Ss the CR has become associated with the CS and for the remaining ¾ of the Ss no conditioning has occurred. The effect of the second reinforcement is to give the unconditioned Ss another chance, and ¼ of these now become conditioned. The differential prediction, then, concerns the probability of a CR on the third test for Ss who made no CR on the second test (and similarly the probability of a CR on the fourth test for Ss who made none on any previous test, and so on). The strength conception requires this conditional probability to increase, whereas the all-or-none conception requires it to remain constant. The test seems quite sharp, for even with allowance for variation in conditioning rates among Ss, a model which assumes that associative strength increases with reinforcements cannot stand constancy of this probability unless its assumptions are so restricted that it reduces to an all-or-none model.

The pertinent results of Gormezano's study are shown in Figure 5, carried through the first four trials, beyond

T_1 R_1 T_2 R_2 T_3 R_3 T_4

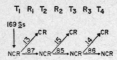

Fig. 5. Trial-by-trial acquisition data from Gormezano's study of eyelid conditioning. Values of particular interest are the proportions of CRs following 1, 2, or 3 consecutive non-CRs.

which the number of cases begins to drop off too much for comfort. Inspecting the sequence of probabilities of CRs after 1, 2, or 3 consecutive NCRs—.13, .15, .14— we find the hypothesis of constancy appearing rather more attractive than the progressively increasing trend required by the strength interpretation. (According to a linear model, for example, the value .15 for a CR after an NCR should have been .24, and the .14 for a CR after two NCRs should have been .34.)

The consistency of these conditioning data with those of the paired-associate situation is almost too good to be true. In psychology we are not used to having quantitative tests of alternative theoretical notions yield such apparently decisive outcomes. Consequently, and considering the importance of the theoretical issue, perhaps we will not yet be accused of beating a dead hypothesis if we look for one more test with experimental arrangements differing from both of those preceding. We would like a situation similar to paired-associate learning in that unreinforced test trials can readily be given without disturbing the learners but one which eliminates the possibility of achieving substantial proportions of correct responses by guessing. A situation which meets these desiderata is the free verbal recall experiment used by Bruner, Miller, and Zimmerman (1955). For our present purposes the minimal experiment will consist of a single reinforcement followed by two recall tests. The reinforcement involves merely the experimenter's reading a list of words aloud to S. On a recall test, S is asked to write down as many words as he can remember (in any order). Then after an interval during which no additional reinforcement is given, S is (unexpectedly) tested again.

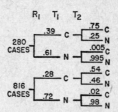

Fig. 6. Results of two miniature experiments on free verbal recall, showing near-zero proportions of correct responses on a second test trial for cases which did not have correct responses on the first test after a single reinforcement.

Results of two experiments[7] of this sort are shown in Figure 6. The upper tree represents an experiment with 35 Ss, each given a list of eight words at R_1. On the first

[7] These experiments, conducted at Indiana University with the assistance of Judith Crooks, will be reported in detail elsewhere.

test, T_1, 61% of the 280 opportunities for correct responses (C) yielded either incorrect responses or omissions (N), and of these less than 1% were followed by correct responses on the second test, T_2. In a replication conducted with some minor variations in procedure, 102 Ss were presented with eight words each on the reinforced trial. This time (lower tree in Figure 6) there were 72% N responses on the first test and less than 2% of these were followed by C responses on the second test. Clearly, if a word is not given correctly on the first test by a particular S, the chances are virtually *nil* that it will be correct on a second test.

This result does not, of course, *prove* that reinforcement has exerted no strengthening effect on the associations in the cases when the correct response failed to occur on the first test. But one whose theory requires him to assume that such strengthenings occur has a taxing assignment in producing a case for the existence of factors or processes which appear in just sufficient force to cancel out the hypothesized increments in response strength under each set of experimental procedures we have examined. Explanations depending on such factors as individual differences are not very prepossessing in the light of control comparisons of the type exhibited in Figure 3 (a similar control, with a similar result, was used for the free-verbal-recall situation). One might appeal to the effects of learning which occurs on the first test trial itself, arguing that an incorrect response which occurs on the first test receives a large increment in associative strength (from sheer contiguity or perhaps from some unspecified source of reinforcement) and therefore recurs with high probability on the next test. One important difficulty with this hypothesis is that the data do not support it. In the paired-associate study cited above, for example, the observed relative frequency with which an incorrect response occurring on the first test was repeated on the second test was only .24. Interpretations which preserve the incremental conception of associative learning should certainly be sought with all vigor; at the time of writing, however, none has come to my attention that seems at all plausible.

RETENTION AS A FUNCTION OF REINFORCEMENT
AND INTERSPERSED TEST TRIALS

The story does not end here. Even if one is ready to grant that associations are made and broken in an all-or-none fashion, this concession, although by no means a minor one, does not exhaust the resources of the strength concept. It is possible that after an association has once formed, associative strength in the sense of resistance to forgetting continues to grow as a function of reinforcements. In fact the experimental situations we have used appear well suited to demonstrate such an effect.

It will not have escaped notice that although the three miniature experiments yielded sharply negative results relative to the conception of learning as a gradual strengthening of associations by reinforcement, they agree only in part with the usual notion of all-or-none learning (as, for example, defined by Voeks, 1955). The formation of learned associations appears to be discontinuous rather than gradual, but once a correct response (or conditioned response) has occurred to a given stimulus, it does not appear with certainty when the stimulus recurs after a rest interval. In fact, "forgetting" as measured by the proportion of shifts from a correct response on the first test to noncorrect on the second test ranges from about 20% in the paired-associate situation to about 50% in free verbal recall. For the eyelid conditioning study, we did not report these proportions since the numbers of observations on which they were based were rather small; but for what it is worth, we might add that the proportions of CR to NCR shifts following the first three tests, despite the intervening reinforcement, fall well within the range given above for the other two experiments.

The minimum set of operations and observations required to test for a dependence of "resistance to forgetting" upon number of reinforcements is exhibited in Table 1. Following either one or two reinforcements, a sequence of two unreinforced test trials is given; and retention is measured in terms of the proportion of instances in which a correct response to a given stimulus on the first of these tests is repeated on the second test.

TABLE 1

Design and results of minimal experiment on retention as a function of number of reinforcements

Procedure	Amount of Retention	
	P-A	FVR
R $T_1 T_2$	.90	.54
R R $T_1 T_2$	.89	.52

Results of two such experiments are shown in the table.

The left-hand column of proportions represents data from a study conducted by the writer with the assistance of E. J. Crothers (Estes et al., 1960). Twenty Ss were each run on six eight-item paired-associate lists under each condition (number of reinforcements). The stimuli were nonsense syllables, and the responses were numbers in half the lists and familiar words in the other half. The right-hand column presents data from the free verbal recall experiment previously cited (102 Ss each tested with a list of eight items under each condition). The pattern of test proportions needs little comment. In each case the difference called for by the traditional conception of associative strength fails to appear.

This outcome is a little hard to swallow. It is well known that retention increases with overlearning. If the additional reinforcements given during the overlearning period do not produce the increased resistance to forgetting, then what does? We may obtain a clue as to the answer by introducing what might a priori seem to be very slight change in the design of our minimal experiment on retention. This variable is illustrated in Table 2.

TABLE 2

Design and results of minimal experiment on retention as a function of a test trial interposed between reinforcements

Procedure	Amount of Retention
R R $T_1 T_2$	.52
R T_1 R $T_2 T_8$	.78

In the free verbal recall experiment cited previously, we included, in addition to the condition shown in the upper row (which is the same as in Table 1), a condition with the same number of reinforcements but with an additional interspersed test trial. The idea was to give an opportunity for correct responses learned on the first reinforced trial to become conditioned to cues which are present only on test trials and not on training trials—in other words to spread the effect of the first reinforcement over more stimuli. Retention is measured in terms of the proportion of correct responses repeated from T_1 to T_2 in the upper row and from T_2 to T_3 in the lower row. In contrast to the lack of effect on retention produced by increasing the number of reinforcements, note the large effect of the added test trial. Two reinforcements without an intervening test yield only 52% retention, whereas two reinforcements with an intervening test trial yield 78% retention from the first to the second test following the second reinforcement.

Although the principle that retention increases with number of reinforcements is exceedingly well established in the lore of human learning, we must face the possibility that this empirical relation, like the classical acquisition curve, is an artifact of the confoundings inherent in the usual experimental paradigm.

CONCLUDING REMARKS

To recapitulate the box score: we have conducted a series of highly simplified experiments especially designed to provide relatively direct evidence for the widely accepted interpretation of learning and retention in terms of increments and decrements in associative strength. We noted that in virtually all contemporary learning theories, the concept of strength is assumed to have at least three different empirical manifestations—the habit hierarchy, the growth of associative strength in the sense of response probability as a function of number of reinforcements, and the increase in resistance to forgetting of once established associations with additional reinforcement. We tested for all three of these effects by means of the simplest controlled comparisons we could arrange, doing our utmost to eliminate the confoundings and the layers of statistical processing that shield the behavioral changes occurring on individual learning trials completely from view in conventional experimental designs. And under these presumably favorable circumstances, all three effects mysteriously evaporated, leaving a picture of unitary associations the learning and unlearning of which proceed on an essentially all-or-none basis.[8]

What is the import of these results for the question raised earlier concerning the strategic soundness of the general methods on which investigators of learning chiefly rely? The concept we have examined in detail epitomizes the intervening-variable paradigm for theory construction that has been popularized by Tolman and Hull, and their followers, to the point of dominating contemporary learning theory. The general technique is to postulate a hypothetical state or entity which is held to intervene in some sense between observed stimulus and response variables. Predictions derived from theories built around such constructs are checked against data from standard learning experiments. Thus the adequacy of the theories depends in turn on the adequacy with which essential aspects of learning are captured by standard experimental designs.

I have emphasized the term "standard" for despite the fact, decried by many critics, that psychologists in this

---

[8] Several readers of a prepublication draft of this article have raised the question whether alternative measures, e.g., response latencies or recognition scores, might yield evidence of learning in cases where the probabilities of conditioned responses or of correct recalls do not. Regardless of the answer, it is important to note that information about concomitant changes in other variables would have no logical bearing upon conclusions pertaining to the one actually chosen for analysis in a given experiment. To determine whether the behavior of recalling the correct response to a paired-associate item is learned in all-or-none fashion, we required an analysis according to the paradigm of Figure 2 with recall score as the dependent variable. To determine whether correct recognition of a previously viewed item is learned on an all-or-none basis, we would need a similar analysis with recognition score as the dependent variable. To determine whether the behavioral change associated with a decrease in latency is learned on an all-or-none basis, we would need a similar analysis with some criterion of change in latency as the dependent variable, and so on.

field have resisted all admonitions to standardize their tasks, situations, and procedures, they have more than compensated for this lack by the degree to which they have standardized their experimental designs. Scanning the reference list of, say, Hilgard's *Theories of Learning* (1956),[9] one can find no more than a meager handful of studies which are not molded into a paradigm that might be termed the groups-by-trials design. The master blueprint requires the investigator to average some type of performance score, e.g., frequency of conditioned responses or of correct responses, over a series of trials for groups of Ss—the groups being differentiated on the basis of conditions obtaining over the series. Going back a few years in the experimental journals, one finds the customary output of this experimental paradigm to be a set of mean performance curves for experimental and control groups; more recently the output is typically an array of analysis of variance tables, perhaps supplemented by some mean criterion scores. These observations in themselves do not constitute a criticism. No one would gainsay that the groups-by-trials design and its associated statistical techniques are useful tools for assaying the effects of various procedures and conditions upon performance. It is easy, however, to overlook the fact that the groups-by-trials design yields only information about relationships and trends which hold on the average over groups of Ss and series of trials. No accumulation of experiments, however large, all conducted and all analyzed in accord with this same general method can provide a sufficient empirical check on concepts and assumptions that refer to processes or events occurring in the individual learner. The findings we have considered in this paper suggest that in point of fact some of the most firmly entrenched concepts and principles of learning

[9] The harvest is even scantier if one consults the more monographic works, e.g., Tolman (1932), Hull (1943), or Spence (1955), associated with systems of intervening-variables in behavior theory; or, for that matter, my own theoretical writings (Estes, 1959). In the eclectic treatise of McGeoch and Irion (1952), deviant experimental designs appear in references with the earliest dates but disappear as one comes down to the contemporary literature.

theory may be in a sense artifacts of a conventionalized methodology.

The laboratory investigator of learning is used to going his own way more or less oblivious to the rattle of criticisms from textbook writers, educators, and other "outsiders." Traditionally the criticisms have always been to the same effect—that the "learning experimentalist" should push on from worn out fields of conditioning and simple verbal learning, where there are really no unsolved problems of any importance remaining, and devote himself to richer, more complex, experiments that come closer to learning situations of real life (as contrasted with the unreal life found in the laboratory). Here we break with tradition, for the criticism generated by our work within the field suggests that progress toward a satisfactory theory of learning requires, not more complex, but simpler experiments. The conventional experiment, far from being oversimplified, represents such a complex and intricate confounding of stimulus and response variables over trials that once it has been done and reported in conventional form, no amount of study of the analysis of variance tables and Vincentized performance curves can disclose the effects exerted by specific causal variables on individual Ss upon particular occasions. Concepts depending solely upon the conventional experiment for support may turn out to belong, not to a psychology of learning, but only to a psychology of the criterion score, the mean performance curve, and the groups-by-trials design.

In concluding, I would like to indicate that I do not mean to offer the experimental findings reported in this paper as a crucial test of incremental vs. all-or-none theory. What does seem clear with respect to the former is that the kind of evidence heretofore adduced in support of incremental theories is inadequate to distinguish them from alternative conceptions. More penetrating experimental analyses are required. We have made a start in this direction, and from the early returns it appears that no extant theory of the incremental type can handle the pattern of results that is emerging. The temptation is great to indulge now in a bit of speculation as to whether the answer to this situation will prove to be a remodeling of one of the familiar incremental theories, or perhaps a quite different theory based on all-or-none assumptions —but this is a step I do not intend to take.

Since the earliest days of associationism, overdependence upon speculation and circuitous inference has impeded the interplay of theory with experiment. While I would not for a moment depreciate the role of imagination in science, I suspect that it will begin to serve us effectively in learning theory only as we begin to accumulate reliable determinations of the effects of single variables upon single learning trials in individual organisms. If by continual simplification of our experimental analyses and refinement of our mensurational procedures we can achieve these determinations, we may find that the long sought laws of association may be not merely "instigated," or even "suggested," but literally dictated in form by empirical data.

REFERENCES

BRUNER, J. S., MILLER, G. A., & ZIMMERMAN, C., Discriminative skill and discriminative matching in perceptual recognition. *J. exp. Psychol.*, 1955, 49, 187-192.

BUSH, R. R., & MOSTELLER, F., *Stochastic models for learning.* New York: Wiley, 1955.

DEESE, J., *The psychology of learning.* (Rev. ed.) New York: McGraw-Hill, 1958.

DUFORT, R. H., & KIMBLE, G. A., Ready signals and the effect of interpolated UCS presentations in eyelid conditioning. *J. exp. Psychol.*, 1958, 56, 1-7.

ESTES, W. K., Learning. *Annu. Rev. Psychol.*, 1956, 7, 1-38.

ESTES, W. K., The statistical approach to learning theory. In S. Koch (Ed.), *Psychology: A study of a science.* Vol. 2. New York: McGraw-Hill, 1959. Pp. 380-491.

ESTES, W. K., HOPKINS, B. L., & CROTHERS, E. J., All-or-none and conservation effects in the learning and retention of paired associates. *J. exp. Psychol.*, 1960, in press.

GOODRICH, K. P., ROSS, L. E., & WAGNER, A. R., Performance in eyelid conditioning following interpolated presentations of the UCS. *J. exp. Psychol.*, 1957, 53, 214-17.

HILGARD, E. R., *Theories of learning.* (Rev. ed.) New York: Appleton-Century-Crofts, 1956.

HULL, C. L., *Principles of behavior.* New York: Appleton-Century, 1943.

Kendler, H. H., Learning. *Annu. Rev. Psychol.*, 1959, 10, 43-88.

Kimble, G. A., & Dufort, R. H., The associative factor in eyelid conditioning. *J. exp. Psychol.*, 1956, 52, 386-91.

Kimble, G. A., Mann, L. I., & Dufort, R. H., Classical and instrumental eyelid conditioning. *J. exp. Psychol.*, 1955, 49, 407-17.

McGeoch, J. A., & Irion, A. L., *The psychology of human learning.* (Rev. ed.) New York: Longmans, 1952.

Restle, F., A survey and classification of learning models. In R. R. Bush and W. K. Estes (Eds.), *Studies in mathematical learning theory.* Stanford, Calif.: Stanford Univer. Press, 1959.

Rock, I., The role of repetition in associative learning. *Amer. J. Psychol.*, 1957, 70, 186-193.

Spence, K. A., *Behavior theory and conditioning.* New Haven: Yale Univer. Press, 1955.

Spence, K. A., Behavior theory and selective learning. In M. R. Jones (Ed.), *Nebraska symposium on motivation.* Lincoln: Univer. Nebraska Press, 1958.

Tolman, E. C., *Purposive behavior in animals and men.* New York: Appleton-Century, 1932.

Voeks, V. W., Gradual strengthening of S-R connections or increasing number of S-R connections. *J. Psychol.*, 1955, 39, 289-99.